Let's go Mad

A YEAR ABROAD IN SEARCH OF

UTOPIA AND ENLIGHTENMENT

ROB BINKLEY

with Murphy Hooker

Skyhorse Publishing

Skyhorse Publishing books may be purchased in bulk at special discounts for sales promotion, corporate gifts, fund-raising, or educational purposes. Special editions can also be created to specifications. For details, contact the Special Sales Department, Skyhorse Publishing, 307 West 36th Street, 11th Floor, New York, NY 10018 or info@skyhorsepublishing.com.

Skyhorse® and Skyhorse Publishing® are registered trademarks of Skyhorse Publishing, Inc.®, a Delaware corporation.

Visit our website at www.skyhorsepublishing.com.

10 9 8 7 6 5 4 3 2 1

Library of Congress Cataloging-in-Publication Data is available on file.

Cover design by Laura Klynstra
Cover photo: iStockphoto

Print ISBN: 978-1-5107-1009-2
Ebook ISBN: 978-1-5107-1010-8

Printed in the United States of America

Dedicated to T.

—Murphy Hooker

Contents

1

Shanghaied into Oblivion

THE WHOLE CRAZY TRIP ERUPTED in a mad burst of psychosis last December when the wild devil of my youth shanghaied me into oblivion.

Before it happened, I was living a fraudulent existence some might classify as the American Dream. I thought I had it all: I owned a successful chain of coffee houses, I had an amazing girlfriend. Life was good, but something was missing—something big I couldn't put my finger on until one Sunday afternoon.

"Are you listening, Rob? They could put you in jail."

"No . . . I was tuning you out."

I was in my lawyer's office in downtown Palo Alto. It was one of those sunny afternoons everyone on the East Coast dreams about when they're shoveling snow. He was laying out my options for dealing with the coming crisis: a surprise audit by the state of California on my "cash-only" coffee bars.

"I just want to know what I did to deserve this."

"They found some discrepancies in your books. They claim you owe them back taxes in the amount of—let me get the exact figure—seventy thousand, nine hundred and sixty-two dollars . . . and eight cents."

"That's ludicrous. I got a hundred grand stolen *from me* by the same CPA who they say didn't pay my state taxes."

"It appears your ex-accountant really embezzled one hundred and seventy-two thousand, nine hundred and sixty-two dollars . . . and—"

"Eight cents. I can add."

"Right."

"I filed criminal charges against the guy six months ago, and the Palo Alto Police Department did nothing. Does the state of California know about this? Tell them to go put him in jail. He's the criminal."

"That's not how it works. In the eyes of the state, it doesn't matter who filed your return; your company owes the back taxes."

"I don't have seventy-three thousand dollars in cash. He cleaned me out—I'm cash poor."

"Then they will seize your cafés."

"If they take them away, how can I repay them? They're squeezing me! This is my livelihood, everything I've worked so hard for."

"I believe you, Rob. You got screwed by this guy, but that's not the issue. With the prospect of a felony tax fraud conviction hanging over your head, I advise you to work with these people."

"I'm not paying for a crime I didn't commit. I'd rather—"

"Refusing payment is not an option."

"What if I just left? Pulled a 'Lex Luthor' and left the country?"

"You could lose everything. They could put you in jail if you're found guilty of tax evasion."

"Not if they can't catch me."

"You're not thinking rationally."

"Because you're not helping! Maybe I need to seek counsel elsewhere." I grabbed my bag and left.

"You'll be sorry you did this."

I walked outside to collect myself when my best friend Brian pulled up in a rental car like he just robbed a bank. "Binkley!" he yelled through the open window. "How would you like to escape from all that's *right* in your world?!" I stuck my head in the passenger side. Brian looked like a mix between the Unabomber and a Blues Brother.

"How'd you know I was here?"

"I called Elena."

"Right. You steal this thing?"

"You don't wanna know. *Get in.*"

I got in.

"Where you been? Thought you were dead in a ditch somewhere." Brian hadn't answered his phone for two weeks.

"I had an experience." Brian was being mysterious as he pulled into the parking lot of one of my cafés. "I've got a story to tell."

"So do I," I said.

We walked inside. Brian had a wild look in his eye as he sized up the crowd. No one bothered to look up from their laptops. Everyone had their heads up their asses—an average Sunday.

Brian followed me to my back office and laughed at the studious café vibe. "We're invisible." We found some privacy behind closed doors. I grabbed two chairs I usually reserved for interviewing hot potential employees and told Brian about the audit.

All he could say was: "You're screwed."

He whipped out a bottle of rum from his backpack and a lime-green candle shaped like a giant phallus, which he lit then placed at the center of the table.

"You should put a hit on that accountant," he said while he carefully poured two shots.

"I tried. . . ." I looked at his candle. "Whatever you've got planned for tonight, count me out."

"Don't worry." He slid a shot of rum to me. "Trust me." These were Brian's famous last words from high school. "Just allow for this idea to wash over you . . . Soon you will see the world like I do . . . It appears I've come at the perfect time . . . Focus on the flame."

I downed my shot and pointed to the candle. "Is this really necessary?"

"Yes. This is for your own good. I want to open your mind to what's possible."

"You know I hate spirituality. And giant green phalluses in my face."

"I know." He stood behind me to make sure I was staring directly into the flickering candle, then he rubbed my shoulders and went into a story about how he had just "got choked out by corporate America" and had resigned from his corporate tech sales job last week. Brian said his fatal error was "telling the truth to a group of clients during a national sales event," which got him fired; the resignation was just to save face.

"Moral to the story is: I'm screwed too." He downed another shot.

After a few hours Brian had filled me with so many shots of that 120-proof elixir, I felt sick. "I need to lay down" was the last thing I remember saying before fading to black. I hadn't blacked out in months.

When I came to four hours later, I was lying on the roof clutching my flip-flop. People were carefully stepping around me. I sat up. Either I was hallucinating, or there was a party going on.

"Here, drink this." One of my employees, Rachel, rushed me a glass of something. I was hoping for water, but it was more rum—the same stuff Brian was totally ripped on now. I wanted to obliterate my pain, so I drained another glass.

Rachel sat in my lap. "You okay? Hope it's cool we're on the roof. Brian said we should hang out to see if you needed your stomach pumped. Do we need to take you to the ER, or something?"

"No. Just haven't been eating lately."

"Poor baby." She got up and went back over to Brian, who was on fire, preaching to my disillusioned wait staff.

"I'm talking about an escape. An out. Run away with me, all of you! I've got life figured out!" Brian squeezed Rachel's butt.

"If you've got it all figured, why are you still here in Palo Alto?"

He roared, "Great question!"

Brian stopped ranting to check in with me. "What the hell happened to you? Your tolerance is for shit, man."

I tried to re-focus. "I dunno. Haven't been eating from the stress."

Brian wasn't listening. He'd gone back to railing on the girls for being "numbed out" to reality. "The point, my lambs, is American consumerism hasn't delivered us into any angelic realm—it's turning us into yuppified zombie shitheads."

He held up his giant old-school cell phone from 1990. "Look. This is how civilizations die. I'm going off-the-grid from consumerism, TV, Vegas, porn, the Internet, whatever—and I'm most definitely going off American women."

Kali, the part-time hostess, let him have it. "If you don't like the Internet or American women, go live in a third world jungle."

"That's not a bad idea," he looked at her name tag, "*Kali.*" Brian plopped down next to me and moved the candle close to my face. He quietly inspected my soured mug like a crime scene investigator. When he got too close, I pushed him away.

"Stop it, will ya? How long was I gone?"

"Who knows? Time is just a concept."

Eventually the party died down, and everyone went home. With no female buffer, Brian set to brainwash me with the fervor of a cult leader with a plane to catch.

"What if you had died from alcohol poisoning tonight?"

"I still may die from alcohol poisoning."

"Can you say you really lived? Fulfilled your pure potential? Accumulating wealth doesn't count. Was your life spent following your bliss?"

"My bliss??"

"Are you your essential self, Rob? Do you even know who that is? While hiking on mushrooms recently, I had what the Japanese call a *satori*—what your hero Kerouac once described as a spiritual kick in the head."

"Good for you."

"Consider this your kick in the balls."

"Kick your candle in the balls. I need to eat!"

"The time is now. I've got a plan, and I'm bringing you with me."

"Bringing me where?"

"To a better tomorrow, away from this *Brave New World*."

"Every time you start conversations like this, we end up on some moronic adventure."

Brian held up an advertisement for some airline hocking an around-the-world ticket sale. "This is the solution to what ails us. Two 'Around-the-World' tickets. We can fly anywhere, anytime, one way for a year, until we run out of planet. The offer expires soon, so we gotta move on this. C'mon. Let's go grab your stuff."

We'd been planning to take a trip together for six months, but that was before he disappeared for two weeks. It was the last thing on my mind tonight.

"You seriously want me drop everything now? Weren't you listening to my predicament?"

"Yes! I was." He poured me another drink. "Weren't you listening to mine??"

Maybe it was the rum, maybe it was the audit, maybe it was me realizing I *was* unhappy with this modern life. But after about the seventeenth shot, I confessed I had not been following my bliss. I felt doomed to die a nameless cog.

"My life *does* feel meaningless," I slurred into his candle, which had burned down to a flaccid nub. "I don't want to die alone. . . ."

He scribbled in a notebook. "Aha. We all die alone. You're afraid of death, are you?"

"Stop scribbling!" I threw his pencil off the roof. "This is our *lives* I'm talking about."

"That's right. *This is our lives.*"

Brian put away his notepad. "Rob, the truth is I'm liquidating my 401(k) as we speak, selling my suits, my car, and even my pornography collection. I'm dumping it all because it's time for us to blow."

"Blow?"

"We're only on this earth for a microsecond. If we don't leave now, *they've already got us.*"

"I could go to jail. I'm in a legal quandary! I'm trying to grow up and be responsible, and you're trying to infect me with your madness all over again."

Brian sighed. "That's just the stress talkin', man. Don't make me resort to extreme measures. I'm giving you a way to escape your 'legal quandary' and this shallow existence we've built for ourselves. You should thank me."

"Look. I love you like a brother, but I love this country, too. And we're both wasted and I could go to jail and I haven't heard from you in weeks. It's possible you need psychiatric help."

Brian blew out the candle. "You already knew *that*. Look, if you're not down to evolve with me, then *say goodbye to your little friend*. I'm cashing in my chips. I may never come back."

"Just . . . wait. Let me puke, and make some arrangements."

Brian put his foot down. "No! Stop purging my lessons! We book our trip now, or never! We have one month to liquidate everything, then we take LA, then *the world*."

"LA?" The world was spinning.

"We leave out of LAX, my friend. If we delay any longer, the machine will eat us alive. We'll both get locked down with mortgages, taxes, car payments, insurance, wives, kids, child support, alimony . . . One of us will be dead or in jail by age forty, trust me. Our departure date is January 7th. You've got exactly one month to get your shit together."

I came to my senses. "Aw man. I need to call Elena! I missed our date night!"

I grabbed for Brian's cell phone, but he yanked it away. "Not in your condition." He dialed Elena's number (my house number), then held the phone to my ear.

I got our answering machine. I mustered a steaming pile of bullshit. "Hi sweetheart . . . I'm alive . . . you won't believe." Brian made some fake static noises into the phone. "I'll explain later . . . you're breaking up . . . I got robbed, food poisoned! Brian's having a psychotic break-down! I'm driving through the canyon. I love—!"

Brian hung up on her. We looked at each other.

"I'm a bad boyfriend."

"Yes, you are," Brian said.

Somehow Brian drove us back to my condo even though we were both completely wasted. We rolled in stealth with the lights off, and parked out in front so we didn't make a total spectacle of ourselves.

Samba music was coming from somewhere inside the condo. This was not normal for a Sunday night.

We stumbled in the front door. The music was blasting. It was con-spicuously dark. Brian raided the fridge. I flipped on the kitchen lights. There was no food on the stove.

Something was off.

I left Brian in the kitchen and went to find Elena. I followed the samba music to our bedroom. I stood there swaying outside the closed door for a minute, then I heard the most awful sound any man can possibly hear.

My girlfriend having sex—with someone else.

I shook the doorknob; it was locked. I didn't bother knocking.

Full of boozy rage, I kicked in the door with all the pent-up anger I had welling inside me from the goddamned audit. It was easier than I imagined; what was not so easy was processing what I saw. My loyal girlfriend was riding some jackoff like it was the Kentucky Derby.

Rage. Sickness. Flames on the side of my face. I wanted to puke, but I didn't. Then I did. All over the carpet while they kept screwing. They didn't even really slow down.

I slammed the door, then broke some shit and stormed outside.

Brian was already sitting behind the wheel eating a cold chicken leg and drinking a can of beer by the time I got to the car.

"Did we just see that??"

I was apoplectic. "She's having an affair?!"

"Told you. You got nothing left here. Your life is a lie. Just like mine."

"I'm gonna kill her!"

"Noooo, you're not. You're already going to tax jail. We don't need any electric chair–type scenarios tonight. Here, have some chicken." He handed me a half-eaten piece of chicken.

"I have a shotgun!"

"No. You have a pellet gun."

I went for the door, but Brian was too fast. He hit the locks and buckled me in with the seatbelt. He tried starting the car. Nothing happened.

He looked at me. "More bad news: you're out of gas."

"I've got bullets!" I jumped out to go commit a double homicide. Brian chased me down and pushed me away from the front door. I ran around to my backyard screaming like a maniac.

The neighbor's lights came on the moment I jumped the back fence. Brian followed me eating his chicken leg; he spotted my two mountain bikes. "C'mon let's go for a ride and cool off!"

Elena's samba music came back on quietly inside the condo. I lost it. "They're still screwing in there!? On my bed! In my condo! Using *my condoms*!!"

"Come on. Let's go before the cops come."

The scene faded to black.

When I came to, Brian and I were pedaling our drunk asses to a nearby park. I was beyond dazed and confused. I heard myself repeating, "I don't know how to deal with this!"

Brian just laughed. "Well, obviously she is a whore."

We pedaled into the park and dropped our bikes on the dirt. Brian cracked open a fresh bottle of rum from his backpack. I threw my bike against a tree. "This is *not* happening. My life is perfect, my girlfriend is perfect. I am perfect!"

"Trust me, there's room for improvement."

I tripped over a tree root and fell down in a cursing heap. I stayed down, silent for a moment. "I know what you're gonna say. 'Just say screw it, Binkley...'"? Don't let this setback bring you down.' Why is life tormenting me?? What did I ever do? Why can't we all just live like the Beat Generation? All I ever wanted was the freedom to live like Hunter S. Thompson—but they won't let me here! There are too many back-stabbing vipers screwing with my head!"

"You've hit on something there."

"I did?" I was out of breath.

"We gotta hit the road to find our true freedom. Just like the Beats, man."

I perked up. "Yeah, yeah, yeah. We could take a year just like we planned and backpack around the world. Backpacking is the new hitch-hiking, right? We could find our souls on the road . . . Self-discovery is freedom—no ties, no guilt. All experience is good experience. Grace before God!"

Brian laughed. "Screw God, man. I just wanna test the limits of everything. I've been driving the speed limit for too long. Our lives are in flames—so what? We fucked up! Let's pour gasoline on our open wounds. What do we have to lose?!"

"*Yeah*! 'The Man, wants us to pay their fines? Play their games? Punch their clocks!?"

Brian yelled, "Yeah! *Eff* clocks!"

We heard the sirens of the Palo Alto Police Department. We shielded our eyes from their lights as they pulled into the parking lot and drove our way. Like good little boys, we got up and fled on our bicycles, but I don't know why—we weren't criminals, dammit.

At least not convicted ones.

The cops just watched us go. One of them yelled over their PA system: "We don't want you here!"

As we raced away, Brian shouted, "'The Pigs' are right. They don't want us here! Let's go! The world's gone bad—let's go mad!" I pedaled like a drunken wino on a stolen bike. "No conformity, Dean Moriarty!!"

The next day I awoke on my front lawn to sprinklers going off around me. I was still locked out of my condo. I'd left my keys inside. The goddamned samba music was *still* playing inside. Brian was sleeping in his rental car.

The hellish sound of Brian's cell phone rang in my head. After the fourth ring, I realized it was actually his phone ringing right by my ear. I picked it up. *"What?! Is this you!?"*

"Um, hello?" It wasn't Elena; it was my lawyer. He told me I had called him at four o'clock in the morning and left an unintelligible message on his voicemail. The only thing he could make out was this number.

"Look, Rob, I just talked to the prosecutors. They'll let you off with a slap on the wrist if you sell all your coffee houses and pay the back taxes in installments. They have bigger fish to fry than you." I told him I'd think about it, then hung up.

I lay there trying to convince myself that my life wasn't in shambles, and that a plea deal was the best option. Brian was now awake and siphoning gas from Elena's car, which was parked in the driveway.

"I need to go sign some papers."

Brian took the gas can and calmly filled his tank. He just smiled. "You're right, man. The world tour was just a pipe dream. You aren't ready to be free. I get it. They've already got you . . . I'll drive you to your lawyer's office."

"Don't judge me. I don't need any of your crap right now."

"No. I feel your pain. Just get in. We got plenty of gas now."

Brian drove us off in silence, eating from a pack of chocolate mini-donuts. He didn't offer me one.

When we wheeled up to my car, Brian finally fessed up. The lying bastard had already bought the tickets. He pulled them out of his back-pack and gave me mine.

"You have to go *now*, Binkley. You can't leave me hanging."

"Okay, okay. Just give me a month to sort out my life."

"Promise??"

I got out of the car. "I promise!" Then I slammed the door in his face.

I never took the plea deal. Instead, I spent the rest of December avoiding my lawyer while quietly liquidating my life. I hocked it all: my cars, my condo, all my earthly possessions. I even gave up my two cafés. But I didn't tell my lawyer or the state of California . . . not yet. I stockpiled cash in a secret Cayman Islands account that I'd created when I opened the cafés.

Brian called me every day to make sure I didn't cancel. He said he was kidnapping me, and if I didn't come he would kill me. But truth be told, I wanted to burn my reality to the ground. I couldn't turn over what was left of my life savings to a corrupt American judicial system. I had nothing to keep me here anymore.

I was dumping it all to be his willing captive again. Brian had been pulling these forced adventures on me since high school, these sneak attacks on the status quo.

I had no idea what was coming next. All I knew was I never wanted to see Elena or Palo Alto again.

By December 31st, Brian and I were drinking heavily on a morning plane to LA. Things were going as planned. We were on our way to our flight of destiny on January 7th. But first, we embarked on some pre-liminary debauchery.

Brian was already recruiting more members of his cult of personality. This one was a tall, redheaded stewardess. "We're running men, Kiki. Running from the law . . . They're watching us now. You're not gonna turn us in, are you?"

Kiki backed away slowly.

I'd been listening to Brian's pseudo-shamanistic insanity all morning, and it was making me crazy. What was left of my rational mind wanted to call off the trip and try to get back with Elena.

Brian just laughed. "That boat sailed a month ago, man."

Then he turned to me and replied to my inner monologue like some telepathic mutant, his lips never seeming to move. "We'll all be dead soon, Binkley. Time to take the ride."

He could still read my mind, and I hated him for it.

I tuned him out and prayed I wasn't making a terrible mistake.

I opened my eyes to a swirl of nauseous sunshine. Our breakfast of champions of six Crown and Cokes had me feeling less than chipper. Maybe it was just nerves, knowing I was slowly becoming a fugitive from justice.

Brian could sense I was a reluctant hostage, so he demanded I let him push me through LAX in a wheelchair to make sure I didn't flee. He kept pushing me faster and faster until we were running through the airport. "Say hello to the City of Angels, Binkley! We got no time to waste. My LA people won't pick us up cause I'm with your lame ass, so I'm looking into alternate vehicles! My license was suspended last week so renting a car is *out,* unless you wanna risk it. It's New Year's Eve, so designated drivers will be scarce!"

We were five minutes into the trip and I was already terrified by his manic energy. "I'm in no condition to drive!"

He sped up. "Me either! I'll find us wheels!"

We raced out of the terminal into the toxic LA sunshine. The goal was to rampage through Hollywood on our way to attending the Rose Bowl—but we never got to Pasadena. He waved down a taxi, and we set out to see LA in a week before our international flight departed to who-knows-where.

Did I really want to go on a yearlong trip with this lunatic? Even though I had liquidated my life, I was leaving my options open. I still might go back and face the music—or defect in the night to Canada or Mexico where I wouldn't have Brian's insanity shackled to my hip. I still wasn't sure.

We took a cab straight to a dive bar in Old Hollywood like two disheveled alcoholic drifters. It was eleven o'clock in the morning. I ordered pancakes and coffee. Brian ordered Irish coffee and stole bites off my plate. The joint was deserted and smelled like stale beer. I wanted to find a hotel but Brian refused. "Not yet! If you wanna sober up, drink coffee. If you wanna get clean, *wash your balls in the sink*."

He pointed to the bathroom.

I stared at his stupid, smirking face. I wanted to slap him silly. I knew I should go home, I really did, and leave this delusional man-child in that dive bar in Hollywood. I went along with the idea of fleeing the country (mostly) to shut him up, but he never did. *He never shut up*. I also had a sneaking suspicion that if I left him high and dry I may never see Brian again. I could tell by the ever-present look of inspired lunacy in his eye that he was on a collision course with death, incarceration, or worse.

Brian started shooting pool badly. He tore the table felt and almost got us kicked out for launching cue balls into the air like Minnesota Fats's epileptic grandson. We spent the afternoon drinking Irish coffees while he laid out his "Around-the-World Bailout Plan" and all "relevant motives" to anyone who cared to listen.

No one else cared but me.

Occasionally I burst his bubble just to wind him up. "Don't you think if we *really* wanted to change the world and grow as people, we should be more productive members of society? Build houses with Habitat for Humanity, or run for Congress, or join the Peace Corps or something?"

"All corrupt organizations. To put it in the parlance of our idiotic times, here in the soulless void, we have no affiliation to God or country; we're living in the age of narcissism, soaking up bullshit from

Hollywood and Madison Avenue and spitting them out like original thoughts. We're slaves, man—conditioned little drones."

"So we're *both* little drone slaves?"

"I suggest you start drinking heavily and stop thinking so much."

After a day of boozy brainwashing, in my twisted-up mind he was starting to make some kind of sick sense again—*way* too much sense. Brian's a master salesman when sober, but he's even more convincing when drunk. He knew how to push my buttons, and he kept pressing mine until I gave up completely. And deep down I knew he was right. I had nothing to go home to now but humiliation and heartache.

My soul needed an enema.

That night, after we took baths in a bar sink, I checked my messages. I had three urgent ones from my lawyer, who was not privy to the fact I skipped town. He kept repeating my "time was running out."

I hung up and turned to Brian, who was pouring way too much rum into a Coke can. "Attention to things isn't fun, is it, Binkley?"

"Not in my current state."

Brian wanted to go to more bars. "I know you're having a crisis, but so am I. Answer all the vultures closing in around you with a smile and a hearty 'screw you' . . . Just have fun with it."

"Just have fun with what? Running from failure?"

"Look at it this way: You got what—at least another week before they issue a warrant for your arrest—right?"

"This isn't a criminal case—yet. I'm just evading back taxes. Temporarily."

"So we've got plenty of time to make our escape."

I will forever remember the New Year's Eve I spent in Los Angeles as the night I finally decided to stop being angry and "just have fun with it." It was New Year's Eve after all. What else did I have to do?

Something inside me told me to show love for everyone I met, so I did. I was on some sideways mission to break down my carefully constructed American ego and be like Thompson and Kerouac—completely carefree.

But it wasn't going to be easy. I had no idea who I really was once I peeled all the surface layers away.

I was determined to find out.

I didn't want to rely on alcohol and sex with strangers to make me feel like a free man, but I went on a bender anyway to keep my mind open and body nimble.

We roamed the Sunset Strip looking for trouble. Brian hooted at all the girls in short skirts. We drank rum from a Coke can to lube ourselves up to all possibilities.

Brian draped his arm over my shoulder. "Binkley, this gift I've given you is my way of proving we can handle a year with no structure! Can we navigate New Year's Eve on the Sunset Strip going *Mach 3 with our hair on fire??*"

I smiled. "Let's drive *fast!*"

All night, Brian kept saying this was a primer for the road, but I knew we were numbing out so we didn't have to think. I was happy to play along. I had to forget Elena and my downward spiral of life. So for one night it was the Summer of Love in my own mind.

Under the influence of the Caribbean moonshine Brian brought with him from Palo Alto, I let go of all my hang-ups. It was the first time I'd let my guard down and opened up to the world since I don't know—never? I showed love for all living creatures: men, women, dogs, cats—even some trees.

We went bar hopping and rang in the New Year I don't know where. I have no idea who I kissed at midnight, but her lips were wet and willing. All I know is we heard Prince's song "1999" about fifty times in a row.

After the bars closed, we meandered through the abandoned LA streets befriending everyone we met, including a group of transient hippie chicks that were in town from an ashram in Antelope Valley. They thought we were wandering hippies, too, since we were wearing backpacks and two-day-old beards. We became instant friends.

At three o'clock in the morning, we finally splurged on an actual room at the Safari Motel Inn on Sunset Boulevard, which cost forty-five dollars a night. We brought every freak we could find back to the room and had a party till dawn.

Brian had no female filter left by four in the morning. At one point, I looked at him surrounded by who-knows-what on this gyrating yellow floatie. All I could see was a mass of cavorting flesh in the middle of the pool. Brian saw me and yelled, "*How's the peeping?* Every woman deserves some love!"

I shook my head. "Why do you have to be the one who gives it to them??"

"Stop thinking and take your clothes off, grab a beer, and get your ass over here. All you girls, meet your new leader. Join the cult of Rob!"

The girls cheered when I jumped in the pool.

When the sun came up, all my worries had melted away. Brian and I were floating on stolen rafts with the ashram girls, who were telling us how they'd recently contracted the same eating disorder from a celebrity guru. Words had ceased to have meaning.

Who knew what was true anymore. We were all lying to each other.

Needless to say the rest of it got weird. We busted out a new "cock candle" in the room, and someone woke up wearing a zebra-striped thong. And it wasn't me. (Probably. I can't remember.)

After spending a day in bed, Hunter S. Thompson–style, we kept the room for one more night and ventured out for another sophisticated evening on the town.

We looked like a couple of homeless miscreants. I was glad I had packed a few articles of decent clothing but it was clear to anyone who looked too closely that Brian and I were two dudes in desperate need of tetanus shots.

Not a lot of people go out in Los Angeles on New Year's Day Night, but we did, and somehow came across a party that seemed to have never ended from the night before. We found ourselves out in front of the Bar Marmont on Sunset, trying to get into more trouble and forget all the randomness of the night before.

We'd come down to meet my old friend Johnny, who was this lunatic ex-Mormon I knew as a kid. He was supposed to meet us the night before, but got lost at a house party in Toluca Lake. I barely recognized the guy. It had been years since I'd seen him last. Johnny had morphed into some LA performance artist. He had a giant red beard and wore sunglasses at night. He gave me a bear hug the second he saw me, and proudly proclaimed that he was the "Pied Piper of the Sunset Strip—a great goddamn LA guide" and to follow him.

Johnny showed off his skills immediately by putting the "Jedi mind trick" on the doorman at the Bar Marmont. Somehow we walked in without having to pay the insanely expensive two hundred dollar cover for the private party going on.

On the way in I asked, "Do the girls have solid gold vaginas in here?"

"Something like that," Johnny laughed.

Inside, the place smelled of high-caliber sex. Soft lights and shimmering bottles of exotic elixirs lit up the main bar; butterflies were all over the place, as were women—lots of them. It was surreal.

The gyrating hips of a brunette wearing a short skirt and a white scarf caught my eye. She was dancing by herself with a "come hither" look. I leaned into Brian: "The best thing about Los Angeles is girls on the prowl who make themselves so obviously available. They're impossible to miss." We watched "Scarf Girl" flirt with the room like she was auditioning for an invisible camera.

We moved in. Brian brazenly fondled her scarf. "Hermès?" She said nothing. "Did I see you at Starbucks this morning drinking a Mocha Frap?"

She stopped dancing. "Are you for real?"

Brian smiled. "I think so . . . wanna pinch me to see?" Scarf Girl walked away. Her words said "Piss off," but she had those permanent "F-me" eyes; it was very confusing to the average man.

I walked over to Johnny, who said, "These girls only come out at night. During the day, they won't even talk to you."

I had to pee.

In the men's room, I heard giggles coming from the closed stall. Some girls had sneaked into an empty stall to do drugs; I could hear them sniffing. Eventually one of them peeked over the closed stall. "Hey . . . we're making a coffee table book called *Hotties Pissing in Dirty Stalls.*"

"Cool."

They asked if they could "take a dick pic for the book." "Go ahead," I said and—*Snap! Snap!*—my flaccid junk was immortalized. I signed no release form. They asked if I had any coke, but were sorely disappointed when I said no. I had a solution.

I led the girls back to our table and told Brian to hook them up with some shots from his private reserve of 120-proof moonshine he had in a flask. Brian obliged.

"What is this?" they asked.

"Don't worry . . . it's good." They knocked back their shots, then coughed like a thirsty pair of Merchant Marines on shore leave.

It didn't take long for the party to start bumping after that. I waded through a maze of dancing girls and got Johnny's attention. "Man, these women are really into us. It's like a room full of sexual predators . . . *in a good way.*"

Johnny roared. "That's cause they're all *hookers, strippers, and porn stars* who've been up for two days! This is a Vivid afterparty!"

I looked around at all the silicon in the room. No *wonder.*

Johnny led me over to his VIP table and whispered in my ear: "I told these girls you're an adult film producer." He pointed at his menagerie. "See these beautiful women? You can have any of 'em you want." He pointed under their miniskirts; all of them opened up for a peek.

Being a good boy from Palo Alto, I was stunned. All I could say was, "Hold that thought," before I fled. I found Brian, who was surrounded at a different table. For some reason they thought he was a porn producer, too. He was on another one of his verbal rolls.

"I advise all you beautiful ladies to escape from complacency now, flee this land of fake plastic trees or watch Rome burn from your box seat at the Hollywood Bowl!" Brian crunched ice. "You're welcome to join us. We're off to see the world before it's too late and we're all hanging from the end of a rope, with no music."

One girl said, "You sure are a wordy asshole."

Brian sighed, "Nobody gets me." Then he leaned back and grabbed the Scarf Chick walking by. "Kiss me. For luck." Brian stuck his tongue down her throat. The Scarf Girl let him kiss her, then kept on strutting and chewing gum like it never happened.

Brian elbowed me. "Told you she liked me."

"They're hookers!"

"Everyone's a prostitute in this town, Binkley." Brian didn't get it, so I let him live the dream. A few hours later, a few strippers offered to treat Brian to a lap dance if he gave them another swig from his private reserve. Brian gave Scarf Chick first dibs since she kept doing drive-bys.

This time, she took a big swig from his flask then kept on walking. Ten seconds later, we heard her fall into a table.

Rational thought had escaped into the funhouse. . . .

The night was getting blurry. The next thing I remember, the girls were dancing in front of us like the Vegas entertainers they most certainly were. We admired their moves. "I don't know how they can dance. I can't even chew gum!"

Johnny deadpanned, "LA is one helluva drug."

When the girls finally figured out we weren't porn producers or anyone related to the Adult Video industry, they danced off into the crowd. "Gone!" Brian just laughed, "More lost souls dance into the night." We went looking for another spot.

We walked up the hill to the famed Chateau Marmont Hotel at one o'clock in the morning. Johnny pretended to be a guest, then used his mind control powers to get us all in.

He informed me, "This is where Belushi died doing speedballs with Robin Williams. Never do speedballs with a man named Mork!" Brian had no idea what he was talking about.

Johnny led us to a tiny bar hidden in a corner under some stairs and ordered expensive scotch from an old bartender named Elroy, who impressed the Pied Piper of the Sunset Strip by dishing on all the old Hollywood lore.

Elroy said, "Ava Gardner used to give blow jobs in this very speakeasy."

Brian chimed in: "Wow. Is she here tonight?" Johnny gave Brian the death stare. Elroy moved on to more enlightened patrons. Johnny called

Brian an idiot for not knowing his 1940s Hollywood starlets. Brian shot back, "I pride myself on things I suck at!"

In the hotel, we were suddenly mixing with women of a much higher social register than the hippies, hookers, and porn stars we'd been associating with for the past forty-eight hours. Brian leaned into me, now in full Messiah mode. "Look around, Rob. Most people today are miserable. They have very little hope. The grand dream of Western Civilization has failed. It's time we pulled out of this tailspin."

I told him everyone at this private playground didn't seem miserable; they were "stoned immaculate."

"This is not reality," Brian said. And he was right.

Then I met Brooke. Having known her for twenty minutes, she became my new BFF. An aspiring actress from an unnamed "flyover state," she said she loved me but had somewhere to go.

"No, you don't."

"But I have an early call."

"Who doesn't?" I begged her to stay. She smiled; she was a sweet doll. I leaned in to give her a kiss.

Then Brian put a flame to our revelry.

In a burst of apocalyptic idiocy, he decided to rip off the "choker" he'd been wearing all night (a tie with a T-shirt—his idea of class) and hold it over a burning votive candle. I tried to stop him, but he was too busy giving another one of his goddamned speeches, waving his flaming tie in the air.

"I've had it with you scenesters! You're all a bunch of slaves! Our civilization is six billion people trying to find happiness by standing on each other's shoulders and kicking each other's teeth in! This whole scene is a perversion! Sexy ladies join *me* while you still have souls to save!"

The room took it in stride. A few drunken beards clapped, two girls in fluorescent tubetops booed, a frat boy belched as rebuttal.

Elroy the barkeep called hotel security. "You idiots are *outta* here!"

Brian bolted for the door. I grabbed Brooke and we split through the back exit, sprinting past the pool and the parking valets. Brian was way ahead of us.

We fled into the night to the soundtrack of a distant police siren. It's unclear what frame of mind I was operating under at this point, but something propelled me to rock on with this mentally unstable drunken degenerate who was still waving his burning tie in the air.

It must have been the moonshine.

We slowed down heading west on Sunset just as we neared The Comedy Store. I was yelling at Brian when we ran into Johnny taking a piss on the front wheel of a parked yellow "Lambo" he said was Pauly Shore's. Johnny had left the Chateau before Brian went nuts, so we told him all about the incident. If he thought Brian was a crazed nutcase before, this removed all doubt. He was not amused.

Brian changed the subject to tell Johnny about our impending gonzo world adventure. Johnny kept saying, "Go man, *go*! You can do anything you want. Go smoke opium in 'The Triangle!'" Johnny just wanted Brian to leave town.

By this time the bars were closed, so Johnny left and Brian hailed us a cab. We paid the cabbie to take us back to the Safari Inn. I convinced Brooke to come back to the motel with us. When she saw we only had one bed (to save on costs), she asked if we were gay. I told her, "Yes, bi-curious?" So we all hopped into bed together. Brian hated when I pretended to be sexually ambiguous, but he was too drunk to care at this point.

Once Brian started snoring, Brooke convinced me to go back to her place on the beach, where we spent the next two nights together. Actresses . . . gotta love 'em.

Brooke had to go to work eventually, so we said our goodbyes and I met back up with Brian in Hollywood. We finally peeled ourselves away from all the random hippies, actresses, and freaks with whom we'd been partying to head down to Manhattan Beach to see how the other half lived.

First we stopped by the FedEx store on La Cienega Boulevard to pick up the documents my assistant Jody had mailed me five days prior to finalize the sale of my cafés. When we walked out of the store, two of Brian's old fraternity pals from Arizona State University came tearing into the parking lot to pick us up, screaming at the top of their lungs.

We piled into their Toyota 4Runner and hauled ass down the 405 to Manhattan Beach ("hauling ass" in that we were in bumper-to-bumper traffic going 7 mph the entire time). It took three hours to go forty miles, which gave me a lot of time to think.

Spending time with these crazy ex-frat boys was the tipping point to me deciding to get the hell away from America for a year. It was clear that, after a week of mindless debauchery, Brian wanted to go completely crazy and be freer than he'd ever been. Now I finally saw what he was running from: normalcy. These guys.

Watching him with his old pals made me realize how little he had seen outside of America, and how very different we were as people. Brian looked normal but he wasn't. I looked weird and I was. I had long hair and wore T-shirts and flip-flops to work, while Brian wore a suit and cell phone as his uniform until two weeks ago.

Brian was a social chameleon who changed colors depending on the crowd, while I was a bit of a maverick. I didn't need to be part of groups unless it was convenient. It's true I had a certain level of contempt for the organized friendship thing—maybe because I went to San Jose State (a commuter school) and lived at home. I already had all my friends and didn't need any more.

In contrast, at the many universities Brian got kicked out of, he always belonged to the supposedly cool fraternity. The word around the 4Runner was that he was a legendary Phi Delta Theta. It occurred to me during our drive that I never experienced Brian's "legendary" fratboy days. I never visited him during those years because I was either out of the country or working on my espresso bars.

All these thoughts ran through my head while I watched Brian hoot and holler and change his stripes before my eyes in that 4Runner cruising down to Manhattan Beach.

The second we arrived at the ASU Phi Delta reunion party at some brother's beach house, the stories of Brian's past delinquency started coming. And coming. Some highlights:

- Pledge Brian was found passed out in the Jewish fraternity, pants steaming with piss. He was delivered back to the Phi Delta house, complete with the couch he was still passed out on and wearing his pledge pin.

- Pledge Brian got caught licking college girls' asses in bars for sport. He set the Arizona State record of forty-seven straight before he went to jail.
- Pledge Brian got busted for driving a moped through the Pi Beta Phi sorority house with two guys on the back. He got a DUI.
- Brian was eventually expelled from ASU for barfing on the dean at a sophomore Tri Delta mixer and had to move back to California and find another school to pillage.

It went on and on.

This is the same guy who'd been espousing metaphysical wisdom like some combination of Allen Ginsberg and Alan Watts for the past week??

On Manhattan Beach, Brian fell back into his college "Belushi" persona. I watched him hold court amid his old herd. His altruistic revolutionary spirit had vanished into thin air. It was fairly disturbing to see his transformation.

What I saw while partying with these investment bankers, stock traders, and corporate "brosephs" repulsed me. I was searching for truth, and all I saw was nothing but twisted Americana.

These guys were the embodiment of everything I hated about this country. It wasn't their entitled conspicuous consumption that pissed me off; I can obviously deal with that. Brian and I liked hot chicks, booze, and a good party as much as the next guy.

And it wasn't their yuppie attitudes that bothered me. We were all children of the eighties, and like all these Todds and Chads we wanted to make a lot of money and overindulge at every opportunity. That wasn't the problem here.

The problem was there wasn't a glimmer of heart or soul or curiosity or compassion in any of them. They were all alpha male aliens from a different planet; they were apes from Planet Frat. Planet Fart. Planet Winner. Where winning meant nothing other than trampling over anything that's standing in their way in a four-wheel drive with monster truck tires.

After a few hours with these guys it was clear, when compared to every criminal locked in prison, the "winners of the world" were committing far more obscene crimes against humanity and getting away with it.

The Hollywood rejects we partied with last week seemed like saints in comparison. They were the Beats I was looking for—the original people, not always the most hygienic and most certainly delusional—but at least they were genuine and on a path with something resembling a heart.

If this was "winning," I didn't want any part of it. I wanted way more than normalcy out of life, much more than just the textbook American Dream. I wanted to be "real" and measure my success by my own yardstick, nobody else's—especially not Uncle Sam's.

Brian was now screaming over the ska music: "I got four black eyes that night and they were all worth it!"

The Phi Deltas gave us hell for not making it to the Rose Bowl like we were supposed to on New Year's Day. They mocked us for wasting New Year's Eve, "partying with the West Hollywood freaks." "You both probably got AIDS! You did! I can see it on your dicks!"

These are direct quotes.

I pretended to laugh then quietly escaped inside to make a call to the outside world. I rang Johnny and begged him to come get me the hell outta there. I wanted to go home.

When the party died down, I told Brian I wanted to leave. The bros fell silent. They could see there was a black sheep among the herd trying to sneak off with one of their own. My painted toenails (which the commune girls gave me back at the Safari Inn) gave me away.

"You leavin' with the hippie!? Screw that, bro. You gone gay on us, Rakow?" The bros roared, then took more shots of Jim Beam. I wanted to escape in a hot air balloon and fly back to Palo Alto.

Johnny finally showed up three hours later in his 1979 purple El Camino. When he laid on his horn, it played "La Cucaracha." I grabbed Brian and said, "If you want to stay, stay. But I gotta find a new scene."

"Rob, wait."

"Maybe this whole world trip wasn't such a good idea. I get it. *You're* not ready. . . . Just exchange those tickets for vouchers and I'll see you back in Palo Alto."

Brian dropped the frat boy act and I saw the real him again. He grabbed a bottle of tequila and stuffed it in his pack. "C'mon."

The freak was back.

We casually angled for the door. While I pretended to laugh about something, Brian whispered, "That was all bullshit dude, a pure Darwinist act of survival. They aren't ready to hear about my *satoris*—'pearls to swine' man. I don't want any part of this American shitshow."

Johnny wasn't exactly thrilled to see Brian jump in the back of his El Camino, but he didn't say anything—he just tore rubber.

We hauled back up the 405 to Venice to mingle with the "other side."

"The irony is we look like frat boys to these Venice Beach misfits," I said as we sat down at a rooftop hotel bar that looked more like a glorified youth hostel.

"But we don't have buttoned-up hearts, man. These cats see that, right?"

"Um . . ."

The place turned into a dance party after sundown. By this time, Brian and Johnny had buried the hatchet and were entertaining themselves by shoving red ashtrays up the asses of all the animal topiaries stationed around the party like they were red buttholes.

"Real mature!" I yelled. Brian stopped and grabbed me. "Thanks for making us leave that douchebag festival!" We jumped up and down like we won the Rose Bowl. We were two grown children gleefully burning our past to the ground.

Venice shut down early that night, and Johnny had no intention of driving us back across town to our favorite motel (the Safari Inn), so he dropped us by the Beverly Hills Hotel to find some chick named Twila who lived in Benedict Canyon.

"See you boys on the other side! Don't bang any trannies over there!" he said.

By this time, Brian and I were fully smashed (again) so we decided to try to hitch and save some money. We walked east up Sunset when Brian threw someone's garbage can at me, then ran off like a kid. He was so ripped he left his pack on the ground. I grabbed it and chased him down. He hid in the bushes, then leapt out at me like some wasted jungle cat.

"You are absurdly high!" I screamed.

"Just think, Binkley. Tomorrow we'll be walking through a jungle! Life is amazing!" He was bingeing on the possibility of youth . . . and it was starting to piss me off.

I corralled Brian and got him to walk back to the Beverly Hills Hotel, where we jumped in line on somebody's cab and took off for the Safari Inn. After a few minutes in the cab, Brian hopped out at a stoplight to pee. The cabbie started cursing; I begged him to wait. The cabbie thought I was insane when I went into some bushes looking for Brian.

He had suddenly vanished up a tree, down a hole, in a gutter. Was this the end of our rampage? If I could lose him in LA, what horrors would befall us in a foreign romp?

Returning to the cab alone, I saw the cabbie had left our drunk asses. Thankfully he had thrown our backpacks out of the car after he ransacked them looking for something of value. I picked them up and started walking east alone. I tried calling Brian, but got his voicemail.

I don't know how long I walked (cursing him to hell), but I eventually got a call from Johnny to come and get Brian, who was now magically with him and Twila at a gay karaoke bar in Beverly Hills.

"Rob! Come get your boy. *He's running amok in Liberace's Slipper!* He's flirting with disaster, man. Get here—this is *serious!*" Johnny gave me the address and hung up.

A gay karaoke bar in Beverly Hills?? How the hell did Brian run back into Johnny so fast? I was almost to West Hollywood; we must have been walking in opposite directions.

Needing a lift, serendipity struck. Out of the corner of my eye, I saw the same cabbie coming up behind me that had abandoned us a few minutes earlier. I flagged him down and acted like it was a life-or-death emergency. The driver cursed me in Farsi but I threw him fifty bucks and he took me in.

A few minutes later we arrived at a karaoke bar called Liberace's Slipper. I immediately saw Johnny running out of the bar with a girl I presumed was Twila. All he said was, "He's your responsibility now!"

I went inside just in time to see Brian get thrown down a flight of stairs. "That didn't hurt!" Brian did a stunt roll to the bottom and skidded to my feet, laughing.

"That hurt."

Two Korean bouncers followed him down the stairs. "You had enough?" I jumped into the fray before they kicked Brian's teeth in. "What's going on here? This is my client. He's a celebrity!"

The bouncers explained they warned "my friend" to lay off the boss's lady (who was a transsexual), but he'd been "cruisin' for a bruisin' all night."

Brian, still laid out at my feet, laughed, "All night?? I just got here!"

I asked the bouncers to back off and explained that Brian is off his medication and his lawyer will call them the next morning with a solution to this "huge mistake." They threw us both out the back door, "Stay outta the Slipper, you piece of shit!"

It was a foreboding start to our magical journey. After a week of complete LA insanity, I still didn't know if Brian was some kind of modern-day prophet or an escaped lunatic on a mission to drag me to hell with him.

Maybe we were both losing our minds.

We called a cab to take us to the airport. Our plane was supposedly leaving in a few hours. By this time I was having serious second (and third and fourth) thoughts about putting my life into the hands of this loose cannon, so I told the cabbie to just keep driving down Santa Monica Boulevard, all the way to the beach. I needed a moment to reassess my future.

I gave the cabbie money to keep the meter running. "Just wait for us, we'll only be a few minutes." We made our way down to the water. Was I going to catch this plane or not? It was decision time.

Brian had sobered up and regained some of his composure. "That beating jarred loose some bad memories, man."

"To be perfectly honest, you don't look or sound mentally prepared for this trip. Maybe we should just call this whole thing off?? My concern is you could easily get us killed over there—wherever 'over there' is."

"Why so negative? I'm the one who just got my ass kicked!"

"*Where are we even going?*"

"That's the fun of it; we'll decide at the airport. We can go anywhere!"

"So, there's no plane in two hours?"

"There *could be*. Our tickets become valid in two hours. Why waste time? We only have a year to fly. C'mon, don't get cold feet on me *now*."

"Just, let me think. . . . You're nuts, you know that?"

"I've been told."

We sat in silence on the beach and listened to the ocean. The sun was coming up. Brian began frowning at his cell phone while mine kept buzzing; my battery was on life support. After a long silence, he came back to life. "You know, wherever we're going, we don't need these slave machines. They must be silenced."

He snatched my cell phone and threw it into the ocean. I watched in horror as it skipped over the water and sank to the bottom of the Pacific. "*Noo!* I never got insurance!" Brian kissed his giant cell phone then launched it into the ocean, too. As he watched his phone sink, he gave it a final salute.

"That's that. . . ."

Believe it or not, this is the moment I finally had my *satori* about Brian—on the beach at dawn watching our cell phones sink to the bottom of the ocean. All my feelings of fear over this trip somehow morphed into an overwhelming sense of freedom. I said, "That was the most symbolic move I've witnessed by a human since the fall of the Berlin Wall."

Brian laughed. "You need to get out more."

I got up and motioned him toward the cab. "C'mon man. We got a plane to catch."

"You mean you're in?" He put his arm on my shoulder as we walked back to the parking lot. "You know, you're gonna miss your court date. There'll be a warrant."

I laughed. "Wouldn't have it any other way."

We hopped in the taxi and told the cabbie to drive us to LAX, and step on it.

While we drove down the 405 at dawn, my heart raced. I couldn't believe I was actually doing this. I started listing things we forgot to do.

"We forgot to call our moms, we forgot to call our friends, we forgot our immunization shots! We might catch malaria or gonorrhea—"

Brian looked at me. "Or *monkey herpes*."

We howled like two monkeys into the rising sun.

Five hours later, I awoke on a Singapore Airlines 757 with the worst hangover of my life.

Where am I? . . . Who am I? The world was spinning. *What just happened?* For the first time in 169 hours, my blood alcohol level dipped below toxic levels. Flashes of my epic truancy came rushing back in a sickening blur. I knew I just made a grave mistake.

When Brian's face came into focus, the only thought that raced through my mind was, *It's that guy's fault!* I lunged for his throat. "What have you done to my life?" I scared the old guy sitting in front of us. Brian fended me off.

"It's for your own good! Here . . . have a cookie. They're *fresh*."

My life was ruined. My best friend had systematically, over the course of a month, brainwashed then shanghaied me. I wanted to jump out of the airplane. Brian ate my cookie. "Save your rage. It's a long flight to Singapore. I suggest you order a drink."

There was no turning back. I ordered a drink.

I wouldn't speak to Brian again for another two hours. I plotted to kill him as soon as we got off the plane, and die in one of those Singapore prisons. It was a small price to pay. I downed a Crown and Coke and faded (back) to black, with an anvil on my head and a sickness in my heart.

I awoke from my epic slumber to a flight attendant checking to see if I was still breathing. It finally dawned on me we were seated in first class. Brian told me the world tickets gives you free upgrades when available.

In a daze, I stared slack-jawed at the full moon as it rose over the Pacific. I had a terrifying thought; I had just committed to marrying a lunatic for an entire year. It was going to be worse than marriage: During a typical marriage, everyone has to work or do something during the day, right? This trip was going to be much worse.

After four more Crown and Cokes, I rationalized blowing up my life on a whim. I looked at my kidnapper chatting up an old lady and realized that Brian shanghaiing me was his way of saying, "I love you so much I'll be with you twenty-four seven for the next year."

I was resigned to traveling with this maniac. I made up reasons we would travel well together:

1. We shared the most important traits of good backpackers—wanderlust.
2. Brian was an expert at corralling the beverage cart so it always sat next to us in the aisle while the rest of the plane slept.
3. I couldn't think of a third reason.

While the normal passengers slumbered we helped ourselves to booze off the cart, watched movies, and plotted our adventure. Drunk on an assortment of exotic beers (at three in the morning in some time zone), we became co-conspirators again. We agreed to immerse ourselves in the raw, unfiltered world, just like Thompson and Kerouac, and learn about ourselves while testing our conditioned beliefs on everything.

We celebrated unplugging from the American grid. Brian had finally won me over for good; I was all in, no longer worrying about anything but experience. Not our safety (although that would be a major problem along the way)—not anything.

Brian would eventually have me speaking in proverbs like him as I re-learned how to live in the moment, all the stuff I had denied after graduate school when we both sold our souls to "God money." I had no idea what was ahead but I knew it was going to get weird . . . very weird. So many things were going to get broken. We didn't care if we got mugged in Indonesia, desecrated in Australia, cuffed and stuffed in Thailand, or punched in the face by Buddhist monks in Tibet—I wanted to have a "personal renaissance." I needed it. We both did, before we became two more doomed assholes with a mortgage to pay.

And that was how this whole bizarre adventure began. The tales of debauchery and spiritual enlightenment to come are too fantastic not to tell. I thirsted for experience and Brian was my ticket to the promised land. In my madness I bought the ticket; I took the ride. I needed to live. I needed to suffer.

I had to go.

2

Wanderlust in Bali

STOCKHOLM SYNDROME IS REAL. I never believed it until it happened to me. After a twenty-hour flight over the Pacific, I was one with my deranged captor. I was never going home. Brian had blown enough LA sunshine (and moonshine) up my ass that I was no longer concerned with the facts, with tomorrow, or with reality.

All I cared about was the possibility of the *now*.

I was still in a dream state when we touched down in Singapore. I needed to get off the plane before I truly believed we weren't landing back at LAX after some crazy circuitous joy ride where Brian had paid the pilot to do aerial donuts all over the Pacific for a day just to screw with my head.

The first sign we weren't in Kansas anymore was when the captain spoke to us in three languages (Mandarin, Malay, and English). Brian informed me we had a short layover before flying to our first official stop: the island country of Indonesia.

"Where are we again?" I asked.

Brian pointed to the Singapore Air logo. "*Singapore* is our hub to all of the Orient."

"Don't say Orient."

"Why?"

"It's imperialist-speak."

"But it sounds so cool."

"Just trust me."

The only thing I knew about Singapore was that it's an extremely controlled, law-abiding society. Brian knew this too, so he was already dreaming about getting jailed in an exotic land. "Never been caned in a foreign country, have you?" Brian asked. "Might be a learning experience for you, Rob."

"How about we don't? Although, now that you mention it, I think I dreamt that the second we got off this plane I put your head on a spike and paraded you through Singapore while chewing gum."

"May want to wait till we get to Indonesia for that. The canings here are *intense*."

We lumbered our bones off the plane and onto *terra firma*. It felt good to be on the ground again. Brian rambled through the airport with his sleep mask dangling from his neck.

"How can I still be hungover?"

"It may take a week to detox," I said.

"We don't have time for that." Rather than checking ourselves into rehab during our layover, we decided to sneak in a few drinks with Eric, our medical student friend from Canada, who was in Singapore working on a sex study involving monkeys.

Eric's company was inventing some new Viagra—but you couldn't mention the word Viagra around him, or he got angry. He told us the poor monkeys didn't even get to co-mingle while they were shot up with the sex drug. "Cruel and unusual punishment," I said.

"All in the name of fornication!" Brian laughed.

Five hours later, we were lubed up and airborne again on our way to Bali, Indonesia. Brian zonked out immediately. Bored, I messed with him as he slept; I inched my stinky foot over and rubbed on his chin—perverse male bonding.

Brian didn't think it was funny. The flight attendant saw us "foot canoodling" and quietly asked if we were on our honeymoon. "We have champagne for newlyweds," she gestured to her cart. This would be the second of many occasions where we would be mistaken for a gay couple.

"Why, yes—yes we are. How kind of you to notice." I drank the split of champagne by myself while Brian snored. Afterward I slept, too, but not well. I dreamt I was following Elena's moans through some sun-drenched city street that had ever-present samba music in the air. Two sounds I'd rather not hear ever again.

I was jarred awake when we touched down in Denpasar, Bali. The jail-break was complete. The fugitives had arrived. Brian and I were on a faraway island in a faraway land with no extradition laws—a comforting perk I researched at an Internet café in the Singapore airport. It was to be our home for the next month.

We stepped onto the tarmac and into a blanket of intense heat. "Where should we go first?" I asked. "Whatever we do, I say we stay a while and relax."

Brian announced he was getting into Taoism. "I want to make a concerted effort to think less to open up more space for *nothingness*." This meant he was nursing a jet-lagged hangover so I was in charge of the planning.

During our flight over the Pacific, we made a drunken pact not to act like typical American tourists who frequented spots like Cancun to see how much they could drink in a week. Though it was in our California DNA to party like maniacs, we were on a mission to evolve into something more by learning about life and the real world outside of America.

To hell with tourists, we were to be *backpackers*—totally mobile travelers who immersed ourselves in foreign cultures and new bohemian adventures.

Of course, the second we stepped off the plane our grand plans went out the window, and we headed straight to Kuta Beach. (A total cop-out I know.) Kuta is not a travelers' paradise; it's more like the undisputed party capital of Indonesia, like a watered-down Waikiki. But young American men looking for a good time had to start somewhere, right??

Whatever we were trying to do, we were doing it our first day in Kuta, evolving *very, very* slowly. Brian was dying for a drink; the prospect of getting one got him bantering again. "Rob Binkley, misunderstood by many . . . envied by many. You take the overwhelming and turn it into a one-hour time slot."

"Compliment or insult?" He didn't answer.

I checked *Lonely Planet* for tips. A religion among backpackers, it's the best travel guide in the world. Published by a couple who began traveling around the world in the 1970s, *Lonely Planet* doesn't tell you what Hilton to stay at—it teaches you how to travel off the beaten path and see things inexpensively by giving tips on the hostels, bars, and best ways to get around. To backpackers like us on an extreme budget, the Book can extend a trip by months.

"Why read about a place we're about to see?" Brian saw my nose in the Book. "Why not just see it, then form your own opinion?"

"Are you taking a stand against reading?"

"You'll miss life with your head down, all's I'm saying."

I ignored him. The Book advised us not to take a taxi or shuttle; instead, it suggested we "walk out of the airport to the freeway and flag down a city bus," which we did. It saved us a few rupiah (which is Indonesian money). I waved the Book in his face. "You'll thank me when you don't end up penniless in the jungle somewhere."

"Whatever you say . . . You're the king of your own world."

We arrived at Kuta Beach and checked in at the Palm Gardens guesthouse for twelve dollars a night, or six dollars each. The Book claimed this was expensive but after twenty-plus hours at thirty thousand feet in the air, we splurged. Brian was happy with the amenities: "Ceiling fan, toilet—this place is great!"

We collapsed in a heap of exhaustion and took a quick nap that somehow lasted eight hours. At three in the morning, we awoke to a thundering rainstorm, not knowing who or where we were. The thunder was so loud I caught Brian doing some form of praying in the dark. Our room didn't have electricity, so I could only see him in bursts during the lightning show. When the storm passed, I fell back asleep watching the largest bug I had ever seen nest on our open window. Life was good.

On our first full day at Kuta Beach, we got up early, excited to experience everything. There was much to see. Bali is a gorgeous patch of archipelagic nirvana sunning itself along the equator in the Oceania region of South East Asia. The beaches were white, the mountains were green, and the valleys were endless. I fled America in search of a Utopian alterna-reality, and this place certainly looked the part.

According to the Book, only a third of the 17,508 Indonesian islands were populated by humans. I wanted to see them all. Brian wanted 17,508 beers, stat. We strolled past the street vendors selling their wares. Kuta was compact and full of mysterious little alleys called "gangs" with restaurants, hotels, and bars just off the beach.

"Crazy," I said. "This place has been plundered by a neverending stream of marauding invaders over the years—from Java Man and Flores Man, two of Bali's pre-historic co-founders, to the Hindu and Buddhist kingdoms of the early centuries, to the seventeenth century European colonialists, to the Javanese ethnic majority of today—Indonesia's been passed around like a *doobie* for its location and resources since the seventh century."

"Fascinating." Brian selectively listened to every fourteenth word I said. "We need to buy some pot. . . . Now *those* are ample bosoms."

Brian had his eyes on some sunbathers. I kept reading from the Book: "Though Indonesia is the most populated Muslim country in the world, here in Kuta "Bacchus," the god of wine, reigns supreme."

I looked up; I was talking to a palm tree. Brian had wandered off to see two topless sunbathers. I strutted up to the ladies and gave them my "cool face." "So, we're new in town, *meine fraus*." Brian was in the middle of busting an awkward move on two German bikini girls who spoke no English. "I hear there's a very rambunctious nightlife here. Can you point us in direction of the Jell-O shot store?"

The topless girls squirted him with a water gun full of suntan oil and laughed. I jumped in to save him. "What my foolish friend is trying to say is, '*Ich bin ein Berliners.*'" The girls kept laughing, though I'm not sure they got the reference. Probably not.

Brian whispered in my ear, "How do you say 'I want to oil your breasts' in German?"

I winked at the girls through my sunglasses. "I have no idea, but let's grab these *fraus* and go visit a temple! It could be a romantic setting."

"And put more clothes on them??" Brian had a point.

When we turned back to the girls, their boyfriends suddenly appeared from nowhere. *Game over.* We gave the bikini *fraus* the "call me" hand signal and kept on strolling. "Oh, our flirting has just begun." I turned to Brian and smiled. "Body language has no language barriers. Now what should we do?"

"Dude." Brian stopped me to explain he wasn't interested in sightseeing; he'd rather meet people than things. "I realize I don't know what I'm doing and that can be infuriating to smart people like you. Just do me a favor and don't tell me where I'm going next. It'll ruin the surprise."

"So you're saying we should just—"

"Go with the flow and see where it takes us. The first step is get a few drinks in you—and unleash the beast." He was referring to my alter ego. Legend has it, "he" comes out after my blood alcohol level reaches a certain level of toxicity. (I've never met the guy myself, but I hear he's a charming fellow.)

I put away the Book and just let the day flow. After seeing the talent on the beach, I knew our hormones were not going to let us go culture hunting no matter how hard my brain tried.

We sat on the sand watching the skin go by while ours sizzled in the sun.

The tourists had come out to play. I heard four different languages being spoken at once, none of them English. Bali felt like a melting pot of all the cultures and religions that came before us, but with a party atmosphere and a Planet Hollywood thrown in for good measure.

Fair warning: Kuta Beach may turn off some travelers who are "looking for Paradise Lost"—and they have a point. People come to Bali for various reasons, but if you come to Kuta Beach, it's for sun, sand, sex, and surfing. There's not much to do besides hang out on the beach, eat *nasi goreng* (chicken fried rice), party in the open-air bars, or have unprotected sex with strangers. If you're not into those four activities, you may want to skip Kuta.

As you can imagine, Brian and I weren't bored here at all. We were still decompressing from America and unloading nearly thirty years of conditioned baggage from our past lives. We made a decision to "let it all go" so our souls could be free to move about the planet without any lingering stress. For the first month, we didn't even mention our lives were in flames back home. None of that resurfaced until we began to run out of money. At this point, we were still just two expatriates starting over, and our journey had just begun.

I spent our first day reading and reflecting on how I got halfway around the world to drink all these Bintang beers before noon. I decided my personal goal for the trip was to get out of my comfort zone, and to test my values to see if they were true or just conditioned responses to life I was repeating over and over.

I think a lot of people come to a point where they wonder, "Is my life really my own, or am I living someone else's dream?" I had to find out. I knew I needed strange and weird experiences to help me understand who I am and what I wanted to become.

Brian, on the other hand, is strange enough of an exotic bird that he probably is who he'll always be: a paradox, an enigma, a man-child in perpetual flux who will never settle down because to do that would be to die.

Or at least that was how he seemed to me on day one.

It occurred to me that I was getting torched. There was a lot of cloud coverage, but the equatorial sun could not be stopped. My skin wasn't used to being attacked with such intensity. After about an hour of tanning, I took shade in one of the many bars on the beach. Brian stayed out on the beach, intent on getting skin cancer, while I worked on my liver disease under a nearby *palapa*.

I watched Brian strut around in his brand new Speedo while Indonesians scampered around him. "If success is measured by free time, we're the two richest guys in the world!" Brian yelled to me. He was high on freedom. Brian would never wear a Speedo back home, knowing his pasty ass looked ridiculous, but here he didn't care. Besides, all the Europeans were doing it.

A quick observation about the locals: They must be ancestors of the prehistoric Flores Man who once roamed these parts and was three-feet tall. All the natives around here seemed to be no more than five feet tall. I never considered myself vertically blessed (at six feet), but here I am a giant. Brian, at five-foot-nine, seems to like his newfound advantage.

When the sun set on our first full day, it finally hit me how amazing it was to be unplugged from America. The pressures of modern life are greater than most people understand. Once you're relieved of all adult responsibilities, life becomes really pleasant. My soul was opening up. With the stress slipping away, all that was left was the capacity for joy and experience.

I wanted to drink in the world through one giant beer bong.

Our afternoon buzz was wearing off. We decided to go forage for ice, Coca Cola, and Jack Daniels for our room so we could have "relaxers" before we went out. The problem was, by the time we tracked down the Jack Daniels, it was so hot our ice had melted. This was our first learning experience: Always buy ice last when shopping near the equator. When we returned to our room, sheets of rain came down so hard it made us double the speed we normally drank our relaxers.

After a day of wide-eyed wandering, it was time to experience Kuta's nightlife. Being two outgoing bastards, we hit all the bars and socialized with everyone we met. We took advantage of one of the most exciting features of traveling—getting to know other travelers and learning from their experiences, attitudes, and cultures. By the end of the first night, we felt like we'd met everyone on the strip.

The following day started late since most people stayed out until four o'clock in the morning here. We got up around two o'clock in the afternoon and had eggs and banana pancakes and juice. Then we pretended to surf or sit on the beach, as close to topless European girls as possible.

Brian was pissed at me all day because I kept dropping the "gay game" on him last night, and ruined his chances with a girl named Simi from Denmark. He told me to "stop salting *his game*," or he would throw me in the ocean. I didn't listen.

Brian walked around the beach introducing us as "two obnoxious Americans" to every attractive woman who spoke English. "We're like *Dumb and Dumber*. No, fun and funner!" Most people had no idea what he was talking about, but Brian had us pegged.

He was getting as red as a lobster, so he skipped the second night out to read *Zen and the Art of Motorcycle Maintenance* and tend to his jet lag and equatorial sunburn. But I knew he really wanted to find a pay phone to call his security blanket of an ex-girlfriend back home. *Sucker.*

That night, I was walking home from the Shari Club with a guy from Vancouver named Ken. It was five o'clock in the morning, and we had just scored some warm beer and low-grade pot. We came upon two enormous frogs having sex. Ken and I sat there staring—should we interrupt them or just watch? I felt like a pervert.

"This can't be normal," I said.

Ken replied, "Ya know, I heard if you lick them while they're having sex you can get high from their sexual excretions."

"*Really* now?"

Ken bet me a bag of weed I wouldn't do it. I took the challenge. I leaned in slowly so as not to disturb them, but when I saw the grotesque sight up close, my tongue recoiled. To save face, I grabbed the frogs and ran screaming up to a couple of Swedish girls. "Look at these frogs having sex!"

The girls were not happy to see a longhaired American holding two copulating amphibians. They ran away terrified; I gave chase and calmed them, but they didn't trust my crazed biologist act. Needless to say, they declined to join us for our afterparty.

Ken and I kept on moving to our guesthouse on Poppy Lane, which was impossible to find. We got lost in the neverending maze of streets that seemed to go in circles. We finally found our way home, and woke Brian to make him smoke a joint with us. Brian sat up eager to get high; he lit up the joint with pleasure. "Why do I smell an Italian kitchen?" I asked.

"I want pizza!" Ken could smell it too.

We were too ripped to realize we had bought a joint of Indonesian oregano. Brian spit it out after two drags. "You woke me for this??"

I looked at Ken then started howling.

"Amateurs. . . ." Brian shook his head. "You really are the dumbest smart guy I know." Brian went back to bed.

It wouldn't take long for this smart guy to learn that in Kuta every shady deal was just a bit shadier than normal. Travelers must develop a sixth sense about these things. I was still on the low end of the learning curve.

The next afternoon we were at a bar called Tubes when some guy asked Brian where the best surf was. Brian came up with a good answer without having a clue. After the surfer left I said, "You have no idea where the good surf is, you idiot."

"He doesn't know that."

"So you just made shit up?"

"No, I . . . read it."

"Where? Tell me. Where did you read it?"

Brian was ashamed. "In your stupid book, okay?"

I smiled. "That's all I wanted to hear."

Later in the day we bobbed on two rented surfboards just off the coast at low tide and stared up at the sky. "Shouldn't we try to surf at some point?" Brian mused. "We're Californians, we should be surfers." We decided to give it a shot. Tomorrow.

Later that afternoon brought magic, one of those sublime moments I will never forget. We swam in the rain with our new friends Kim, Omar, and Josephine. Surfing illiterates, we bodysurfed on one-foot waves while lightning storms crashed down around us.

Torrents of rain came so Dede, a four-foot-tall Rastafarian guy we met on the beach, invited us back to his hut. He made us milk and honey tea. It was a great place to hang out while the lightning passed. I felt like I was among friends even though we hardly knew any of them.

"Dudes . . ."

Josephine interrupted Brian, "I'm not a dude. Don't call me dude."

"Correction—dudes and *dudettes*—this has been such a great day with all you good people. Are we, like, forming a new subculture here?" Brian laid on the comic naïveté.

"We would if any of you *Yanks* had any culture," Omar said, which always drew a laugh. The stupidity of Americans is a punch line that never gets old, no matter what country you visit.

We all shared our unique perspectives with the group while we rode out the storm. I didn't know it then but, after a short lifetime of travels, I've discovered times like these are what backpacking is all about. Traveling is not about the high you get from attending huge parties or experiencing seminal moments of glory like "running with the bulls" in Pamplona or bungee jumping off the Space Needle in Auckland. The satisfaction comes from the joy you take from small bonding moments like these—sipping milk and honey tea in a rainstorm with good friends.

This is what you remember.

After a week in Kuta, we were watching our rupiah. Brian came up with an idea "to bridge the gap with the locals." He decided to get a job to pay for our drinking habit. Brian flagged down a Wells ice cream vendor walking by with the standard greeting.

"*Apa kabar*?!" (Translation: What's up?) "Can I buy that shirt off your back?"

The ice cream vendor knew enough English to be bribed. Brian bought his shirt and offered to switch places with the vendor. He gave him his seat on the beach and a tumbler full of Jack and Sprite.

The vendor agreed. "*Terima kasih!*" ("Thank you!") He happily took a load off.

Brian grabbed the cart and walked up and down Kuta Beach selling ice cream; I rang the bell. We sold frozen delights to all the sunbathing Europeans and Australians. Brian even used his disguise to hit on the ladies, including one of the topless German birds we met our first day on the beach. She flirted back, buying the largest phallic-looking ice cream stick in his cart.

Brian served it up with a smile, "On ze house, *schöne frau.*" ("beautiful woman")

"We've got a candle back in our room that looks just like that thing," I said. "You and your friend should stop by."

The moment was ruined when her fat, drunk boyfriend in a thong emerged from nowhere to claim her. The upside was Brian got a tip from him. "If you can get a tip from a German, you know you're doing great." I patted him on the back and we kept on moving.

That night, on our way home from another party, Brian and I ran into a little Indonesian boy that wanted to sell us magic mushrooms. I had read somewhere they could either be poison or crap, but they had to be better than licking frogs. The mushrooms didn't look like any I'd ever seen, so we asked the little fella if he would eat some first.

"If you start tripping, we'll buy them."

The kid got scared, probably because we were towering over him trying to shove his own product down his throat. In broken English he said, "Men who aren't safe, aren't safe here," and he ran away into the night. We just stood there and watched him.

"Was it something we said?!" I yelled to no avail.

"An ominous warning," Brian said. "Take heed."

"Oh well . . . no mushrooms for us."

We called it a night.

Our dreams of enlightenment were drowning in a sea of Arak Attack cocktails (made with a rice liquor that's eighty percent alcohol) and bottles of imported whiskey. Our days were blurring into one long party haze with our new Aussie friend Felix, who had coerced Brian and I into getting blotto every night. He had become a fixture with us, a gregarious devil of a man who didn't give a crap about anything. Felix was even crazier than we were. He had a hearty personality and a penchant for binge drinking (like us) and all things fun.

At first sight, Felix appeared sane. We ran into him one night at a country and western bar on Kuta that had a brothel in back. He was a normal-looking bloke who ironically (or insanely) dressed himself up like a tourist from the 1980s with a Hawaiian shirt, hat, and camera around his neck. He looked like Hunter S. Thompson.

I first laid eyes on him when he bumped into our table on the way out of the brothel's back door. He nearly knocked over our table full of drinks. "Next round's on the klutzo!" He threw down some change and we were off.

He sat down at our table and went into his life story. "The first thing you should know is I don't normally bang hookers!" He inserted a two-dollar tip into the assless chaps of a prostitute walking by. "That's the cherry right there!" The Chaps Girl kept walking unfazed; her chaps were full of tips much larger than his.

"Got my heart stomped to bits by my future, now never-to-be wifey. Left me at the bloody altar in front of God and everybody. . . . It was public brutality!"

Felix said he was heartbroken and looking to drown his sorrows with booze and women. "The order is not important!"

Brian was into him immediately. "At least you have a reasonable life goal set for yourself." And that was that. I never dried out enough on Kuta to know exactly when we veered into dangerous ground, but it was around the time Felix joined our gang.

A few days later, the Muslims on the island were fasting for Ramadan. Although Indonesia is mostly Muslim, here on Bali the vast majority of the natives practice Hinduism. The ones who prayed to Allah were easy to spot.

When the sun set on our island paradise, the local Muslims came out to eat just as Felix, Brian, and I ventured out to our favorite bar, The Bounty. There we befriended two Swedes named Nick and Lars.

Lars, who amazingly worked at a 7-11 back home, mentioned "slam dancing was still a big craze in Sweden," so we did some male bonding on the dance floor. Everyone smashed into everyone while the girls stayed on the sidelines. It was great if you're an idiot into masochistic fun. I kept falling down but the Swedes would pick me up and throw me back into the air.

This lasted until three in the morning. Worn out, I abandoned Brian in the mosh pit to drunk-dial girls back in America, with no success.

The next night, the gang was back at The Bounty where it was the usual debauchery. I spent hours talking to a Danish girl about the Great Dane, who I totally guessed was Macbeth. My second guess would have been MacGyver. She told me everything about "ladle laws." I had no idea what a ladle was, so I just kept smiling and nodding.

Brian was holding court in the middle of a group of Danes, who were humble people that were very proud of their culture in which everyone has a responsibility. Their government advocates traveling two years after high school to better understand what they want to do as adults. America seemed out of touch in this regard.

After our educational talk, one of the drunk Danish gals told us she had soaked a tampon in tequila earlier and was wearing it around to get a buzz. "Are you for real?!" Brian roared. "Can I stick one up my ass and get drunk?"

"Bend over!" She called Brian's bluff.

The longer we stayed in Bali the clearer it became that some of these island lunatics would *sniff a bee's butt to get a buzz.*

The Bounty was offering two-for-one drinks until midnight. Brian ordered twenty shots to get all the Danes drunk, then he gave me the bill. We all got so blasted Brian and I ordered another round and began throwing shots in each other's faces, making a general nuisance of ourselves.

By two o'clock in the morning, I had all the liquid courage I needed to leap up on the dance podium where I boogied like an epileptic off his meds. I would never pull a move like that in the States, but here inhibitions were out the window. It didn't take long before I was yanked off the pole.

When I was pulled down, I saw a roomful of faces frowning in my direction. Even in my inebriated state, I could tell the locals didn't appreciate our exhibitionist American attitudes. We didn't know it yet, but we were accumulating a growing legion of silent enemies just waiting to pounce.

We left The Bounty and staggered to our other favorite haunt, the Sari Club (which years later would be blown up by terrorists with 202 people inside). We jumped up and down on the dance floor screaming, "Let's go mad!" with Felix leading the way.

I grabbed a policeman named Danny and we went around the club talking to everyone. I bought Danny a few drinks. I thought now that we're friends I could buy his police shirt from him, but he refused. Later, Brian came back wearing Danny's police shirt—he said he gave him "an offer he couldn't refuse," but I never found out what that was.

I warned Brian that impersonating a police officer would get him caned, but he didn't care. "I want to see how many laws I can break!" He was getting stupider by the minute.

By four in the morning we were all hammered. A group of us decided to go for a swim. Brian jumped in a motorcycle cab and took off with some Australian girls. Felix and I came out of the club just in time to see him flying down the boulevard, screaming, "*E mayya hootsy cosa!*" (which I'm sure means something obscene in Indonesian).

A few seconds later Brian jumped from the moving cab and almost ran into a post in front of a couple arguing on the corner. He started talking to the couple. Brian said he asked the girl if she was okay when— *bam!*—her boyfriend hit him over the head with a beer bottle.

The first fight of the trip erupted.

I ran toward the commotion and saw Brian in the center of the melee (he was the tallest one and the only one wearing a white police shirt). Then one, two, three, four, five, six—*seven* guys charged him.

Brian took off and ran a block into a dead end alley. When I turned the corner, I could see the seven Indonesians showing off their karate moves as they closed in to throttle Brian, who had nowhere to go. Brian covered his head as the gang kicked and punched him everywhere. By the time Felix and I arrived, the gang had vanished. Brian was a mess. His head was bleeding. His arms were turning purple and an inch of meat was gone from his thumb.

"This is what they call an 'Indonesian drive-by,'" Brian moaned. "Was it something I said? I got jumped by the tiniest gang *ever*." Brian tried to laugh but could only cough. They pounded him really good. The two Aussie girls who were first responders were no help. I'm sure the guys targeted Brian for being obnoxious or impersonating a police officer. Or both.

The crowd dispersed; no one had answers. Brian wanted to go looking for the guys but one of our rules on the trip was to avoid fights since the outcome would never be good. On the walk home, I asked Brian if he taunted them with slanderous jokes.

"I may have mentioned I screwed one of their mothers."

He was kidding . . . I think.

The spectacle of our idiocy got even more foolish the next night when we went out again, this time on the Kuta strip. Brian was still wearing his bandages from last night's beating like some American POW on shore leave.

At some point, a two-hundred-pound Swedish woman named Inga attacked me on the dance floor to the tune of "Baby Got Back" from Sir Mix-A-Lot. I danced with her but feared her horniness. She could have picked me up and taken me home with her so I went into critical inebriated-thinking stage.

I proceeded to tell her the sickest things I could think of as a form of repellant. That didn't work. My filthy talk turned Inga on more. She whispered in my ear that she wanted to take me home and do disgusting things to my orifices. She was fondling me everywhere. This is why women are afraid of aggressive men who get too grabby.

I needed a buffer so I grabbed Brian, who was more wasted than me, and threw him at Inga while I fled for the bathroom. When I came back, Brian had disappeared.

Uh oh, I thought. *This is how serial killers nab their prey.* I scanned the dance floor; Inga was nowhere. I assumed Brian probably got lost outside, so I collected Felix and the Swedes for an Indonesian style search and rescue mission.

We hailed a taxi, bought six large Bintangs, and began driving around. I offered the driver every other sip of my beer to get him on our level, but he wouldn't have it. Since there were only so many bars in Kuta, once the beers were done we called off the search and I went back to our guesthouse. When I arrived home at four o'clock in the morning, our building had no electricity. I staggered in the dark.

I heard ABBA coming from our open window. I crept up and peeked in. The lime-green cock candle was burning inside. In the haze of candlelight, there Brian was tied to my bedpost in his underwear like a rag doll. Brian appeared to be out cold.

I tried to get his attention. "Pssst! Wake up, you kinky bastard." No response. "I hope you don't have Inga in—"

I heard a Swedish baritone gargling mouthwash in our bathroom to the tune of "Fernando." It was Inga. Did Brian actually sex her up? How drunk was he?

From the zebra-striped overnight case on the bed, it appeared Inga was planning on staying a while. I threw a bag of Skittles at Brian's head and whispered, "Dude! Wake up!" I stayed crouched in the bushes. No way was I walking in there, or Inga might have me for dessert.

When Brian finally opened his eyes, I could see the horror wash over him as he realized his search for experience had gone horribly wrong.

The warning from the Indonesian kid echoed in my mind: "Men who aren't safe aren't safe here." Covered in what appeared to be Balinese guacamole, Brian tried to wriggle free but Inga had tied him down good.

Brian and I locked eyes. I could see tears running down his face, silently pleading for someone to save him.

Brian nudged his head toward the bathroom. I saw the reflection of Inga in a mirror coming our way. She looked angry, like a rabid Kong. My heart was pounding; I had seconds to free him. I wondered how would his mother take the news? Our first month on the road and he's already a sex casualty. He'll be humiliated postmortem.

This was the motivation I needed. I flew through the open window and untied Brian from the bedpost just as Inga walked in. She stopped dancing when she saw me. "You here to join ze party too?!"

"I don't think so, Inga!" I fought off her advances, using our backpacks as shields as Brian crawled out the window.

I was left in a Mexican standoff with the hulking Swede who was totally naked. I tried to talk sense into her. "C'mon, fun's over. Time to go home, darling. Let's make this easy on both of us."

While we stalked each other around the room I managed to stuff all our belongings into our packs. Inga hurled a litany of Swedish curses at me for ruining her afterhours party. She wasn't leaving; the woman was out of her mind. As soon as I had all our gear packed, I blew out the cock candle; it was suddenly pitch dark. I bolted for the window. Inga stumbled around in the dark screaming unintelligible gibberish.

I grabbed Brian, who was lying on his back in the courtyard, and we took off running. We didn't stop until we saw ocean. I finally got a look at Brian and busted out laughing. He was in his underwear with *rambutan* fruit (a local delicacy) smeared all over him.

Brian was gasping for air. "Did that just really happen?"

"I didn't know whether to hug her or tackle her!" I gave him a bottle of water I had in my pack.

"We will never speak of this again." He guzzled the water and collapsed on the beach.

I inspected the jelly all over his body. "What the hell is all this?"

"Stop asking questions. Must forget."

"Did she penetrate you? I saw an apparatus."

"Mock me in the morning—can't talk."

"It's morning now."

The sun was coming up. I pulled towels out of our bags and made a bed. I laughed myself to sleep while Brian moaned with a towel over his head. Good times.

We never returned to Palm Gardens.

The next morning I awoke face down on the beach with a host of mosquitos sucking blood from my sunburned back. I forgot to grab our mosquito net (which never worked anyway) during last night's hotel exodus.

The island was spinning. I looked around; our stuff was strewn everywhere. Tourists were on the beach sunning themselves around us. Brian was washing himself in the surf, scrubbing away last night's residue.

I shouted, "I wanted to take a picture before you cleaned up!"—not trying to cheer him up. Brian walked back to our beach spot and plopped down on a towel.

"I need to chill today. Isn't that what we came here to do?"

I couldn't remember. My mind was scrambled eggs.

We didn't move from our beach spot all day. The plan was to detox, just drink Sprite and rediscover our souls. Our friends Nick and Mag showed up and were disappointed we weren't drinking; they thought we were alcoholics for some reason. Their disappointment waned when they saw our Sprites were loaded with Southern Comfort that Brian had hidden in the sand. Brian needed to drink away the memory of last night. He didn't say a word all day.

Everyone said we were getting ripped off at Palm Gardens anyway, so we spent the end of the day wandering around town looking for new, cheaper digs where Inga would never find us.

We had each budgeted twelve thousand dollars for the trip (one thousand dollars a month), which we still thought could get us around the world in a year. "As long we stick to third world countries and don't develop any habits harder than alcohol, we should be able to make it."

Brian, Felix, and I decided to share a room to save money; also, there was safety in numbers. We only needed three small beds with a fan. Air-conditioning was out of the question. Soon we found a place called Kedin's Inn that was in our price range. It was basically a thatched hut with two beds in the front room and one in a back room. We went to the front desk to pay for our room. I got them down to twelve dollars a night, four dollars per person.

We became friendly with the teenage boys working the front desk. They said we would get a free night if we "put on a show" for them.

"What kind of show?" Brian asked, rubbing his bruised body.

"If you bring home a girl and do naughty things to her, will you let us watch through the open window? You can have that night for free." These kids were little pervs!

Felix thought this was hilarious. "Do you like big Swedish girls?" I told them about last night's adventure; they were rapt by my story. The memory was too fresh for Brian, so he went outside to find a pay phone to call his girl back in the States.

While Brian was gone, we shared a few beers with the horny weasels at the front desk, and Felix and I agreed to give them a show—somehow, someway.

That night, after our day of semirecovery, the Southern Comfort was getting dangerously low so we ventured out again with Felix, Nick, and Mag. Brian said if he spotted Inga, he was "getting the hell outta town"—with or without me.

"What are the odds we see her again?"

"This is a small island. I'd say pretty good."

Fate must have been smiling on Brian that night. Once it became clear Inga wasn't going to surface, Brian relaxed. He partied hard to forget his pain and did such a good job he never made it back home. I was concerned he had forgotten where our new room was or that he was dead in Inga's closet until he showed up around ten o'clock in the morning with a huge Bali Hai Beer in his hand and a fake mustache glued sideways on his cheek.

"How's that mustache workin' out for you? You look like a Picasso painting."

"I'm still alive, aren't I? Rakow shoots, he scores!" He laughed then tried to kick his empty beer bottle into a nearby trash can, failing miserably.

The next morning we committed to bringing girls back to our new digs at Kedin's Inn to save some money on our room. That night, I somehow managed to bring home a nice, svelte Swedish girl named Olivia. We walked through the front courtyard and the little perverts followed us to our room, keeping what I thought was a subtle distance. Olivia picked up on it. Our sick little jig was up.

We were determined to save the twelve dollars. so we went out on a serious prowl the next night. We all got separated. Brian and I never even made it home. I ran into Brian staggering home the next morning. We found Felix waiting for us in our room wearing a big Aussie grin. "Where you two idiots been?"

Brian looked at his bed; it was a mess.

Felix looked disappointed. "You ruined the surprise!" He explained he brought us home a "gift" last night. Since he was getting over getting dumped, he thought he would "treat us" all to an Indonesian hooker. He assured us she was female. "I paid good money for her. I can't believe neither of you came back."

Brian said, "I have two questions: Did you open the window and make sure the boys got a peek?"

"The window may have been open," Felix said.

Brian picked his sheets off the ground. "And why are my sheets on the floor?"

"You don't expect me to screw a hooker in my bed, do you?"

I busted out laughing.

Brian shook his head. "You're a very sick boy."

We were running home in the rain that night when six prostitutes on mopeds attacked us. They shouted, "You owe us two dollars!" in broken English. Apparently Felix never paid one of them for last night's sex show. We ran for our lives in flip-flops, which was hard to do in a down-pour. Brian yelled as we ran, "You didn't pay, you idiot!!"

Felix screamed, "I paid! I just didn't tip!"

The prostitutes tried to run us down repeatedly with their mopeds, but we dove to safety into some bushes. We lay low for a while. They cruised by a few times with flashlights but never found us. When the coast was clear, we crept home, totally caked in mud.

From then on, we were marked men in Kuta. I couldn't believe it.

"So you're saying a gang of hookers wants us dead because of a two-dollar tip?"

Felix rationalized, "I broke custom . . . and it's the Indonesian economy, mate. It's rainy season, times are tough."

"Yeah, yeah. Things are tough all over."

I tried to pay Felix's debt the next day when I ran into the only hooker from the gang who would still speak to us. She said her pimp hated arrogant foreigners who don't tip because his father was a pale, freckled bastard from Amsterdam who abandoned him.

"Rico's poppa never tipped his mama." And Rico the Pimp never forgot.

I ratted out Felix. "Listen lady, the bad tipper wasn't us; it was actually a freckled Australian, so . . ."

The hooker chewed gum and smoked. "Rico don't care. You all look de same."

She gave me the universal "throat slit" sign, then flicked a lit cigarette in my face and hauled ass on her moped, spraying mud on my shorts.

Our days in Kuta were numbered; I knew we had to start moving if we were going to avoid pimp retribution, another run-in with Inga, or round two with the tiny gang who beat the crap out of Brian.

Back at Kedin's Inn, I told Brian and Felix the story while cleaning moped mud off my clothes. "No wonder they call streets 'gangs' here; the streets are full of them!" I kept messing with Brian as he packed his stuff. "This place has a gang problem, get it? The gangs are full of gangs."

Brian was clearly disturbed by our legion of island haters. "What if they all ganged up? Look at me. I can't take any more abuse. We've got to pace ourselves if we plan to survive this trip."

"Now you're talking like me. C'mon, you look fine. So you'll have some mental and physical scars. That's a part of *being young*."

"I, for one, am not waiting to find out what happens next." Brian convinced us it was finally time to motor. We loved Kuta Beach, but we didn't love Rico the local pimp who was out for our heads. Felix wasn't interested in "staying around to die" so he tagged along.

We kept pushing ourselves forward into the unknown. Bali suddenly was full of too many people who wanted us dead. We decided to dry out on some remote island and avoid chaos. Brian, Felix, and myself (the newly minted threesome) threw on our backpacks and got out of town.

We took the bus to Candidasa, a small fishing village that was only a two-hour ride from Kuta on the other side of the island. It was a perfect, serene spot that was also a jumping-off point from Padang Bai to some of the smaller islands we wanted to check out.

We spent our days hanging out on the beach, reading and napping in our little *palapa*. There could be no debauchery as Brian and I shared a bed in an attempt to get back on budget. Felix took the other bed.

We were thankful our nights were uneventful as we had a chance to regroup and catch up on our reading. Part of this so-called "personal renaissance trip" was expanding our minds in every direction; reading was a part of the plan. We had lost focus on our plan somewhere along the way, but now we'd found it again.

After two days, we took a *bemo* (a jalopy bus on three wheels) to Padang Bai, then hopped a three-hour boat ride to Lombok Island where we spent the night in Senggigi, which was a beautiful little town. Our room was ten dollars, but we had our own beds. It had an amazing pool and bar. Naturally we fit right in at the bar, our natural milieu.

The following day, we took a boat to the Gili Islands, three heavenly little desert islands with white sandy beaches and coconut trees. Each island had a unique vibe: Gili Air had the cool local character; Gili Meno was the lovely little island you wanted to spend a day on with your girlfriend; and Gili Trawangan (known as Gili T) was the most developed island, with bars and a happening party scene. Gili T was also the largest of the three islands so we stayed there; we felt it probably wouldn't sink if a tsunami hit.

Surrounded by coral reefs and beautiful hues of blue water, Gili T is the stunning palm-fringed island of your dreams. It took us two hours to walk around it; we found beautiful seashells on our hike and climbed coconut trees to get coconut juice.

The next morning, Brian, Felix, and I jumped on a tiny open-air dinghy with three girls and a guy. We were all going to check out Gili Meno, the smallest of the Gili Islands. As luck would have it, the dinghy was so small we got a chance to get to know the girls.

Due to close quarters, my leg had the pleasure of brushing up against one of the girl's leg when the boat swayed—her name was Kelli. After a chat, we realized we'd struck gold; we were sharing a dinghy with probably the only Brazilian girls in Indonesia, and they were stunners. Their accents were incredible. Granted, our bar was slightly lowered but these girls—especially Kelli and her sister—could have fought for a seat at any nightclub in Rio and won.

One thing I learned from my travels is some cultures raise their young ones to be skilled socializers; the top of that list has to be Brazil. By and large Brazilians show everyone a great time, even here on a remote island in the middle of the South Pacific. Brazilians will smile their beautiful smiles while drinking you under the table and dancing you off the sandy floor, always laughing and chatting you up so you feel like the most important person on earth. Their beauty and charm is bewitching.

We had our eyes on all three girls. I was already plotting how to dump the guy overboard but nothing drastic was necessary; it turned out the guy was Kelli's brother. We asked the girls questions that required long answers and just listened. We became fast friends. Amazingly enough, Kelli was carrying a bottle of champagne, a rare libation in these parts; it happened to be her birthday. Brazilians and champagne—travel nirvana!

The boat ride cemented the start of a wonderfully crazy night. When we reached the smallest Gili Island, we all got adjoining rooms.

That night we all went to dinner and had a great meal with many, many drinks.

After dinner, full of exotic bubbly, Brian, Felix, and I were staring the girls down like three ravenous wolves. I was playing footsie with Kelli under the table. I judged it was definitely on between us. I thanked Allah (after all, it was still Ramadan!).

We hit the dance floor with Felix leading the way, yelling, "Let's go mad!" It was our mantra now; we were bound to do it everywhere we went. Whenever we got crazy we chanted it no matter our location (but usually it was on or near a dance floor). By this time, we were loud and loaded; the restaurant owner asked us to quiet down, but we threw him in the middle of our dance circle. Two minutes later he was jumping up and down with us screaming "*Ole, ole, ole!*"

Felix magically produced a bottle of *mezcal* that he cracked open at eight o'clock to keep the party going. By nine-thirty the bottle was gone. "Who brings the party? We bring the party!" Felix chanted as Brian drained the last of the bottle, eating the worm. Seconds later, Brian realized what he did and puked all over our busboy. "I swallowed the worm!" Since we weren't in Mexico in the 1800s, I think he must have swallowed a caterpillar that crawled into the bottle.

It was clear by the vomit-covered busboy that we were having too much fun. So we left to go "clubbing," which consisted of dancing on the beach in a thatched hut with an old boom box that was blasting music from crappy speakers. We were all going *loco*, our brains as distorted as the speakers on the boom box.

The whole gang left the club at four in the morning and walked the beach until the sun came up, careful not to walk through anyone's thatched hut homes. We kissed our Brazilian beauties goodnight (even though Brian had puke-breath), and collapsed in the hammocks in front of our cabana. I think Felix passed out on the beach with some Rasta dudes while smoking weed.

Brian was snoring in his hammock when my prayers were answers. Kelli came outside to surprise me. She was wearing her blue bikini and had a chocolate and cinnamon cupcake she'd gotten at the restaurant for her birthday. She was drunk and sad to be twenty-five. She thought her life was over; I told her it was just beginning.

I invited her into my hammock and comforted her quarter-life crisis by busting out what was left of Inga's candle to make the cupcake more festive.

"Nice candle," she said with a laugh.

"It's a novelty," I said. "It's become a bit of a talisman on the trip; rub it and it will bring you good luck."

"Like this?" Kelli asked and gently stroked the candle—then she laughed that amazing Brazilian laugh of hers. The candle dwarfed the little cake but she blew it out while I sang "Happy Birthday." Then we fooled around in the hammock while Brian coughed and yammered in his sleep a few trees away. It was absolute heaven.

The next day we were in recovery mode. "Today's world revolves around yesterday's bodily damage," I announced to Kelli, who was almost as hungover as Brian. Felix was nowhere to be found.

Kelli had to meet back up with her friends. She told me they were leaving for another island, so we said our goodbyes and promised to write even though we knew we wouldn't.

Brian and I spent the day reading and hydrating. We tried to run around the island to detox but that didn't work out so well. We were still fairly fit, but jogging in equatorial, salty air while hungover was ridiculously difficult; our lungs were burning. We ran into Nick and Mag from Kuta Beach, who laughed at us. "Look at the two drunk American crazies running barefoot around the island!"

We spent the day exploring the little villages, climbing palm trees, and visiting thatched houses where the natives lived. Later in the afternoon, we decided to eat some of the local magic mushrooms since we were taking a vacation from booze.

We dropped 'shrooms with our old friends from Bali: Felix, Kim, and Josephine from Denmark, Omar from England, and Sarah from Sydney. It was a drugged-out United Nations consortium; we never got around to talking about world peace.

We walked around after the drugs kicked in. It was a mild psilocybin high—not so intense that you stopped to stare at bark on a tree for five hours straight, and not so mild that the stars in the sky didn't start attacking you (they did). It was just right; so was the setting. The island had no roads. There was only one village that (sometimes) had electricity, so we tripped in the dark in environs unknown.

We kept bumping into shadowy strangers I couldn't see until I was practically kissing people who didn't speak English. It was like a surreal psychedelic trust exercise. At the peak of my trip, I felt a rush of hot air approaching; it was Brian, who ran into me higher than Hunter S. Thompson.

"Rob! Oh my God. Life is *so carefree.* The world is *so beautiful.* Life is amazing! My mind is so dirty from all this glorious freedom!" He whispered in my ear, which was really my eye, "*I want to do dirty things to all these women I can't see.*"

"I know you do, *amigo*!" I calmed him down and we wandered toward holiday lights in the distance, thinking Santa may be blowing off some post-Christmas steam in the South Pacific. He wasn't.

It was a bar on the beach called DeDe's, where we climbed coconut trees and did handstands out front. We met a guy inside who told us about his friend who nearly died from getting "the bends" (a decompression sickness) while scuba diving that day.

We were so high; our collective empathy meter went to eleven.

Everyone on mushrooms got into his story, all of us circled around, staring with dilated eyes at the concerned fella. Kim kept repeating, "Sa, sa, sa, sa," for what felt like hours. My ears started ringing so loud, all I could hear was Brian and Felix laughing like maniacs in the background about God knows what. Their laughter made me laugh.

Everyone listening to the guy's story thought I was an insensitive dick. I couldn't help it; it was impossible not to laugh. My trip was surging; I had to get out. I grabbed Brian and Felix and we went outside to watch the imaginary shooting stars.

We came back to earth around four in the morning. Felix was starved so we tried to raid some of the thatched huts we could find in the dark. We got busted a few times by angry natives. We should have been arrested, but there were no cops on the island.

We tried the polite route by knocking on some doors and kindly asking people if they could spare some rice, but seeing three foreigners at your door at five o'clock in the morning with a bottle of sambal hot sauce in their hands was too scary for the locals. No food for us, so we went home.

When we got back to our room, we were so wasted we couldn't find our key, so we ran down the row of rooms knocking on doors asking if we could borrow their key. Eventually, Felix broke into a vacant room and passed out on the floor.

In the morning, I realized my key was in my pocket all along.

Our trip kept going south, geographically and metaphorically.

We booked a small boat to southern Indonesia to explore more remote islands. We were to travel with a group of other backpackers. I suckered Felix into coming. I told him he'd enjoy this frugal adventure. "You Aussies are a rugged bunch!"

I had no idea how rugged the trip would be.

Our goal was to end up on Komodo Island, where we could frolic among the Komodo dragons, an ancient species of giant lizards that have evolved over forty million years. They only inhabit this island, so we were excited to see them in the wild. "They say Komodo dragons are cannibals and can grow over ten feet long if they are not eaten by one of their friends," I recited from the Book.

I looked up at Brian. "I'd eat you if we were starving." Brian grabbed the Book and threw it into a nearby palm planter.

The next morning, we started our six-day voyage. The trip was remarkably cheap, which was a warning sign I should have heeded but I was too busy high-fiving myself for cutting a sweet deal. The boat people told us we had to sleep on deck and "to bring our own sleeping bags," which sounded nice—sleeping under the stars—but it turned out to be a nightmare of monolithic proportions.

When we boarded the small wooden motorboat, we saw they weren't kidding; the only thing below deck was the engine room. "So much for our berths," Brian said. "This could be the beginning of a brain-scattering experience."

On board we encountered ten backpackers from around the world, five chickens, five ducks, enough unripened bananas for a forest full of monkeys, and rice for all of Southeast Asia. The first day we motored six hours to a small island called Salt Lake, which (surprise) had a salt lake. It was a chance to stretch our legs and snorkel. All seemed well.

Then the rains started our first night on the boat. It rained on us all night, the boat leaked everywhere, and we had no shelter. Being young and dumb, we were still happy for the adventure. The mood would not last.

The next day, we sailed for thirteen hours through torrential rains. Everyone got seasick. We asked the Captain to skip all the other stops and get us to Komodo Island because we were all starving.

The tour people failed to mention our all-inclusive meals would be tiny bowls of runny rice; the bananas were for the monkeys. Being the petulant brat that I was, I went on a hunger strike.

By day three, I was slurping down runny rice to stay conscious. The travelers from Europe were about to mutiny. Seasick passengers were limp from puking over the side of the boat.

The European men were in a predicament. They foolishly brought their girlfriends, who by this time were all freaking out. Brian and I could only look at each other and laugh at the unfolding horror. Felix had grown sullen and wasn't talking; I think he was pissed I talked him into this trip.

It got so bad we tried to squeeze into the engine room; we were all freezing to death in the rain. Problem was, there was only room for six to eight people below.

Brian went below to check it out and came back laughing. "It's a horror show with many pitfalls." The room was full of toxic diesel fumes mixed with burning incense wafting from the captain's shrine to Allah. "The boat floor is covered with two inches of water that reeks of alcohol, plus many other wonders."

Brian said the rain was the better option, so he plopped down for the night. Felix and I tried to sleep below. After a few hours, the petrol fumes and leaky roof finally lulled us to sleep. Once we fell off around four in the morning, the loud engine started up again and blew toxic fumes all over us.

By day four, we thought we might actually die on this godforsaken boat. The women were crying rivers; the trip was turning into a nautical version of the Bataan Death March. We sailed another thirteen hours with no land in sight.

Brian confronted the captain, who didn't speak English. He demanded that he "let us off this stinking deathtrap!" The captain shouted "You go!" in broken English. Brian looked around; there was no land to be had, just endless blue ocean. He sat back down.

That night, I dreamed I was in a prison camp.

By day five, everyone was waiting for the fumes to put us out of our misery. Just as we drifted off to something resembling sleep, the captain started the engine and the fumes blasted us again. We were in Dante's Inferno, waiting to die in some concentric circle of tropical hell.

Then at five o'clock in the morning, all the circles of hell broke loose. A rogue wave rushed through the portholes, dousing us with hundreds of gallons of salt water. Felix's backpack and electronics were destroyed. He sat up from a deep, petrol-induced sleep and started swearing. Soaking wet, he stomped up to the captain (who never slept) and demanded he let us off.

When I got aboveboard, Felix was shaking the poor man by his collar; I stood by ready to save the captain in case he actually dropped him overboard. The captain went to his old standby; he called his bluff, "You go—*go!*" He pointed at the ocean.

We seriously considered jumping overboard since we were now passing islands and some of them looked inhabited. The water was dark blue and looked beautiful enough to swim in, but our backpacks would have been dead weight.

Felix let the captain live. We all sat back down.

Brian, the confused Taoist, began praying to Allah below board, burning incense at the captain's shrine. He spent the rest of the night chanting, all the while hacking out the diesel fumes.

We were losing our minds.

Then, by the grace of God, our prayers were answered. The sun came up and Brian shouted, "Land ahoy! Komodo Island, dead ahead!"

We all rejoiced like stowaway rats on the Mayflower. We asked the captain to drop us in the harbor where we all dove into the lagoon. No one waited for the boat to hit shore.

We crawled onto the beach and kissed the ground. Then we toured Komodo Island to get our land legs. We found the visitor center. I was so happy to be alive I wrestled with a three-foot lizard who approached us. I couldn't catch him. He was strong, but not a full-sized dragon.

We gobbled down *nasi goreng* at a local restaurant like apartheid victims who'd stormed the Big House. Brian inhaled food so quickly he went to the bathroom to throw up—then kept on eating.

Refueled with food and a few beers in us, I talked Felix and Brian into hiring a walking tour guide to show us the natural wonders of the island. "We've come this far and nearly died; I'm getting my money's worth out of this bloody place."

Our group's guide spoke limited English; he inexplicably thought the English word for Komodo dragon was "chicken." During the first half of the island walk, he said in hushed, excited tones, "Look, chicken, chicken. Careful, careful." Since our only language was English, Brian, Felix, and I were the first people on our tour to pick this up. We went to our guide and pointed in the bush. "I think I saw a chicken that way. Should we run?" It was good fun.

Eventually someone corrected him but we thought the idea of deadly chickens was hysterical. We hiked further into the brush and crept up on one of the big, ancient dinosaur lizards that moved so slowly we felt comfortable getting close. We tried to leap over a few while they weren't looking until we saw how fast they ran, then we kept our distance.

After the day tour, we dared to get back on the hellboat, only because we could see the next island in the distance, which had a proper village.

We docked in Labuan Bajo on Flores Island. It was paradise found. Everyone was so relieved to get off the sinking hellboat for good, all the other backpackers fled in different directions without saying goodbye. The three of us holed up in a shack for five dollars a night and went straight to the village watering hole, where we drank beers until we were happy again.

We met two Aussie girls from Adelaide who went on a rant about how their city was the best in the world. I think everybody should have a favorite city, but they had never been to another country besides

Indonesia and Australia. I said, "Maybe you should see a few more countries before you pass judgment," but it was no use. It was their opinion, so I guess they were right.

After surviving the hellboat, we were determined to catch the next plane out of Flores back to Bali, the island that almost killed us, which was now our savior and land of civilization.

The people at the little airline shack told us there might be a plane tomorrow or the next day. "Your lack of exactness terrifies me," I said.

The airline lady explained because airplanes were hard to come by we "should probably go to the airstrip and wait." The prospect of going to a landing strip and waiting for days was a new form of hell. We were desperate to get back to Bali then onward to our next destination, Australia.

I tried to work my magic on the airline lady. "Look ma'am, we don't mind if we can't get a seat. We'll sit on the floor. Or with the pilot, even." She said it "wasn't a good idea to fly with the captain" because "planes have a hard time clearing the jungle floor on takeoff as it is."

I stepped up my game, "But ma'am, we *have* to be on the next plane. Can't you see my colleague is deathly ill??" I pointed to Brian, who looked like absolute hell. She was unmoved. "Also," I mustered up some tears, "our families just perished last night . . . in a horrible group bungee-jumping accident while vacationing in Australia. We have to identify their bodies or they'll be buried at sea, which as a fellow Muslim, you know is against our religion."

She said nothing; she just stared at me with narrowing eyes.

"Come on!"

I eventually talked our way onto the next flight. Two days later.

After we landed at the Denpasar airport, we headed back to Kuta Beach. Although we were "wanted" men, it felt like home. The day was pleasant. We got a room at Kedin's Inn and slept until midnight. Then we dragged our asses back to the main drag for what seemed like the 200th time in the past month.

Yawn. I needed to drink more to enjoy this, so we drank Arak Attacks till we keeled over. Once we were all trashed, we made a point to say farewell to every person we met who hadn't punched us in the face or assaulted us. By the end of the night, two bars' worth of friends knew we were headed to Australia. I ended the night chasing frogs down the streets for old times' sake, catching two and bringing them home to Brian and Felix. Brian licked them both. Nothing happened. He probably gave some girls warts on our journey.

The next morning just wasn't Brian's day.

Ominous signs were everywhere. A stray dog attacked him the second he stepped outside. I wasn't privy to the attack since I was in such bad shape I didn't drag myself out of bed until six o'clock in the evening. I woke to Brian packing. "That's it! This place is cursed!" Brian said he'd had his fill of paradise. I convinced Brian he was imagining things and to venture out for dinner.

When we did, we immediately saw Inga on the beach harassing the Wells ice cream man. Brian freaked out and made a beeline for the street, where he almost ran in front of six native girls cruising by on mopeds. Fearing Rico the killer pimp was just around the corner, Brian ducked under a watch vendor's table to hide.

This particular vendor was an aggressive solicitor who didn't like us because we never bought his stuff. Brian watched the vendor yell at some tourist from under the table. When the tourist wouldn't buy a watch, the vendor threw his own products to the ground, cursing like a sailor.

When the vendor bent down to pick up his watches, he saw Brian and snapped. With one swipe of his hand, he cleared his entire booth of watches, shouting and stomping on his own goods. This was the first time we had witnessed a native lose his mind.

Our Indonesian adventure had definitely come to an end. We walked over to the travel office and booked our flight to Australia.

After a month on the island, we had the rest of the night to relax and lay low before our flight the next morning. We splurged on *good* Indonesian pizza; it was terrible but we loved it. We had officially lowered our standards so "what didn't kill us was amazing."

Over dinner, we heard Heinrich from Sweden got knocked out during a bar brawl a few nights back. Felix said, "I guess the natural progression of absolute madness is the world around you goes 'mannie' too."

I thought about it. "That's a profound statement." Brian tried to laugh but he was too rattled. He kept looking over his shoulder all night.

Despite the bumps and bruises, we enjoyed going crazy in Indonesia: the sunburns, the friendship, the hangovers, the unadulterated debauchery, getting beaten by a tiny gang, tied up by a kinky Swede, menaced by a gang of hookers, licking frogs, jumping chickens, making sexy with Brazilian girls, the dog attacks—we even enjoyed the boat from hell now that it was over.

It seems a lot of people travel to places, find what they like, then do it a million times. This is a backwards attitude, if you ask me. To enjoy every country for what it has to offer, you have to free your mind from all preconceptions, "be here now" and "go with the flow." These are the keys to a good travel experience. But what the hell do I know.

After dinner we went back to our guesthouse and listened to Elvis on the radio I lifted from Inga in our exodus from Palm Gardens. We reflected on our journey and anticipated what was to come. Brian blew out our lucky candle and let the tree frogs serenade us to sleep. "Get ready, Rob. Tomorrow may hold the greatest surprise so far."

I closed my eyes and envisioned Australia. "Can't wait to see what happens next."

3

Getting Down Undah

WE KEPT PUSHING OUR GONZO adventure to the limit.
Our dreams of escaping the tsunami of unbridled capitalism
in America had led us into a hurricane of debauchery overseas. "This is
not how I envisioned this trip turning out," I said as we boarded our
flight out of Bali.

"Don't worry." Brian smiled. "We still have eleven months to turn
it all around."

After nearly a month exploring Indonesia, we departed for Singapore
on our way to Australia. I breathed a sigh of relief as I watched the islands
vanish beneath us. Brian was already wearing his sleep mask. He didn't
look back, he just mumbled, "We're lucky they let us leave with our limbs."

"I don't think I learned a damn thing from that place."

"I learned never try to outdrink a three hundred pound Swede with
a suitcase full of sex toys."

"No, I mean real stuff, personal renaissance stuff."

"Oh, *that* . . . Did you really think we'd leave California and suddenly be magically healed of all our fatal flaws?" Brian asked.

"I dunno. Maybe."

"At least while you're *living the question*, you're living like your heroes."

"What the hell does that mean? Living what question?"

"The meaning of life, dumbass. You know, Dr. Thompson and Captain
Kerouac would have gone on an epic drunk if they were in our flip-flops."

"But they were writing about it. I barely remember half of our gonzo exploits."

"That's on you. Do some memory exercises, brother. I'm going to watch the inside of my eye flaps."

Brian went to sleep and I took out my journal and started to write my first complete sentence of the entire trip: *In the end, Indonesia was a lovely place, full of two hundred and fifty million small, friendly people with a few insane ones (Brian did get beaten and nearly raped), with many beautiful islands full of traveling lunatics. . . . But it was time to go.*

Then my pen ran out of ink. Still, it was a start.

Our flight took us to Singapore, where we had another brief layover. Since it was our travel hub, we wanted to explore it during our short stays. Our Canadian friend Eric, who watched monkeys screw for a living, picked us up from the airport and took us to a food bazaar to try the Singaporean cuisine, which I quickly dubbed the "Best in Asia" before even visiting the other countries. We devoured spicy swordfish, squid omelets, and Tiger Beer, then went back to the airport to catch our plane to Sydney.

On our flight over the Indian Ocean, I played Nintendo golf while Brian snored incessantly. Somehow Brian had talked us into first class again. He was good for something. Seven hours later, we landed in Sydney.

Brian and I didn't know much about Australia other than what we'd learned from repeated viewings of *Crocodile Dundee* and the traveling Aussies we met on the road. From our encounters, they all seemed to be fun-loving and full of wanderlust. The ones we partied with were always quick with a laugh and had wonderfully entertaining drinking problems. We always seemed to fit right in with them.

Besides their charming alcoholism, all the Aussies I knew were constantly traveling, which at first made me think their homeland wasn't all that great but I would soon discover Australia is a lot of fun—*too much fun*. It's beautiful, dangerous, wild, and free—kind of like Texas meets California meets New Orleans. The only problem is, Australia is so far away from the rest of the Western world I couldn't imagine myself living here, which makes sense since it was originally founded as a British penal colony, like a giant Alcatraz.

Now that Brian and I were finally here, we were ready to explore their turf like the Aussies did the world—with reckless abandon. We found a traveler's kiosk in the airport that was set up for backpackers like us, then headed for the tourist mecca Bondi Beach, a few miles from Sydney, where we shacked up in the thick of things at the reasonably priced Hotel Biltmore, right on the beach.

We settled in, then did a half-ass jog along the beach. The scenery was jaw-dropping. Later we hung out on the beach all day and worked on our color, which was coming along nicely. Brian pointed out Bondi Beach had an underwater shark net; he was interested in the marine life. He was using someone's binoculars to see if he could spot pods of whales or the warm water fairy penguins that sometimes swam close to shore among the many surfers.

After a while, I noticed his gaze drifted to all the bikinis around us, which were more appealing to his eye.

That night Felix took us to the Bondi Beach Hotel to "go mad" again. Later, we found a small casino where Brian won two hundred Aussie bucks, which we blew on expensive shots of Louis XIII cognac. After way too much money won, lost, and spent—the drinks proved more expensive in a first-world country no matter what we ordered—we cursed our high tolerances and fled back to our hotel to drink the cheap hooch we had stashed in our rooms.

The next day, Felix took us to a secluded beach where we spent the day jumping off ridiculously high cliffs into shark-infested waters. Before our first jump, I was gripped by sheer terror.

"You know, Felix . . . I noticed some of the other beaches have shark nets to keep the sharks away. But not here." He just laughed and jumped into the sea, giving off a crazed Mohican yelp. It took two seconds for Brian to follow suit, "See you in the emergency rooooooooooooooooooooom!" *Splash*! *Splash*! They both popped up laughing, then mocked me until I jumped in, too.

On our way home, we magically found two unopened bags of marijuana; the goddess of travel was finally smiling on us. Brian was elated, "Dude, high times! We're the lucky strollers."

I was less enthusiastic. "Stay cool, this could be some kind of Aussie sting operation."

Brian agreed. "Right . . . . No more Ingas." We crouched behind some shrubs and waited.

"You wankers been watching too many Scorsese movies," Felix said, then he walked over and picked up the bags and speedwalked away. Brian and I looked at each other. "Hard to argue with that."

We spent the rest of the afternoon high, stumbling around Bondi Beach laughing at how trendy it was. It was a surreal contrast from a week before in the deserted jungle terrain of Komodo Island, where our idea of fun was leaping dragons. We sat down at an outside café and watched all the pretty girls walk by.

"Australian girls win the world contest for best-looking legs," Brian observed.

"Hands down," I said.

Felix piped in. "I prefer the California birds."

"You always want what you can't have," I mused, like it was some kind of original thought.

"You should write that proverb in your journal." Brian was mocking me for writing stuff down now.

"Better watch out. This journal's gonna be Exhibit A when they finally lock you up."

"It won't be admissible. You're an unreliable narrator."

"Didn't know you were a writer, mate." Felix seemed impressed.

"He's not—but he patterns his life after Charles Bukowski."

"Dr. Thompson, man. Hunter is my god. . . . C'mon, let's go get weird."

That night, inspired by all the gonzo writer talk, Brian and I reverted back to our old habits. We ran amok at Kings Cross; the locals call it "The Cross" even though there was nothing remotely holy about it. It was dominated by bars and strip clubs. We danced all night at the Soho Bar with two girls named Heidi and Amy who were going to a wedding the next day. I tried to talk them into letting us tag along, but couldn't convince them we'd act our age.

"We respect holy unions!"

Brian chimed in, "He's lying."

We ended the night getting kicked out of bars thanks to Felix, who couldn't handle his liquor. When it was near dawn, I said goodbye to Heidi and Amy and took a cab back to our hotel. I lost Felix and Brian somewhere along the way.

I woke at three o'clock in the afternoon the next day with a sour anvil on my head. I got up and walked around Bondi Beach with a hangover and tried to soak in the beauty. It was a small beach community with little houses on cliffs that overlooked the ocean. Charming . . . I needed to sit down.

I slinked into a café and had a cappuccino. I sat in a slumped stupor watching all the beautiful legs walk by until sunset. Brian was still passed out back in our room; he missed the entire day. I tried to write in my journal but it hurt. All I could manage was one sentence: *"I'm turning into a drunken vampire. . . ."*

The next morning, we were once again down at Bondi Beach licking our wounds from a two-day-old hangover.

Brian was semi-conscious with his head on the table. "We gotta keep movin'," I moaned. "We've been gone a month and half and have only been to two countries? If we don't see at least twenty countries this year we are total losers. . . . What is wrong with us?"

Brian tried to lift his head off the table but couldn't. "We both know the answer to that question."

"I need to find sweet Utopia," I mumbled to myself.

Brian had no idea what I was talking about. "Is that a strip club?"

I'd never really talked about it with Brian, but I'd been dreaming of Utopia my entire life. Call it what you want—Utopia, Xanadu, Oz, heaven on earth—I yearned to live someplace free from all the trappings of the modern world.

Does it exist? Did it ever?

I have a feeling it did and still does, somewhere, but where? Maybe I was just naive, but I didn't think it was such a crazy idea. I wasn't looking for some easy way out of reality—I didn't want to bask in hedonism in some land of milk and honey where beautiful women fed me grapes all day (though that would be nice). I just wanted a purer way of life, free from all the fake plastic trees and fake plastic people that seemed to have spread everywhere, like some vapid virus. Maybe that's why I drank so much. I've been caught up dreaming some outdated hippie fantasy.

When I told all this to Brian, his only response was, "And look what happened to the hippies—they're all driving Volvos."

I was lost in an existential haze and needed guidance, so I dug out my old friend: the *Lonely Planet* travel book. It recommended we flee the city on a famous backpacker bus called the Oz Experience.

I perked up, "Oz . . . That sounds like heaven." After paying a fixed price, the Oz Experience would take us north up the eastern coast from Sydney to Cairns for around two hundred dollars. The best part was we could get off wherever and whenever we wanted. This was a brilliant concept for any backpacker.

Brian and I staggered down to the Oz office to lock up our transportation. I bought us the entire eastern Australia option for two hundred and fifty dollars. After I got the tickets, I found Brian outside. He was still staring into the void.

"God is dead . . . . God *is dead*, Rob. *What chance do we really have?*"

"Dude, snap out of it! They said we can jump on and off. And get this, you can drink on the bus!"

Brian turned to me like a lobotomy patient, then he smiled like he'd been awakened by the devil. "Sounds like . . . the best bus *ever*."

The night before we left Sydney, Felix got all his "friends" together and threw us a going away bash. My first mistake of the evening was drinking half a bottle of Bundaberg Rum before we even left the hotel. Bundaberg is fifty-seven percent alcohol and will sting you in the butt, especially when you chug half a bottle in two hours.

Brian said, "You drink like a combination between Bluto Blutarsky and Charles Bukowski. Your new drunk nickname is Blutarsky Bukowski."

I just looked at him. "I have no response to that."

The sun went down and we met up with Felix's "friends" down on Oxford Street at the old Paddington Inn, one of our favorite haunts. I walked in glowing from the Bundaberg, and had the strangest conversation with an attractive girl named Pippa, who told me she liked to get "choked out" when she was having sex.

I asked Pippa—whose drunk nickname became "Choke Out"—all sorts of questions. "What happens if he does too good of a job?" When Pippa finally ended our conversation, I said, "Nice to meet you. Maybe someday I can choke you!"

She said, "That would be great." I almost ran after her, but decided against it.

Later, I met a girl named Missy, who was extremely drunk and belligerent. By this time I was hammered, so I proceeded to provoke her belligerence with a stick. I asked Missy provocative questions, and she started throwing drinks on me. I thought this was awesome. Her friends, however, were horrified at her behavior.

So for fun, whenever her nice friend wasn't listening, I'd whisper obnoxious obscenities in Missy's ear and she would erupt like clockwork. Then her nice friend would come over to yell at her again while I sat there innocently. All this happened while a cockatoo was perched on my shoulder.

This asshole game I was playing reminded me of an old high school friend who liked to get girls very angry with him, then he'd try and turn things around and sleep with them. I was amazed at what he was capable of; he was more successful than not.

He later became a psychiatrist.

After the Inn, we went to a nightclub and it got ugly. This is when I officially began to regret taking Felix under my soused wing. On the outside he seemed to be one of those classic Beat characters, a soiled angel with a broken heart and a shady past, which was intriguing at first. When we met him he was mourning his lost love, so I thought, why not let him tag along?

Turned out Felix was a little more broken than we thought he was. The first sign of trouble was he kept getting us kicked out of everywhere. The second sign was he kept running into "frenemies" who wanted him to pay for past delinquent debts, which he assured us were figments of their imaginations.

Felix kept getting booted out of bar after bar. The night was turning into a creep show of skeletons from Felix's closet, all of them screaming, "Break your pawkets," a phrase they must have picked up from American gangster rappers. When Felix did "break his pockets," all he had in his waterproof Ocean Pacific wallet was twenty-eight Aussie bucks, a condom, and a picture of his lost girl, which didn't get him far.

His antics had me drinking heavily. Every time a new frenemy came out of the woodwork, I pretended I didn't know Felix. Brian had no such decorum. He just stood there pointing and hooting, "I've never seen one guy's closet full of skeletons come back to haunt him all in one night!"

The Bundaberg helped me black out the rest of the unpleasantness. When I regained consciousness, I was back in my room—I thought. Then through the darkness I heard a strange voice in my ear, "You Yanks are the best lovers." Even in my blurred state, I found that quite odd. I mean, this mystery woman's voice sounded a bit too gravely for my usual taste. Maybe she's a smoker. Then I felt something touch my crotchal region. It was a hand, a bit too calloused and large for a woman.

A cold chill came over me as I opened my eyes into my new reality. I was in bed with no woman. It was some dude on top of me. I heard myself screaming like I was being screwed by the devil, *"Get off!"*

Brian woke up screaming, *"Inga!! Intruder!"* He began wildly swinging a walking stick. Then he flipped on the lights. We saw someone rolling around mummified in my sheets. It was our intruder alright, but it was no Inga.

It was Felix on the ground, giving me the death stare.

Who am I? What was in that Bundaberg??

Felix didn't say a word; he just dashed out of the room into the night wrapped only in a sheet, leaving his empty Ocean Pacific wallet behind. Brian eventually stopped swinging the walking stick, went to the open door, and watched Felix run off into the distance.

He quietly closed the door and sat back down on the bed. "You don't see that every day."

"He was trying to steal third base when I woke up!"

Brian smiled. "Oh I'd say he stole it clean."

I dragged myself into the shower and let the cold water pour down. Nothing against homosexuality, I love the LGBT community, but I had been violated. I spent an hour scrubbing my body looking for my lost dignity to the sound of Brian laughing like a hyena. I never found my dignity in that shower. Felix left me regretting I ever trusted a stranger. I reemerged from the bathroom and guzzled a bottle of water, then fell onto my sheetless bed. Brian just smiled.

"Just . . . *don't.*"

Brian laughed. "What? My name is Paul and this is between ya'll."

"Dude, I regained consciousness during mid—whatever. If anything happened, he was having sex with a corpse."

"Whatever man; I believe you. I mean . . . he *was* hotter than Inga."

It had taken six weeks for both of us to get violated overseas. I turned off the lights and put my pillow over my head. "Is the world just as corrupt as America?"

Brian busted out laughing, "Obviously, *yes!*"

"Has everyone's soul been sucked to hell?"

Brian rolled over in his bed, "Try not to think too hard."

The next morning, I packed my stuff. Sorting through the remnants of last night, I muttered, "This trip is getting ridiculous."

Brian looked at me. "You said you wanted new experiences." I could tell he was trying to keep a straight face.

I was never going to live this down. The Felix thing was screwing with my head. I had been searching the world over for real-life Beats, even though Brian kept saying it was a fool's game. The reality was, I wasn't finding any "saints of the streets" on the road. I'd been swan diving into the depths of the food chain, looking to find the purest of filthy souls and had found nothing but deeper holes of humanity.

I'd befriended freaks, fiends, and drunks, and after much research, it appeared they weren't holy beatnik saints untainted by capitalism after all. . . .

They really were insane freaks, fiends, and drunks.

The Felix incident taught me I couldn't get by on just having blind faith in humanity anymore, not in a world out to hustle people like me. I also couldn't drink Bundaberg Rum anymore. Christ, I couldn't black out anymore! It scared me to think of myself during a blackout just letting go of the wheel and hoping my car wouldn't drift into oncoming traffic. But I had done it hundreds of times. My luck has to be running out.

I made a resolution not to black out again. I didn't want to end up in bed with another man . . . unless I was sharing a bed with Brian to save money.

The time had come to finally leave Sydney after two weeks of fun, fondling, and felonies. We left knowing we had experienced the best and worst of a great beach town full of awesome and horrendous people.

We left Bondi Beach on the Oz Experience Bus on our way to Dog Sheep Ranch where Brian and I would spend Valentine's Day with thousands of sheep. Our plan was to travel up the eastern coast from Sydney all the way to the Great Barrier Reef and Cairns, where we would fly out. We estimated it would take about a month to complete.

We walked to our pickup spot on a corner and, sure enough, a brightly colored Oz Bus pulled up that looked like it once belonged to Ken Kesey.

"This is like *The Electric Kool-Aid Acid Test* bus," I said.

"Happy now?" Brian said.

"Yes . . . yes, I am." We shuffled onboard with a bunch of other like-minded lunatics.

Our magic bus ran into a snag just outside Dog Sheep Ranch. We couldn't enter the property because heavy rains had flooded the river and road.

"This is unacceptable. We can cross this thing ourselves." Brian jumped up. "C'mon!"

Back in America we'd probably be arrested for endangering ourselves or forced to sign a waiver, but "down undah" the driver just laughed and said, "Go on ahead!"

We balanced our packs on our heads and waded across the flooded river. Seeing two idiots like us survive inspired the rest of the backpackers to follow suit. We didn't think any of the others would follow us after we spent the past four hours forcing everyone to watch *Dumb and Dumber* on repeat, which no one found funny. But they did.

When we all finally slogged our way up to Dog Sheep Ranch, we were greeted by a menagerie of wildlife. Bouncing kangaroos and screeching cockatiels were everywhere. The valleys and plains seemed endless and green. It was gorgeous. Just at that moment while looking out at this wonder, a cockatoo flew down and landed on a bunk next to me.

After we settled in, Brian and I took a tour of the sprawling one-thousand-acre ranch with the other backpackers. When we toured the main operations, I had to keep an eye on Brian; he seemed to be staring at the sheep a little too fondly. "We did say we wanted to try new and strange things on our world adventure, right?"

"Keep it to yourself, Rakow," I said.

The head rancher announced, "Now we're going to shear the sheep. Who wants to give it a go?" I didn't want any part of it. Grabbing a poor screaming sheep and shaving it is a lot harder than it sounds.

Brian raised his hand. "Why do we have to 'share' the sheep when there are so many? It's Valentine's Day, and you guys have thousands." All the backpackers laughed. The ranch hands looked like they wanted to shear Brian from head to toe.

That night after dinner, we sat around drinking with three gals from New Zealand who were very open about their sexuality. The girls talked about how horny they were and how they masturbate every night and wanted to get shagged constantly.

I asked them if their boyfriends ever cheated on them with sheep. They all said it has happened with some of their boyfriends but "a proper beau wouldn't do that." I asked if sheep sex was cheating or not, since "it wasn't even a human."

They all agreed it still was.

Later, Brian and I left the girls to venture into the paddock to roam around the rollicking hills. We didn't have a torch, so we used the moon as our guide. We wanted to go cow tipping but we didn't know how.

We tried to sneak up on some cows but they realized what we were up to. This was either a regular occurrence, or we were too loud.

These cows would never let us near them, so we decided it was not nice to push over sleeping animals. So we tried to catch a sheep.

Call us depraved idiots, but we wanted to see if there were any sparks between these four-legged sex sirens and us. The girls said if you put their hind feet in buckets of water they wouldn't run. But since we didn't have any buckets, we tried to chase down one of the nimble little buggers. Every time we thought we had one cornered, it would jump a ravine or race down a cliff.

After an hour, we gave up our romantic endeavors and headed back to our dorm, where we could fantasize about the Kiwi girls (or the sheep) in private.

Good times?

The next morning, we were off for Bingara, an old mining town in the interior of Australia, in the state of New South Wales. Our driver said it was one of the only places where diamonds had been found.

"This could be the answer to all our money woes," Brian said.

"Not bloody likely."

The first thing we noticed when we got into town was the people of Bingara seemed to be a very close-knit group. Very few foreigners ever stepped foot near here. It felt like the Mississippi of Australia; the entire place had a very *Deliverance* feel to it.

We checked into the Imperial Hotel then found the only bar in town. It was small but had a pool table. The problem was the natives were already drunk and it was six o'clock on a Friday evening. You could tell the place was going to fill up with belligerent locals very soon. After a few beers, we learned you didn't want to beat any of the locals at pool. They were all cowboys who were looking to fight some fancy-pants Yank, so we played it cool and lost a few games on purpose just to get in their good graces. Then I started kicking their asses and things got testy.

Trouble finds Brian, so it didn't take long for him to get into a skirmish in the bathroom. After a few toilet-related run-ins, Brian asked me to watch his back while he was pissing, so I did. And just like he described, the cowboys came barging in to bump us and make snide remarks.

I tried to defuse the situation. "Hey fellas, we're just like you—you like beer. We like your beer. You like women. We like your women, too. Can't we all just get along?"

They stood there seemingly stunned by my idiotic speech, then shoved me into a bathroom stall and left laughing like a pack of jackals. We should have gone back to our room, but we didn't have any booze waiting for us.

"I'm not sacrificing my buzz on account of a few sheep lovers," Brian said, so we kept drinking till they closed.

By the end of the night, the cowboys wanted to fight so bad they resorted to aggressively hitting on all the Oz Bus girls we were traveling with. The final straw was when one of them came up and flipped me the bird. After staring at his dirty cowboy middle finger for a few seconds, I knew it was time to turn in before we got strangled to death by the grubby meat hooks of one of the local cowboys.

We hopped the Oz Bus to Byron Bay the next morning and got the hell out of Bingara. When we arrived in Byron, it was a totally different vibe—hallelujah. It was an earthy beachside town that had a cool downtown district. Byron felt like the opposite of Bondi or Kuta Beach; no high-rise hotels or chain restaurants had invaded yet.

"This place is like hippie surfer cool, man," Brian said as he busted out his empty weed pipe and took off his shoes to mingle with the rest of the alternative hippies roaming about. The locals we met told us if the billionaire developers had their way, Byron would turn into Bondi Beach or even Surfers Paradise, which we kept hearing about, but the town was dedicated to preserving its funky small-town soul.

"I think I want to braid my hair," I said while I watched all the cool surfer girls walk by.

"That's probably not a good look for you," Brian said.

"Is anything a good look for me?"

"How about a paper bag on your head? I wanna find a drum circle and get all tribal on someone's ass!"

"Please don't become *Bongo-Playing Guy*. I hate that guy."

"That's exactly who I'm gonna become!"

"I wanted you to go all beatnik, so I should have expected this."

I ordered a gyro from the local food stall and sat down to watch the groovy scene while Brian went looking for a bongo and some weed. A cool girl named Jade, a typical name for the area, chatted me up on the park bench. She gave me a really good feeling about Byron. I couldn't resist asking, "Is Jade your real name?" For all I knew it could have been her stage name. No such luck.

After we walked around town, we went back to our hostel, called the Arts Factory Lodge, and hung out with the other backpackers. The Arts Factory was set in an overgrown plot of land on the outskirts of town. It had bunkrooms, tepees, camping spots in the jungle, and huge tents. It was like a hippie commune. Everyone at the Factory looked like they just came from a Grateful Dead concert. We were with our people.

That night we went to the Railroad Bar, a pub by the railroad station with outside seating. At four in the morning, I lost everyone and ended up walking back to the Arts Factory in the dark. I went frog hunting, a carryover from Indonesia, and caught a big one, which I brought back to the hostel and presented to these two Danish girls.

"Looooook, pretttyyy," I said like the creepiest kid in your seventh grade biology class, which scared them. Wielding the amphibian, I chased the girls around and woke up the entire hostel. Then I let the frog loose and couldn't find him until the morning.

When Brian found out what I did the next day, he said, "You realize you're a complete jackass."

"Dude. I'm not evolving . . . I'm *de*volving."

"No shit. Have you tried drumming?"

We went to the beach that afternoon, and I got a terrible sunburn even though I was already tan. Every Aussie we met said their "island has a bloody sunroof" in the form of a huge hole in the ozone layer, which explains why Australians have the highest skin cancer rate in the world.

"The way my life is going, my liver is going to explode before I die from skin cancer," I said, before I realized I was flamebroiled.

Brian was barely awake in his chair. "Don't worry. You'll probably get killed by an angry mob first."

We hung out at the beach all day and listened to people talk about sharks. There seemed to be a lot of sightings up the coast and some people, like the English girls we met last night, wouldn't step foot in the ocean. Brian piped into the conversation. "This whole shark attack problem sounds a lot like malaria to me. It probably never occurs but it's the fear of the unknown that scares people."

I looked at Brian. "Have you noticed *this guy* has *no arm*?"

The guy telling the shark story held up his arm stump. "You bloody well *know* it happens here, mate. A great white bit my arm clean off, right out there." The one-armed Aussie pointed his stump at the ocean.

Brian rolled over, unimpressed. "Whatever."

We bought some dope from an English mate named Waldo to ease my sunburn agony, then Brian talked me into taking a drumming class in the rainforest. Simba was our instructor. I must admit it was pretty invigorating sitting outside with people from all around the world beating out tunes. Drumming my mind out, I looked over at Brian and he never looked happier. We both smiled marijuana smiles at each other as we drummed the rest of the day away.

Life, you are awesome.

Maybe it was the joy of discovering a cool new town, but it felt like we were finally learning something at this point on our journey. Maybe we hadn't rid ourselves of all our fatal flaws, but our eyes were opening to the real joy in the world around us. I had accepted the fact that real joy doesn't come from buying stuff or partying your brains out, it came from these moments when you feel truly alive.

While I drummed it occurred to me that maybe we should spend more time doing things like drumming in jungles with hippies and less time in bars. Rather than ponder that question too deeply, I kept on drumming.

At eight o'clock the next morning, the Oz Bus showed up again. We had fallen into the laid-back lifestyle of Byron and completely lost every shred of discipline in our lives, so the early start was a rude awakening. As we piled onto the bus half-asleep, I said, "Well, we've completely lost all structure."

Brian was full of coffee and raring to go. "And it feels great! Congratulations Rob, you're finally off the grid!"

We were soon on our way up the coast to the dreaded Surfers Paradise. We lost street cred with many of the backpackers on the bus who frowned on the place because of its reputation as a tourist trap. "Byron is radness, Surfer's Paradise is *shite*!" That's what we heard from the cool set, but Brian and I didn't care. We kept our promise throughout the trip to experience everything.

We arrived at Surfers Paradise and checked into the Surf'n'Sun Beachside Backpackers hotel. Surfers Paradise wasn't nearly as cool as Byron Bay, but it wasn't horrible; it was like a cross between Waikiki and Kuta Beach.

Mike, our buddy from Canada who was travelling with us now, heard about a party the next night for all the backpackers. Each bar in town held weekly costume shows where the new people from each hostel got on stage and performed some weird act. This would not normally interest me, but the winning hostel team got a free bar tab for the night so we were in.

Mike hatched a bizarre plan. He said, "Since we were surrounded by douche-bag tourists, why not act like one?" He proposed we go dressed in Depend adult diapers and piss our pants onstage. It sounded like something a moron would plan. Naturally, we loved it.

The night of the contest, our first stop was a strip club where Mike, Brian, and I enlisted a French stripper named Nashda to come play with us. Brian thought she would help us win the contest. Nashda was in when she heard we were a bunch of weirdos wearing Depends.

When it was time for the stage shows, which took place at each bar, we had stiff competition. Every time our crew got on stage and did our drag show, the astonished crowds didn't know what to think of us wearing Depends. We never won jack.

After we'd fully humiliated ourselves, Nashda and I left Brian and Mike at the bar and went to drunk dial my mom in the middle of the night. Don't ask me why I thought this was a good idea. If I remember correctly, mom and Nashda had a lovely twenty-minute conversation about dolphins that cost me eighteen dollars.

After five nights of crapping our pants in this tourist hellhole, we realized we had to get back on the road if we wanted to retain any brain cells.

We jumped on the next Oz Bus and headed to Noosa, a posh resort town with the most crystal blue waters I'd ever seen. Noosa is where the upper crust go to get their sun. You could tell we were in an expensive resort town by all the fancy cars, boutiques, and high-end restaurants.

Of course, we couldn't afford any of the luxuries being offered so we stayed at Koala's, a backpacker hotel, in a room for five. It was just four of us travelling together now: me, Mike, Brian, and Gillian, a gal we met from England. We spread out in our large room.

We met some Norwegian girls on the bus ride over, so we made plans to go out with them that night. After dinner, we ended up at one of the upscale bars that actually required shoes, which we hadn't anticipated. They wouldn't let us in in our flip-flops so we snuck around the corner and swapped out our flip-flops with our girlfriends' shoes and tried to get in again. But the bouncers didn't buy it, even though they let the girls in wearing our flip-flops.

The bouncers made it clear they didn't like "men in heels."

Brian wouldn't take no for an answer—being the foolhardy idiot that he is, he pulled five hundred dollars out of his pocket, which equaled about half-a-month of his backpacking budget, and waved it at the bouncers. "Don't you want our money?!" As you might imagine, this obnoxious act didn't go over well. The bouncers glared at Brian, who was now dancing around them like a turkey with his wad of money fanned out over his head.

I heard a police siren in the distance. Drunk and paranoid, I looked at Gillian. "They're calling the cops. Let's go." I grabbed her hand and we left Brian dancing like a turkey in front of the bar. It hurt like hell to run in Gillian's tiny high heels. After we ran about a hundred yards, we heard Brian screaming for me so we ran back to the bar just in time to see Brian and Mike get pounded by four bouncers.

I jumped into the fray, yelling, "Everyone calm down! I'm responsible for these boys!" After a few seconds, the fighting stopped. Then Brian ruined the peace by leaping up and tackling the biggest bouncer, which took things to Defcon 1.

All I could think of during the melee was I was trying to be a peacemaker in women's shoes. I didn't want to fight. My shoes wouldn't go over well in jail. Just then, some random Aussie with big knuckles gave me a cheap shot across my chin. All I heard was a loud *crack*! Somehow I didn't go down.

"What the hell'd you do that for?!!" I yelled, lunging at Mr. Knuckles as he walked away. The police sirens were getting close so the bouncers took mercy on Brian and stopped pounding him. Gillian was cursing a blue streak while I yanked Brian up from his protective fetal cocoon and dragged him away. Mike (being a Canadian pacifist) had smartly vanished in the dustup.

Last thing I heard was the bouncers laughing, "Go home, you Yankee poofters, you're drunk!"

So we went home.

We limped back to the hotel in pain, where Gillian tried to tend to our wounds. Brian held a can of beer he picked off the ground to his swollen eye. He put his arm around me. "Sorry for doing the turkey dance. It's good to know you can take a punch."

"It's disturbing to know you're a complete idiot. You're lucky they didn't rob you."

Brian laughed. "C'mon man. That's just the pain talking."

The next morning, my jaw felt shattered. Black-eyed Brian brought me some Australian Rice Krispies in bed to apologize. He inspected my swollen face and said he felt bad since he was the cause of it, being the "king smartass and all." I just sat there looking at my bowl of cereal.

"Snap, crackle, pop goes our bones, am I right?"

I didn't smile. "It's turning into the theme of this trip." Brian gave me a courtesy laugh, "Haha, yeah."

Later, as I inspected my swollen face in the mirror, I had an epiphany. "You realize we have to change our trajectory before we both end up in body casts, right?"

I waited for Brian's response. All I heard were snores.

After our high class, high-heeled pummeling in the fancy resort town of Noosa, Mike, Brian, Rana, Monica, and I got out of town.

I asked Brian, "Doesn't it seem like we're always getting run out of town?"

"Yeah. This bus is our getaway car."

We stopped for a night at the Dingo, a thirty-five thousand acre cattle ranch out in the middle of nowhere. There was another Oz Bus in the Dingo car park when we arrived. Black-eyed Brian was happy to see that the ranch was already full of backpacking crazies. "Let's get this party started!"

I tried to be the voice of reason. "C'mon, man, not again . . . I'm in triple-traction here."

"Let's just go in for a peek-a-loo."

We mingled with our new friends and met the owner of the Dingo who said, "Welcome to the Dingo, boys! The only rules here are wear a condom if you screw my dog."

That statement summed up the Dingo energy. There was no avoiding the debauchery tonight. We'd veered into the eye of another party hurricane and there was nowhere to hide.

That night, the Dingo crew threw a party for all the new arrivals at the bar. Brian said, "If I've learned anything on this trip, it's Australia is one big bloody party," as he watched our new friends drinking, singing, and dancing on tables.

"Emphasis on the bloody," I said, rubbing my swollen face.

The only thing that made us forget our bumps and bruises were the libations and Emma, a good-looking redhead from England who was a ranch hand. We heard she had "meetings" in the back all the time, and would occasionally mess around with some of the backpackers if you were lucky. I struck up a conversation with her, hoping to arrange a meeting for later, but she proved elusive. Maybe it was because I looked like a two-bit stuntman on holiday with all my injuries.

At the end of the night, there was a striptease show. "Just another night in the Outback!" Emma said to me as she got up to lead the nude dancing event. After the striptease, which was an eye-opener, we all drank cheap wine out of a box and danced around in the dirt to bad music until everyone fell over or passed out.

I was the last one standing and it seemed Emma had disappeared in the back with someone else. So with no companion but the owner's skinny dog, I decided it was a good idea to strip naked, put on a trench coat, and run around everyone's sleeping quarters while singing like a drunken cowboy. I remember nothing other than I was feeling no pain. (So much for my blackout pledge.)

The next morning, I woke up outside with no pants on, no Emma in sight, and a huge headache. My only cuddle buddy was the ubiquitous skinny dog that was quietly farting in my face.

I found my bearings and hobbled into my sleeping quarters. Everyone was already up. I didn't take long to notice all my new "friends" were giving me mean looks. When Brian saw me all he could say was, "Duuuuuuuude," like I was in some kind of trouble. I was too hungover to remember my offenses, so Mike took pleasure in reminding me. He said my Mad Flasher routine didn't stop until I ran into a tree and knocked myself out. "I heard a loud 'smack' then you hit the ground, said 'bollocks,' then you were snoring. So we just left you out there."

"Ugh. . . . Did I screw the pooch?" I asked. Mike said, "You mean Emma? She stayed with me last night. But you may have screwed Vegemite, the owner's dog, though!" Then he laughed and walked away. It was appropriate the dog was named after a disgusting Australian breakfast paste. His farts smelled terrible.

Shamed and friendless, except for Brian and Vegemite, I dragged myself onto the next Oz Bus. Late that night, we pulled into Airlie Beach, one of the main points of departure for the Great Barrier Reef. Everyone on the bus had been talking about how Cyclone Justin was on the way, but like morons Brian and I didn't pay attention.

The next morning with Cyclone Justin lurking, we decided to sober up for a few days and enroll in the PADI (Professional Association of Diving Instructors) Open Water Scuba Diving program. We passed the two-day class then went to the Great Barrier Reef to earn our PADI Open Water Certification. Located in the Coral Sea, the reef stretches across nine hundred islands and is composed of nearly three thousand individual reefs. It's the largest living organism on earth, which is built from billions of tiny organisms known as coral polyps and is home to many other life forms. It's so huge that it's one of the few natural wonders that you can see from space.

Brian and I boarded the Anaconda yacht, a ninety-five-foot sailboat, and headed out to the Great Barrier Reef, the world's largest coral reef system and one of the best diving spots in the world. It was remarkable we could even afford the trip on this amazing skiff, but it was inexpensive—maybe because the cyclone was about to hit and all the sane people were heading inland.

We made two dives the first day, but the waters were stormy so the visuals weren't great, matching our minds. That night, we were so tired from all the nitrogen our body had absorbed that after dinner we went to our bunks and crashed.

We dove thirty meters the next day as a part of our deep-diving training. We were warned about getting nitrogen narcosis, which gives you the feeling of euphoria and drunkenness right before death. I piped up, "How will I know I've got it? That's how I've felt the entire time in Australia." Brad, the dive instructor, didn't laugh. He was dead serious, so I stopped joking around and paid attention.

Cyclone Justin hit the final night of our dive training. We waited it out at the local pub. I went back on my promise and bought a bottle of Bundaberg Rum and drank the whole thing with Brian, Mike, and Paul and Brad, our two dive instructors. With the Bundaberg coursing through our veins, Brad and I danced around the bar while everyone that wasn't with our diving crew wondered what the hell we were celebrating during this hellacious cyclone attack.

We went to another bar and met two guys, one named Beauty, who was a lunatic, and the other, Roger, was from Holland. Beauty got sloppy drunk, so we left him to go outside into the cyclone and howl into the night like a bunch of idiots in a hundred mile-per-hour windstorm.

Brian almost got stabbed through the forehead with a flying blade of grass that ended up impaling a wooden fence. When we witnessed that amazing feat, we ran back into the bar.

I was on a mission to dive on the Barrier Reef if the cyclone would just pass, so the next morning Brian, Mike, the Norwegian girls, and I took the bus to Cairns, another beach town on the eastern coast in Queensland. We lost Brian to amorous intentions with one of the Norwegian girls, who finally fell for his charms.

Cairns is the end of the road for many backpackers because it's where the other international airport is located in Australia. It's a great spot to hang out with other backpackers because there are always people coming and going. I was hoping to dry out and just dive for several days while Brian was away, but as it turned out the damn cyclone followed us up the coast.

No diving for me. We were trapped inside, so I was resigned to sleep in, read a lot, and then poison myself silly at night at a bar called the Woolshed. I couldn't escape the Aussie party even when I tried. *Every time I think I'm out, they pull me back in.*

When Brian caught up with us two days later he was full of energy and ready to binge drink. "I'm back, baby! I'm a new man, I finally got to wet my beak!" he announced right before he got naked at the Woolshed while two rugby players carried him around on their shoulders with a piece of cardboard crammed in his ass. This ritual had a name: They called it "The Landshark." I thought it was a big joke, but apparently everyone has done it once or twice in these parts. The entire bar was laughing at Brian. I just shook my head. All I could think was, "Is this what we came here to do? Get things crammed up our butt?"

Our spiritual quest had bottomed out in an Australian party bus. After the nonstop bacchanal that was the infernal Outback, Brian and I were mentally wrecked. I was probably sober only twenty percent of the time I was in Australia, and it had taken a toll. I knew I had lost complete track of time when I saw a calendar and didn't know what month it was. "Is that calendar right? What month is it?"

"March, I think." Brian said.

"March *what*? How long have we been here??"

"I don't know. . . . Two months?"

"You've got to be kidding. I thought it was still February."

"Dude . . . you need help."

When I finally sobered up long enough to realize we had not just had a "lost weekend" in Australia, we'd had a lost two months, I felt like an idiot for wasting so much time rampaging around the eastern ass of the Outback like a couple of blotto outlaws.

Brian spent the next hour going on about how his brain cells were melting with every passing day we stayed here. "I forgot what I ever wanted out of this trip . . . I need to start over. I need to go back to kindergarten, man."

We didn't know where to go next, but we agreed we had to flee to a country that would challenge us in some way. Australia we understood; the formula here was adventure, party, friendship, party, fight, party, pass out, party, try not to screw the pooch, and party some more. Although I still love Aussies to this day with all my enlarged heart, we never once got out of our comfort zone—unless you count me possibly getting raped.

I needed more. My liver needed less and I still wanted to be shocked and amazed by life.

"Where should we go next?" I asked him.

"I dunno," Brian said, "but wherever we go, we're back to square one on the evolutionary scale."

While we thought about our next move, for symmetry purposes we spent our last nights in Cairns wasted out of our minds. I have no idea where Brian disappeared to—I was with Lea, my Danish girlfriend who had traveled with us for the past two weeks.

One late night in Cairns on the way back to Lea's hostel, we stopped at a phone booth. You've probably noticed I have this strange personality quirk where I want to talk to my mom when I'm drunk. I can't say that she ever wants to talk to me, but it's something I've done my entire life. I know drunk dialing your mom is bizarre and probably Freudian, but it's even worse when you bring your barely legal girlfriend that you promised to travel with for the next month in Australia into the phone booth with you. You definitely don't want her to overhear you telling Mom that you're leaving for Singapore tomorrow, which is what happened. When I let it slip, I tried to backtrack but Lea flipped out.

After I saw how hurt Lea was, I felt like a complete jerk for misleading her. I apologized and promised I would stay two more nights to say a proper goodbye. I genuinely liked Lea and had vowed to make a real effort not to treat every woman I met on the trip like a transitional woman after the way things ended with Elena, even though that's what they might've been.

I mean, what were the odds Brian or I would find *true love* on this yearlong escapade? What are the odds anyone does? Ever? When I posited this to Brian, he said, "Gotta live the question, man. Gotta *live* the question."

He kept repeating "live the question" so damn much it became our private mantra, the one that really defined our trip. "Let's go mad" was the public mantra we shared with the rest of the world in times of extreme revelry, but in private we had a deeper quest. No one else we met on the trip knew this, but us "stupid Yanks" had a few tricks up our sleeves yet.

I bid Lea farewell two days later. We promised to stay in touch, but in the end (spoiler alert) we never did. I went looking for Brian, who I found passed out in our room. He looked like warmed-over shit. He mumbled something about running into "our Depends stripper from Surfers Paradise at the end of the world" last night.

"You mean Nashda?"

"Nasty Nashda . . . You just missed her." He said she spent the night with him in my bed. I felt a twinge of jealousy since I still had a thing for Nashda, but what did I have to be jealous about? She wasn't mine. No one was anybody's on this global gallivant.

Brian bringing a stripper into the dorm at night sure got the gossip going at the hostel. Not only was it against their policy, but the word trickled down to a few of our lady friends who had become slightly attached to us. By the end of our final day, it was clear we had to get out of the country since we had promised several girls we would travel with them to four different countries—none of which we planned to actually visit.

We mercifully departed Australia on the 25th of March—a month too late. I watched another country vanish beneath us. "We always leave when the shit's about to hit the fan."

Brian smiled with his sleep mask firmly fastened. "It's the first rule of showmanship: always leave 'em wanting more."

With no idea where we were going next, we flew into Singapore and spent the night at the apartment of one of my parents' friends.

The apartment had all the modern amenities. Brian and I wasted a day doing laundry and watching TV, neither of which had been done in a month. While staring at the tube and catching up on American sitcoms and the news, I realized how easy it was to step outside of the spinning world and not miss it. I turned off the TV and looked at Brian, who was splayed out on the couch. "Well, nothing happened in the world in three months."

Brian yawned. "I can't remember half of what happened either."

I pulled my clothes out of the dryer. "I guess it's a wash then. . . ."

Brian yelled, "So, I hate to ask, but where should we go next??"

"Well, I've given this some thought. Since we've been run out of every country we've visited so far, maybe it's time for a slap in the face."

Brian didn't like the sound of that. "Slap? Dude I'm still healing. I can't take anymore—"

"A metaphoric slap, a forced wakeup call . . . something to snap us back into reality. Something to make us think."

"Like visiting the Cambodian killing fields or Auschwitz or something?"

"Maybe . . . but how about we go visit Jack's ghost first?"

"You're blowing what's left of my mind."

"We're really close."

"Why now?"

"I think I have to . . . with or without you."

"You don't *have* to do anything. Your psyche is already fragile—and my head is as soft as a newborn's. Why jeopardize our sanity with a giant bong hit of reality? We haven't even gotten to the nude beaches of Thailand yet!"

"Will you just listen? You've been driving this ship for nearly three months and look where it's gotten us."

"You're blaming all this on me? You said you wanted Utopia, so I brought you there. It's not my fault we can't control our animal impulses."

"Well, it's partly your fault . . ."

"Point taken. All right." Brian was too tired to put up much of a fight. "I'll let you drive. I'm reasonable. I want growth as much as you do."

"Then it's settled. The 'Cirrhosis Tour' stops now."

4

Philistines in the Philippines

BRIAN AND I WERE AS sober as we'd been all year when we packed up our belongings and hopped a flight to Luzon, the largest island in the Philippines and one of the most populated islands in the world.

"Really think Jack's still hangin' around here?" Brian muttered while sipping his first virgin Bloody Mary ever.

"There's no place he'd rather be," I said.

I was dragging Brian to a bittersweet reunion with a past I could no longer ignore. We were returning to the "scene of the crime" where my childhood ended—the place where my family was torn apart and I developed my thirst for whiskey and women. This is the part of the story where you find out why I call my mom when I'm drunk. It's a habit born from one man; he had many (good and bad) habits, and they were all passed down to me.

Brian didn't seem to mind. "Have you noticed we're doing nothing but island hopping?" he said. "Indonesia, Australia, now this."

"Australia's a continent."

"Technically. But who are they kidding?"

"I love islands. When I was little I always told Jack I'd retire to one. Maybe I still will."

"*Now* I get it . . . Jack's just a red herring. We're going to the Philippines to find Utopia."

"Maybe. Hadn't thought of it like that. But if Utopia exists it would have to be on an island, right? Cut off from the rest of the corrupt world."

"You may be on to something."

I didn't let on how conflicted I felt about this leg of our trip, but Brian was right—we were island hopping on our sideways hunt for Shangri-la. We were going to the perfect part of the world for this kind of quest. Like Indonesia, the Philippines is an archipelago country made up of more than seven thousand islands.

It's broken up into three main geographies: the mega-islands of Luzon and Mindanao and the many small and beautiful Visayan Islands. If you're a diver, surfer, big-city culture junkie, or just love to vacation on heavenly beaches, there is an island in the Philippines for you. Divers and beach bums should head straight to the Visayas, where island-hopping and diving is king.

We planned to scour the Visayas for our Xanadu eventually, but we had some business to attend to first.

We landed right in the heart of the action in the swarming capital city of Manila where we ran into a mass of holy mayhem the second we touched down. "The Book calls Manila the 'Pearl of the *Orient*' . . . Should we file an anti-defamation lawsuit?" Brian closed the book and handed it back to me. "So racist."

"Very funny. Drink it in, Rakow." I gestured to the swirling chaos around us.

"Will you stop mentioning drinks? I'm tryin' to dry out over here." He set his gaze on the insane scene. "Why is the entire world at the airport today?"

"Hate to break it to you, but we've landed in the vortex of this country's love for Easter. Everyone's leaving to holiday in the provinces."

Brian laughed. "Great. Is the Savior in the building? I'm Catholic! Everyone go crazy at once!" he shouted, waving his arms at the swarms of Filipinos rushing to catch their plane.

I can't remember whose plan it was to fly on Easter weekend, but it was a terrible idea. The country's overwhelming Catholic population had stormed the airport at once, the result of three hundred and fifty years of Spanish rule. Western religions may seem incongruous with this part of the world, but the Philippines is a very different animal from their neighbors in Southeast Asia like China, Korea, Thailand, Cambodia, and Vietnam. Instead of Hindu and Buddhist, they're Catholic and Muslim. Instead of the pervasive Asian cultural influence you find on the mainland, the "PI" is very much rooted in Pacific Islander, Spanish, and (yes) American traditions.

"You know more about this place than your stupid Book," Brian said.

"That's cause I used to live here," I said.

This was Brian's first visit to the Philippines. Not mine. The "PI" was my second home when I was a teenager. Being back felt like déjà vu all over again.

We settled into a long queue for a taxi. Brian fell asleep on his feet and I got lost in my thoughts. I couldn't stop thinking about the old man. Dad was a complicated guy who I never fully understood. He retired on Luzon, near the Subic Bay Naval Base, when he was in his early forties. He seemed like some character out of an adventure book when he told me he bought a trimaran sailing boat in Hawaii and was going to sail it for six weeks to the Philippines.

Back then, I thought Jack was so cool, so glamorous, having this second life away from home. However, Jack seemed slightly less heroic when he never came back home to the States.

He had a heart attack and died in the Philippines when I was twenty-one. He was only forty-eight; it was his second heart attack. He smoked, drank, and never exercised, so his debauched lifestyle finally caught up with him. By the time he croaked, I was already out of university and making my own money independently, so it was my job to fly over and get all his stuff. That was seven years ago.

Here I was, back again. Ironically I'm at my lowest point in life and succumbing to all my fatal flaws at once. Guess it's only appropriate I pay a visit to the place that created them. I don't know what I expected to get out of this, but I felt I needed to say goodbye to this place and put old memories to bed that I'd blocked out ever since Jack said "adios" to the world with a beer in his hand and a cigarette dangling from his mouth.

"What are you thinking about?" Brian asked from his trance-like state.

"The great and powerful Captain Jack, who had a heart attack," I said.

"Why'd he leave you and your mom to come *here*?"

"I asked him a few times but he never explained. All I knew was Dad docked his trimaran at Subic Bay, bought a bar, and that was that. I didn't ask too many questions. Didn't want to make Jack angry."

"But they *stayed* married . . . Who does that?"

"It wasn't a conventional setup. I didn't have a normal childhood."

"Yeah, no shit. Neither did I."

After waiting in line for hours amid the throng of traveling Catholics at the airport, we finally caught a taxi to the bus station. The drive normally took fifteen minutes but it took us two hours. In the taxi, Brian marveled at how our cabbie jockeyed for space in the congested, narrow Manila streets.

"There are absolutely no road rules here except the driver with the biggest balls wins!" Brian kept ordering our taxi driver to "punch it!"—which, of course, our guy didn't understand since he spoke no English. So we inched our way past all the familiar skyscrapers that jutted into the polluted Manila haze, slowly scooting our way through all the shantytowns and past all the new, shiny shopping malls with all their American stores.

We were snarled in traffic for so long I almost told the driver to pull over so we could spend the night in Manila and Brian could experience all the city's many speakeasies I used to drink in. But I was feeling selfish. I was on a mission to see my old home on Subic Bay. I didn't need to keep Brian entertained all the time.

We finally arrived at the bus station and waited for three more hours with what seemed like another million Filipinos. Eventually we snagged a bus to the city of Olongapo, which bordered Subic Bay and was a two-hour trip that took us six. At this point, Brian was not feeling very chipper about the hellish commute (he'd been sober for far too long to enjoy anything), but I knew what to expect. I leaned into the punishment. I was here to pay my dues.

Olongapo felt like a ghost town. The Subic Naval Base, a relic from World War II was long gone. There were still things to do, but all the hotspots from back in the day (Olongapo, Barrio Barretto, and Subic) had fallen into hyper-attrition. Everything had changed since the Navy boys left. The sixteen thousand servicemen who used to run amok here when it was the world's largest naval base had all gone back to their wives. All that was left were locals, drunks, go-go dancers, and lost ex-pats.

There were still large hotels opening up; it looked like more Filipinos were vacationing here. But when I was a kid, there were over a thousand bars within ten miles of each other. It was beyond madness to a fourteen-year-old like me. In my mind, it was like the USO scene from *Apocalypse Now* every night. At least that's what I told my friends back home. Every bar had its own stable of girls. It was quite an eye opener—especially since my dad owned one of the bars.

We checked into the Marmont Resort Hotel, where I used to stay when I was a teenager, then went out to see what was left of the town. We were both dragging so we decided to break our hiatus from drinking to avoid any hardcore delirium tremens.

"Maybe just a few beers to keep us going?" I said.

"I thought you'd never ask. Beer's not really drinking anyway," Brian said.

My internal compass led us straight to my dad's old bar, Jack's Tavern. It had closed long ago, but a new one had opened in its place. Perched on beautiful Subic Bay with the white sandy beach as a backdrop, it was surreal to step inside the building and smell the new air that smelled like the old air, full of stale cigarette smoke, beer, body odor, and cheap perfume.

"I must've drank a million rum and Cokes in here when I was a kid."

Brian ordered a Singha, the only beer in town; I walked around the joint touching things to see if they were real and not part of some dream.

"Where are the go-go girls? You promised women." Brian was testy. I could smell the girls' perfume in the air.

"Must be on a break," I said.

Brian was not impressed. "This place could use a thousand air fresheners."

"Isn't it great?"

"I've smelled better."

"I have a certain nostalgia for this place," I said as I nursed a beer and got to talking about the past.

"Dude," Brian interrupted, "will you finally tell me what the hell you've been yelling about in the middle of the night?"

I admitted I'd been having what some might classify as "recurring nightmares" ever since Jack died. Brian had no idea this had been going on until we embarked on the trip and started sharing rooms.

"He only comes around when I'm sleeping off a night of binge drinking. Guess my scrambled brain conjures him like some twisted side effect from all my years following in his tippling footsteps."

"C'mon, you're no tippler, Binkley. You're a semi-successful entrepreneur on the lam who occasionally dabbles in the *depraved arts*."

"That's a nice way of putting it. Point is, Jack's been visiting me on our Cirrhosis Tour. He came to me in LA and then again in Bali—and on our last night in Australia."

"I thought you were haunted by Felix the amorous Aussie."

"I'd *almost* deleted that from my memory bank. *Thanks* for the reminder."

"What are friends for?" Brian smiled and then looked up at the ceiling fan. It was hardly moving. We were jetlagged and lethargic; the extreme heat kept us stationary so we kept talking. I told Brian the whole story about Jack's unique setup here.

"Since Dad and Mom never divorced, she'd fly in from California to visit him a few times a year. She knew what was going on. I was the only one in the dark."

"Why didn't you invite me over here when we were kids?"

"I wasn't allowed to bring friends. I was kind of embarrassed by the whole thing—but Mom seemed at peace with it. She even made friends with the go-go girls who worked for Jack."

"Shut up."

"Sex workers can still be nice, church-going girls."

"She is an amazing lady."

"She's a saint. It's funny how you take after your parents . . . you adopt their flaws without even realizing it. I followed in Jack's footsteps traveling the world . . . I still drink like him, still travel like him, and seem to have the same moral backbone."

Brian laughed. "You have a backbone, Binkley, but it's not always full of morals." He got up to go to the bathroom.

"What's that supposed to mean?"

He didn't answer so I let it go and stared into my lukewarm beer. I tried to talk to the bartender. "Do the bars here still compete for who has the coldest beer in the village?" The bartender looked at my warm beer, shrugged, and walked away. Guess not. When I was a kid, Jack made sure his beer was always the coldest. He was that kind of guy—competitive like me.

I looked up to him even though I was confounded about what he was doing. He never asked me to keep his secrets; everything was hidden from me. I don't think there was a lot of deception going on between he and Mom. I was the one that didn't understand. I was young and never wanted to challenge the situation. I knew they still loved each other; they were just stuck in an outdated institution that doesn't really work. . . .

Marriage.

Over a few more Singhas, I told Brian about the times I went fishing and drinking with Jack and the village elders.

"Wanna know how Olongapo got its name?"

"Not really, but I have a feeling you're going to tell me."

"Jack told me warring tribes once lived here, and the only peace-maker was this wise old man named Apo. He was like the Martin Luther King or Gandhi of his time."

"Go on," Brian said sipping beer.

"The warring tribes didn't like Apo, so one day he disappeared . . . They found his headless body in the jungle. The tribesmen went looking for Apo's head, but the search was eventually called off—until one day when a boy, who had never given up the hunt, found the elder's head on top of a bamboo pole."

"Apo got James Earl Ray-ed."

"Legend has it, the boy went from village to village to alert the town, kinda like Paul Revere. He cried, '*Olo nin apo! Olo nin apo!*' which means 'head of the elder' in Tagalog."

"I'd have been pissed if he woke me to tell me *that.*"

"But once the warring tribes made peace and were wondering what to name their new town, they decided to honor Apo, and the Paul Revere kid . . . And that's how this place got its name, Olongapo."

"Cool story, bro." Brian was itching to go back to the hotel.

"I can't sleep yet. I want the nightmares to end . . . I need to wander. Maybe I'll feel his presence somewhere. Maybe being here again will finally quiet the ghost of the old man," I said.

"Maybe." Brian sighed. "All right, you talked me into it."

We left Jack's and walked around in Barrio Barretto (an area of Subic with a slew of bars). I ran into some old friends. I saw Casey, an old pool shark who had been here for ten years. "Hey kid, the son of Jack is back! How long's it been?? We all still miss that scallywag! You're all grown up now. Wanna shoot a game?"

Brian almost fell for it until I warned him: "You don't want to bet Casey at pool."

On our way to the next bar, we ran into an old rummy I used to drink with on the beach behind Jack's bar. I couldn't remember his name because I never knew it. We slapped backs and kept moving. Brian looked at me. "It's like a reunion of old debaucherers. Is that a word?"

"It is around here."

Later we ran into Pany, who was still the bar manager at Midnight Rambler, which was right across the street from Jack's Tavern. He hadn't changed a bit. Pany was this gay, bodybuilding Filipino, very eccentric—awesome guy.

"Shame what happened to Jack," Pany said. "So sudden. Hasn't been the same here . . . You miss him?"

"I try not to think about it too much."

"He's an emotional compartmentalizer," Brian said.

"He wha?" Pany's English wasn't too good.

"Don't listen to him, Pany. I remember the last time I saw you. I was here selling all his crap and shipping everything else back on a US naval carrier . . . I was drunk for thirty days straight. . . ."

"I remember," Pany said with a laugh. "You go loco in head."

"How'd you sell all his stuff wasted?" Brian asked.

"I lived on energy drinks during the day . . . I never slept," I said.

Brian replied with something resembling genuine concern, "You have PTSD. You need grief counseling."

"I did seek counseling. I took my loss out with the local female dancers!"

"You're still doing it," Brian said. "What's the definition of insanity?"

"Listening to you?"

"Repeating a failed action over and over and—"

"Will you please stop psychoanalyzing me?"

"I'm just sayin', man. Think about it."

"All right. Enough about Jack, you guys. This is the time in the night when I think about other things!"

Back in the compartment Jack went.

The rest of the evening got extremely fuzzy. Maybe Brian was right. Maybe I was insane to be looking for solace at the bottom of a bottle. Maybe I was still running.

All I know is Brian and I broke our "beer only" rule and shared two pitchers of Mojo with Pany, which was so strong Brian and I couldn't remember any more details. I think we did a Subic City run, which was the shady bar area where anything goes. I remember it got wild—it always does here—but I have no idea how wild thanks to the Mojo. Brian assured me the next morning we had a great time at the Main Attraction, the new go-go bar in town. He knew fun was had because he "woke up with an eight-ball from the pool table" in his pocket— whatever that meant.

That afternoon we hauled our bodies out of bed and checked into the Samurai Hotel, which was extremely cheap. We were trying to conserve our nest egg since we blew through too much of it going crazy in Australia. But you get what you pay for here—and we did. Our room had only one small bed, which was not a pleasant proposition, but at least we both knew we wouldn't try any funny business.

We spent the rest of the afternoon looking for a money exchanger. After getting our hands on some Philippine pesos, we were in no condition to be walking around in this tropical environment with extreme hangovers. So we hired a Jeepney, which are leftover American Jeeps from World War II that people still use for public transportation; they were everywhere. Our Jeepney cost five cents every twenty minutes.

I had the driver take us to a swimming hole that was under a waterfall in the jungle; it was hard to find but I knew the way. The driver had to cut through some farmer's fields to get there. He thought we were crazy because there weren't any signs, but we finally made it.

It was still the same beautiful waterfall and swimming pond I remembered. It looked a little smaller, but after tasting the seedy side of Subic City, it was a much-needed slice of paradise. "Now, this is what I'm talkin' about." Brian was finally impressed by something in Luzon.

"Jack took me here. This is what I always envisioned Utopia to be."

"Is *this* Utopia?" Brian asked.

"Nah . . . too much temptation. We'd never live a simple life. I'd die of alcohol poisoning in a year."

"Or a venereal disease." Brian dove into the pond.

The next day, it was Easter morning. Back in the States all the good Christians were going to church then off to brunch with their families—not us depraved philistines. No, we were already sinking back into our old bad habits. Vice was everywhere and we couldn't look away. It was sickening.

Brian and I wandered over to the go-go bar next to our hotel for breakfast, then (like a couple of sheep) went where all the other barflies were going: the cockfight arena.

"Wanna pray at the altar of the cock?"

"Wouldn't be the first time," I said.

"What would Jesus think of our cock worship on his holy day of resurrection?" I could tell Brian was testing the waters to see if my new-found "moral backbone" had turned to jelly.

"At least it's not cock-and-balls worship . . . Let's go. It's what Dad would do."

I was using Jack's debauched rap sheet as an excuse to sink to new lows; I was powerless to stop myself. Was this my gelatinous moral backbone, or my genetic fallacies at work? I didn't know anything anymore.

Going to a cockfight on Easter Sunday in an extremely Catholic country may sound blasphemous and insane, but it's the national sport of the Philippines and a very popular Easter pastime.

The fights were already underway when we taxied up to the open-air arena. Somehow we got great seats for the gruesome gladiator event. Brian was totally into it while I felt nauseous. I was having flashbacks to when Jack took me here when I was a kid. I used to enjoy them, but I'd grown up.

I had to temporarily put aside my hatred for animal cruelty by drinking lots of San Miguel, the most popular beer in the Philippines. Brian handed me one. "Once the San Miguels take effect, you'll ease into the horrific scene!"

Brian made a habit of advising the half-blind Filipino next to us which cock to bet on even though he had no idea what he was talking about. It was not an exact science. We were just betting on which one was bigger, or which one our bookie told us to bet on. Everyone in the bleachers were screaming bets and using hand signals I couldn't understand; it was utter chaos.

Sometimes a person wouldn't pay up and a fight would break out, which got everyone riled up more. "Can't we all just get along?!" Brian yelled through the fisticuffs.

I could only laugh. "When you throw a thousand Filipinos in a cockfight arena and give them five hundred beers on Easter, every peso counts!"

Midway through the fights, we ran into my old bodyguard, Bong. I used to pay him (in drinks) to watch out for me when I was running the streets alone as an underaged kid. "You Jack's boy! All grow'd up!" We hugged and reminisced as best we could in the crazed scene. We laughed about all the times we got thrown out of bars together, drunk and disorderly.

When the dust settled on the event, I won over a thousand pesos, mainly because one of Bong's friends was placing bets for me. My haul paid for everyone's entry, lunch, San Miguels, and transportation back into town. After the fights, Brian, Bong, and I went back to Barrio Barretto and spent Easter evening at a go-go bar to celebrate our winnings.

Praise the lord.

The next day our altruistic journey for truth went off the tracks and into the muck. I don't know what happened, but we were a long damn way from the paradise I sought. A *long* way. The heavenly trip Brian and I made to the secret waterfall seemed like a lifetime ago. Now our fatal flaws were leading us further into the circle of Hell.

We somehow got talked into going to something called the "Rat-O-Dome" with a rowdy herd of old expatriates and Marines who my dad knew back in the day. Just the name of it made my stomach turn, but when a herd of Marines invites you to a gladiator event, you better say yes.

The Rat-O-Dome was not for the faint of heart. It was this spot on Capalones Beach where a bunch of expats got together to party over the mass murder of rodents. For the second day in a row, I was peer-pressured into setting aside my lifelong affinity for animals to join in the bloodthirsty commotion. I felt horrible.

We all jumped in some old trucks and headed out to the remote beach for the day. On the way out, I noticed the large cages of animals in a few of the trucks. Once we arrived, it wasn't long after I drank my eighth San Miguel that I saw an expat bring out the first cage filled with a very large rodent.

"Oh Christ, what are they gonna do to that poor disgusting rat?" Brian asked.

"You don't wanna know." I felt ill, so I kept drinking until I felt nothing at all.

I should have seen the warning signs—one being the fact that no women were allowed at Rat-O-Dome. I asked one of the Marines where all the girls were, and he said all the go-go girls had to stay away. "No tips for them today!" he shouted. I don't think any woman in her right mind would have wanted to attend anyway, unless they were Green Berets.

At the Rat-O-Dome's makeshift arena—chalkboards were brought out on the beach—we were instructed to place bets on which rat would get eaten by the "friendly" pit bulls. They brought out the pit bulls and marched them around like prized ponies so we could see the cut of their jib.

"It's like Thunderdome . . . but with rats." Brian was horrified. Then he started placing bets. The goal of the game was to bet on the exact time it would take a certain pit bull to track down and play ragdoll with a rat. The good news was that, while you watched, for six dollars you got all the food and San Miguels you could throw down your throat.

So there we were sitting around the beach watching the rats scurrying out of their cages. A timer would go off and twenty expat Marines would yell and cheer, rooting on their bets. Inevitably, a poor rat would scurry the wrong way and the pit bull would tackle it and tear it to shreds. It was a gruesome and sobering sight if one weren't drinking many, many San Miguels—and even then it was pretty unsettling.

It got even weirder between the death matches. While they prepared more rats for slaughter, the drunken Marines fired off rocket launchers and various weapons into the water and jungle for fun. It was our own tropical fireworks show.

I was afraid the booze-fueled light show might get even uglier than it already was when one of the tattooed expats, who was holding a rocket launcher, looked down at my toes through my flip-flops and asked, "Hey, son . . . are your toes colored purple?"

"Uhhh . . ."

"You some kinda goddamned fruit boy!?"

I had to think fast. I couldn't tell these insane men some crazy old hippie painted them in Australia while I was drumming on the beach one morning. So I whipped up a lie, "Some chick in Australia painted them! I did it to cover my toe fungus from trekking across the Outback!"

The Marines processed the lie and then busted out laughing. "You California boys!"

Brian just looked at me, shook his head, and smiled.

Night fell; the go-go girls couldn't take being ignored any longer. A few of them emerged from the jungle at the other end of the beach giving off catcalls in broken English. They wanted to come see their "sexy boooooyfrieeeeends."

The drunk Marines were not so happy to see them. They pivoted their weapons in the girl's general direction, cackling like mad.

"This will not end well!" Brian yelled.

These poor girls probably should have known better. This was a testosterone-fueled event, kind of like football back home. So like any drunken football fan would if he had access to heavy artillery, the expats started shooting various machine guns and rocket launchers straight down the beach.

"What the fuck!! They're shooting at them!" Brian laughed. In my Marine pals' defense, they were aiming high, but the women didn't see it that way. They were pissed off and fled, cursing everyone to hell while the Marines laughed like the drunken sailors most of them were.

After the bloody beach bacchanal, we drove back to town and partied at all the go-go bars. We got so inebriated I lost, then found Brian at my dad's old bar with a bunch of girls.

"There you are!" Brian shouted while holding onto three of the go-go girls from the Rat-O-Dome who were nearly shot by rocket launchers. "I told these girls the only thing I'm gonna fire at them is my 'sea men'!" And then he fell over laughing while the girls giggled. I told them I had seen a similar rocket launcher–type scenario unfold while tailgating at an Oakland Raiders game a few years back. Then I left and went back to the hotel to pass out.

The next day, we took a bus to Angeles, a city not far from Olangapo in central Luzon. On the bus, it occurred to me I never dreamt of Jack while I was in Olangapo. Was the old rogue still lurking in my subconscious? I mentioned it to Brian. He said, "Jack's got more deserving people to haunt around here. This place is trouble with a capital T. Not exactly the ideal place to get our shit together."

"A huge error in judgment on my part. But this place is still home to me," I said.

Brian rolled over to try to sleep. "That explains a lot."

The ride was absolute hell since we were hung over and tired from the Rat-O-Dome. I don't know why I chose to visit Angeles other than it used to be the old Air Force city where all the "flyboys" and their groupies used to party. This was another huge error in judgment on my part, but I wasn't thinking anymore. I was just reacting with what limited brain cells I still had sloshing around in my pickle jar.

While Brian was licking his wounds, a cute innocent-looking girl sat down next to him and started rubbing up against him. Brian was somehow smitten. They held hands all the way to Angeles. I had never seen Brian hold hands with anyone, not even his mom when he was a little boy. He's not a big PDA guy.

After an hour into the bus ride Brian looked at me. "This is a very friendly country. You can develop an amorous relationship without talking, and while crammed between five people, no less . . . I think I'm in love."

I had to break it to him. "Dude, she's a prostitute."

"How dare you say that about . . . what's-her-name?"

"Just wear a condom."

"C'mon, those are for sailors."

"Uhh, to be used in places *just like this*. . . .It's your life."

We arrived in Angeles City, a large urban metropolis known for its casinos and go-go bars. "Every city here looks exactly the same—the *opposite* of Utopia," Brian said as we got off the bus.

He hugged his bus girl and we went looking for accommodations, which we found in a cheap hotel called the Park Inn. "So, did you get her phone number?" I had to ask.

"She doesn't have a phone."

"Did you get her name?"

"Apparently she doesn't have one of those either. The only word she said to me was *lovey*."

"Sounds like the perfect woman," I said.

"I have no idea how to find her . . . I need to find her."

"It's a small town," I lied. "I'm sure you'll run into her again."

The first night out, we walked the main drag and stopped into any bar that had a door. We had thrown our beer-only rule overboard and were back to our wicked, wicked ways.

Every time we walked into a joint, the go-go girls would scream "Tom Cruise! Brad Pitt!" and come on to us immediately. Brian enjoyed the attention. "They're trying to sit on our laps while we're standing up!" They, of course, wanted us to buy them drinks but we didn't care; we felt famous simply because we were Americans.

One dancer ran up to me and played with my long blonde hair, "It's sexy-man Brad Pitt! Buy me drink?!" There seemed to be no other backpackers in Angeles City—only old expats, drug dealers, and pimps. Brian and I smiled. We were young, fresh meat for these girls, and we liked it fine.

By the end of the night, since there were twenty bars on the main drag all bunched together, we had over four hundred "friends" who wanted to have their way with us. We drank in the adoration; we poured Red Horse down our gullets (the high octane beer of the Philippines) and bought way too many drinks for way too many go-go girls. This was a big no-no, but the beer was potent and cheap.

Right before I went into complete blackout mode, something magically horrific happened. We ran into Brian's "bus princess." It would have been a fairytale encounter if she weren't gyrating on the pole at the Y Bar. But there she was, much to Brian's dismay. "Oh my God." Brian pushed whatever dancer was sitting on his lap off him in order to get a closer look.

His worst fears were realized. His innocent sweet thing was in fact another go-go dancer in a sea of them. I, of course, being a horrible friend, laughed in his face. "At least she has a job!"

Brian was crushed. "Shut up."

I tried to console him but couldn't stop smiling. "So much for true love."

"You really can be an asshole sometimes." Brian skulked out of the bar, pulling away from the go-go girls who wanted him to stay. I tried to process what just happened. Out of all the girls we had met on the trip, Brian seemed to like this one girl he never spoke to the best.

Love works in mysterious ways.

The next day we decided to switch to a nicer hotel for the same price called the Americana. At breakfast, Brian admitted he made a terrible mistake last night trying to get over his "bus princess."

"I think I had some extracurricular activities with the local go-go girls and forgot to protect myself." This, of course, is another big no-no.

"What did I tell you on the bus?"

He explained what he remembered of the hours after our mutual blackout, which involved some sort of stripper orgy. He said, in a heart-felt manner (which was strange for him), that along with the "hangover and broken heart," he had "buyer's remorse."

"My loins burn like the dickens."

I quietly took in Brian's news over the morning paper. It didn't help that I opened the paper and saw the front-page headline screaming, MORE AIDS CASES THIS WEEK.

I shoved the paper in Brian's face. "I told you! You're probably going to die now."

"Shut up man!"

"I can't be seen with you . . . I've gotta go." I pretended to get up and leave. Since I was much safer the night before, I kept rubbing it in pretty hard over coffee.

Brian sulked. "My bus girl does not have AIDS. What bar is she at? I'm going to marry that woman tonight!"

I laughed, "Y Bar. You better hurry. Your 'Rodney' will probably fall off by sundown."

That night, Brian and his Rodney went out alone, soberly looking for his bus angel at the Y Bar, then other strip clubs . . . then at the pier . . . then at the bus station. He never found her. Love can be cruel.

After Brian's quasi-STD scare, we took it easy the next few nights and tried to regain what little composure we had left. "As much as you liked that girl, we're never gonna find what we're looking for between the legs of a go-go dancer," I said.

"I know," Brian said. "I need to look between my own legs. Look within. Restart my spiritual journey. I've totally ignored my soul the past few months."

"Join the club."

How do you rehab the souls of two man-children? We decided to get far away from all these cities of sin and start looking for paradise.

We found a driver to take us across Luzon to Batangas Pier, which was the jumping-off point to the other islands with Utopian possibilities. The six-hour private ride was infinitely better than the bus to Angeles. It gave us room to think about what we were going to do with the rest of our lives.

There were thousands of people swarming about when we pulled up to Batangas Pier. By now, we were fairly savvy travelers so when all the "touts" approached us to say, "No ferry! You take special boat!" we weren't biting. Touts are always trying to scam stupid tourists by directing them to other piers where they corner you and try to make you pay ten times the price for a private boat. Not this time. Being two seasoned travelers, we just slid through the crazy crowd and found a pier that had a sign reading, MINDORO ISLAND.

While we waited for the ferry to Mindoro island, which is the seventh largest island in the PI, just southeast of Luzon, we played pool with a few local girls who were amazing players. After a few hours of losing our ass to these pool sharks, we got on the ferry and crossed over to Mindoro island.

Mindoro has a mountain range called the High Rolling Mountains that splits the island into two very different provinces. If you're on vacation with some money to spend, go east to the province called Oriental Mindoro. If you want to backpack through rugged terrain, go west to the province of Occidental Mindoro.

We split the difference and went to the dive mecca: Puerto Galera on the north coast of Oriental Mindoro, which is famous for its beautiful beaches and diving, and not as expensive as some of the other resort towns.

The first thing I did to better myself was sign up for a rescue diver course to continue my education. My instructor was named John, a big English bloke who taught me how to save people in all diving situations. Our first dive was incredible. We saw a ton of triggerfish, corals, butterfly fish, and turtles.

After my dive class, an old lady named Mama Lopez helped us find a room in Sebang Beach. It was one room with a kitchenette and bathroom for ten dollars a night. It had a ceiling fan and a refrigerator, so it wasn't bad. It was definitely better than the flea-ridden hotel where we stayed the previous night, at which a cockroach ran up Brian's body in the middle of the night and he totally freaked out.

That night we went walking around Sebang Beach and watched a comet scream through the sky while we relaxed with the locals. Life was beautiful again.

The next day, Brian hiked around the rocks and I went diving again.. The program was very laid back. Since I was the only student, I'd meet with John for classroom work around ten in the morning, then go for a pleasure dive around two o'clock where we did a lot of wreck dives and swam over amazing coral. It was usually a three-day course without dives (just rescue work), but John turned it into a six-day course since he liked me and it was just the two of us.

It was cleansing after all the damage we had done to ourselves. It was nice listening to the waves break while doing my book work on the beach. Of course, the second I finished my course, Brian, John, and I went out and polluted ourselves all over again. (A few years later, I heard John died while diving. This was discomforting news since he taught me everything I knew about dive safety.)

The next day Brian said he was ready to get moving. We hadn't done much in Sebang, and Brian was bored. "At least we dried out," I said.

"Dude, we got hammered *last night*. How long do you really think it can last?"

We took another Jeepney across the island to Roxas. The ride was a lot of fun. We rode through green valleys full of palm trees, waterfalls, and wildlife, and got to sit on top of the jeep and feel the open air in our faces like a couple of dogs without a worry in the world. Brian looked as happy as he had drumming in the Australian jungle. "We're gonna live forever!" he shouted.

We arrived in Roxas and didn't bother getting a room. We were so blissed out on nature we just spent the night on the pier and waited for the *banca*, which is a canoe-type boat that would take us on a six-hour passage to the small island of Boracay, located in the western Visayas region of the PI.

The Visayas was ground zero to our Utopian aspirations. It's where all the beautiful little islands were that I loved as a child. Boracay has become a tourist mecca so it's not the same if you visit now, but when I was young it was paradise—an amazing sight to behold.

We took in the beautiful white sandy beaches and tropical jungle backdrop. Turquoise blue waters surrounded the island, and dolphins swam with us off our bow. Maybe this was the utopia I'd been looking for. Brian was thinking the same thing.

"Is this paradise?"

I smiled. "We may never go home, my friend."

I'd been searching the world for Utopia and, to my surprise, my travels had led me back to where my wanderlust began. "My journey has come full circle," I said breathing in the clean air. "Let's stay awhile."

We checked in at the Tin Tin hotel at the end of the touristy section of the island called White Beach. We met a lot of cool people the first night out. We drank too much, but that was to be expected.

On our scenic walk home from the bar, my dream of Utopia began to fissure. Deranged dogs were barking everywhere. "Did someone spike our Red Horse?"

Around every corner there were black dogs threatening to attack. Was this another nightmare? Was Jack lurking around the next corner? The black dogs appeared on every sand road we walked down.

"This is not good." Brian said as we confronted a gang of slobbering dogs glaring at us through a chain metal fence.

"It's a pack of Cujos," I said. They appeared to be a mix of pit bull and rottweiler.

"Are they from the Rat-O-Dome?" Brian had forgotten where we were.

"No . . . These are the hounds of hell."

Brian gulped. "I thought we were supposed to be in heaven?"

We picked up our pace. But the dogs kept stalking us from behind a long high fence.

"Thank God for that fence," Brian said.

We hurried around the next corner; they kept following us. They were hungry and pissed off.

Then our luck ran out. The fence suddenly ended and there was nothing between the barking beasts and us but air. Even the dogs seemed surprised; they stopped barking to sniff the end of the fence like they couldn't believe their luck.

"Where'd the fence go?" Brian was sobering up quickly.

"No sudden movements," I whispered.

The dogs set their yellow eyes on us. I could see drool dripping from their mouths. Brian and I were fresh meat (again) on an island full of hungry natives. But these weren't go-go dancers licking their chops.

"I knew we shoulda got rabies shots," Brian said. "*Run!*"

We took off. The dogs gave chase in a full ravenous sprint. We scaled a rickety wooden fence and landed in the backyard of an abandoned shack. We were safe momentarily. Brian, lungs wheezing, watched in terror as the fifteen dogs banged their bodies against the fence like battering rams. "Cujo's hungry and that fence is rotten!" he yelled over their barks. "It's gonna go down!"

"This isn't heaven, this sucks!" I yelled. "What now??"

We were about to jump the fence and run for our lives when out of the dark a small puppy emerged from the backyard. The pup was trying to bark like his brothers on the other side of the fence.

"It's a puppy . . . it's a baby panda!" Brian yelled over the barks.

The pup did have the markings of a panda; the little fella couldn't be more than a few weeks old. Brian picked it up and held it up to the moonlight; it looked like it was starving.

Brian was losing his mind. "Let's throw Panda over the fence, sacrifice it to the pack, then make a run for it!"

"What are you, nuts?! We're bringing him with us!"

"You carry it then! That fence is coming down! "

Two seconds later the rotting fence collapsed and the pack of dogs came charging in. I scooped up Panda and we ran the other way, leaping over the fence on the other side of the yard like two jackrabbits.

We ran like lightning down a sandy road, past an old drunk who was staggering the other way. The drunk just looked at us two Americans who were carrying a baby panda like a football while zigzagging down the road with fifteen feral dogs snapping at our heels.

I never understood why the dogs didn't go for the old man.

The good news: When we got back to the hotel, the trauma and long run home had sobered us up. We slammed the door and laughed like idiots. It took a minute for us to hear the baby barking sounds from inside my shirt.

"Oh . . . I forgot we had this little guy." I pulled him out of my shirt.

"Congratulations. It's a boy." Brian collapsed on his bed.

The first night Panda slept with me on my chest. He peed cute little puddles all over the bed and gave me a horrendous case of fleas, but I didn't care. I was in love, maybe for the first time in my life, which was a frightening notion to ponder while I drifted off to sleep.

The next day we woke to the sound of Panda barking. Since we had fed him nothing but beef jerky, we went looking for some real food. We paraded him around White Beach. He was so cute; everyone who saw him immediately wanted him.

"This must be how proud parents feel," Brian said.

We went searching for dog food but there was none on the island. Apparently the natives don't feed their dogs—and sometimes even eat them.

"This philosophy must be why dogs are so angry here," Brian said.

We found Panda some milk and raw shrimp, which he ate like the ravenous mongrel he was. Then we took him down to the vet and got him some flea medication and lathered him up. All clean and pest free, he was even cuter. A fuzzy little baby bear. We took him to the beach to frolic.

Maybe this was heaven after all.

A week later, we were two happy expats-in-training, wallowing in our newfound paradise. Brian and I had seamlessly slipped into the idyllic life of the beach bum. All was right in the world.

I spent the days playing with Panda, reading, and hanging out with the locals. Panda was one happy dog, and all the girls walking up and down the beach loved him. I spent many afternoons scuba diving. I finally saw my first shark, which was unnerving until I realized it was a white tip reef shark that couldn't care less about humans.

Panda had become the hotel mascot. Since we were still staying at the Tin Tin hotel, whenever the owners were around, I called him "Tin Tin" to grease the wheels a bit. It worked; they didn't evict him or us. They loved the little furball like everyone else, even though they'd probably prefer to broil him over an open flame.

Panda learned how to swim and loved going in the ocean with me, which we did every day as part of his flea bath. I was happy as a child again teaching him how to swim. I'd throw him into the surf then help him navigate all the waves. After a while he was doggie-paddling like a pro.

"Doesn't get any better than this," I said to Brian one night while Panda was sleeping in my lap.

"You said it," Brian said. "Forget California, I'm never leaving."

One day we were wandering the beach and finally ran into some young female tourists. I had actually forgotten Boracay had an international airport nearby on a neighboring island. It had been a long time since we'd seen any cute girls that were not go-go dancers.

"I'm feeling a stirring in my . . . *you know*," Brian said.

"Puppies are the best wingmen in the world," I said, then let Panda loose in the new girls' general direction. Of course, he led them directly to us.

"What a chick magnet," Brian said while scratching Panda's ears.

"Welcome to paradise, ladies," I said in my coolest voice. "I see you met our little friend here. You new in town?"

Panda helped us get to know the girls roaming the beach. We made plans to go out with them that night. My date for the evening, a Canadian from Toronto named Mandy, was all jacked up to go to the local party bar called Coco Mango's Place and do the "Cocomango Dare" which always spelled trouble for the uninitiated.

Brian and I explained. "We've already lost many brain cells at both of Coco Mango's locations," I said. "We barely remember the one in Byron Bay. They nearly killed Brian by overserving him until he passed out on a homeless aboriginal tribesman."

Mandy laughed at our stupid banter, "God, I miss American men! You guys are freakin' awesome!" She was a fun bunny ready to rampage. "I'm stoked to lose my brain! Let's go!"

"Shouldn't we eat dinner first?" I asked, trying to be a good guy.

"It may make the stomach pump less painful," Brian chimed in.

"*Eff* food—I'm thirsty!" Mandy replied, which made the girls cheer. For the first time in paradise, we had run into a fun hurricane ready to hit shore.

I looked at Brian, who whispered, "Screw our sobriety. That's the sorority girl's *mating call.*"

"All right, if you say so. See you girls in the emergency room!" I said and off we went, willingly swept up into their high Canadian tide.

The five of us sidled up to Coco Mango's open-air bar at sunset. Coco Mango's claim to infamy was it dared people to slam fifteen different shots in one hour. If you do it and don't die of alcohol poisoning, you get a free T-shirt and your name engraved on a plaque. Brian informed the girls that your country of residence also gets one more notch added to its total on the "World Wall," then pointed out the United States only had 246 people who had done "The Dare," which was only good enough to get us to fourth place.

Brian looked at me. "Dude . . . do it for your country." So we did.

"It's a drink-off!" I yelled. "Canada versus the United States—may the best alcoholic win!" They rang the bell and Mandy and I proceeded to knock back fifteen shots each while everyone at the bar cheered us on. She talked a good game but was clearly an amateur and no match for me since, at this point in our world drinking tour, I had the "tolerance of twelve Bukowskis." Knowing my superpower, I was cocky during the contest, and I chased all fifteen shots with beer. All my alcoholic literary heroes would have been proud.

When the hour was up, both our names were engraved on the wall and Mandy was swaying like a palm tree. We celebrated our victory by dancing on the bar wearing our new T-shirts, then Mandy fell off the bar and it was clearly time to call it a night.

I left Brian and the other Canadian girls at the bar to help Mandy back to her hotel. When we got back to her room, we both passed out and woke up in extremely rough shape the next morning.

Good times in *paradise*? I was beginning to have serious doubts.

The downward spiral continued the following night when Brian and I made the foolish decision to return to Coco Mango's without the Canadian girls, who were smartly holed up in their hotel recovering from last night's near-death experience.

On night two, there were no eligible bachelorettes around so we hung out with Sheila, our first transsexual of the trip. The Filipinos call them *backlas*, but Sheila said they call each other "ladyboys." We spent the night dancing with our new friend and had a blast. It seemed all the ladyboys we met on the trip were extremely good dancers; Sheila definitely was. She had us cutting a rug with no inhibitions, which was rare for us.

"If she doesn't give a hot damn then why should we?" I yelled while dancing like an idiot. "Let's get Sheila drunk!"

"Red Horse it is!" Brian grinned and started ordering Sheila drinks, which turned the dance party into a class-five rager. By the end of the night, we had the whole bar rocking. The locals and travelers loved Sheila, who owned the room. At some point, a random girl tried to slap me; I have no idea why. I was drinking way too much to keep track of anything. Maybe it was Sheila's girlfriend.

At two in the morning, we said goodbye to Sheila, and Brian and I walked back to our hotel along White Beach. It was a long, sobering walk, which got us talking about reality.

For the first time, we talked about leaving Boracay. Brian brought it up first, "I don't want to burst your starry-eyed bubble, man. I love it here in 'heaven' and all, but even heaven on earth can get a bit . . . repetitive, ya know?"

"No, you're right. We can't stay here forever," I said. "We're too young to settle for Utopia anyway. Are we really gonna leave paradise?"

"I hate to be the bearer of bad news, but there's no such thing as paradise, man. I think—and this is just my opinion—but we need to keep testing the limits of our insanity. That's what this whole trip was about."

"I was actually trying to have a personal renaissance on this trip."

Brian laughed. "My personal renaissance involves insanity! It's all about deconditioning ourselves, man."

After a long talk, we agreed it was time to go. Were we crazy? Was Utopia too good for us? Or were we too bad for it?

A few days later, the time had come to leave Xanadu.

Like all children must, Panda had grown up. We rescued him from certain death in the island's "dog Darwin system" and now he was eating like a little horse. Good thing for him he was cute. The day before we left, I asked the owners of the Tin Tin hotel if they would watch Panda, aka little Tin Tin.

"I can't backpack around the world with a little Panda," I said rubbing his ears. The husband and wife hotel owners conferred for a minute then agreed to take Tin Tin. "Thank you. You take good care of him now. I'll be back to make sure he doesn't become an entree on your hotel dinner menu."

The owners laughed and said they'd come to like him for more than his cuteness. "Tin Tin run off roosters that crow all night, slows crowing down!" Once I heard that, I knew he would have a good home here.

"Feels good to leave Panda with a job," I said to Brian, who wasn't as emotional about giving Panda up for adoption.

He just yawned. "At least one of us does."

We said our final goodbyes to Boracay and chartered a *banca* to nearby Panay Island and its international airport in Aklan. On the ride over, the reality of leaving the only place I could truly call "home" and "heaven on earth" at the same time started to sink in. I was more confused than ever about my place in the world. If we found paradise and it wasn't good enough, then what was the purpose of this trip? What am I searching for? My naive quest for meaning the past few months felt like a fool's errand. A child's dream. The temptations we had found flourishing in the rest of the world sure looked a lot like America to me.

"People are the same all over," Jack used to say every time I complained about having to spend summers in a third world country. "The surface doesn't matter. You gotta dive deeper. In the end, the only thing that matters in this crazy world is what's *in here*—Jack pointed to my heart—"and *in here*"—Jack pointed to my head.

"I don't understand," I often said when he was pontificating.

"Here's a puzzler for you: What kind of man are you going to become? You're old enough now to be thinking about how you want to turn out. Don't pattern yourself after me. Genetics are an excuse. We all have free will. Find *yourself*. . . . Have a goal. Then make a plan to be the best version of *you*. That, my son, is the meaning of life—and your homework assignment for the summer. Don't look so worried. Your entire life only depends on it."

Then he winked at me. That was Jack.

"Dad," I said to the ocean skimming by, "if you can hear me . . . I'm still working on that homework assignment."

Boracay was disappearing behind us. Brian could tell I was having a "Jack Moment." I told him I needed a minute. "Sure." Brian patted me on the back and went to the back of the boat to give me some time alone.

I never let myself admit it back in the States, but I missed my dad so much. But I wasn't going to cry. *I will . . . not . . . cry.*

I found Brian sitting on the other side of the *banca*, staring out at the water, lost in his own thoughts. I put my arm around him. "You okay, man?"

"Never better. You okay?"

"Dad always got philosophical on his trimaran. Guess it's in the blood."

"How're the nightmares? Haven't noticed you having 'em."

"They've stopped, for now."

"That's a breakthrough. What do you think it means?"

"Does it have to mean something?"

"Yes. Think hard."

"Well . . . we haven't been drinking as much. Also, I think I finally understand why I have them. They're my subconscious showing me what I don't wanna see when I'm awake."

"And what's that?"

"My future self."

"That is some excellent psychoanalysis."

"I think Jack's my 'Ghost of Christmas Future' . . . My dreams are a mirror showing me what I'm afraid I'll become."

"You don't wanna be like Jack—even a little?" Brian was playing devil's advocate. "He seemed like a cool dude."

"Yes and no. But, I will admit . . . Jack may have left me and Mom back in California, but . . . *he was a legend.* I wouldn't mind being a legend, too."

"You already are a legend, in your own mind."

"You keep saying that."

Brian smiled. "So . . . where we going next?"

"You're asking me?"

"Yes!"

"I don't know, man. . . . But it feels like Jack's telling me, '*Keep going: Don't settle for Utopia—it's just an illusion. Don't make the same mistakes I did.*' I think settling for paradise eventually killed him."

"Self-satisfaction is the beginning of the end," Brian said. "That's some profound shit."

"I'd like to think Jack's started moving again . . . on to the next world, and the next adventure, wherever that may be."

I cracked open two warm beers I had in my pack and handed one to Brian.

"To Jack," I said and lifted my beer for a toast.

Brian smiled. "To Captain Jack." We both drank our beers in silence the rest of the ride. I'm not typically an emotional guy, but I will admit I got misty-eyed leaving the Philippines. But I never cried.

Jack would have been proud. The old man never cried either.

5

Torn Up in Thailand

THE DREAM WAS OVER. PARADISE was lost.

Five months into our adventure and Brian and I were nowhere closer to finding ourselves. We were still two American man-children lost in a haze of debauchery living like a couple of demented gods. *Island-hopping* was no longer just an affectation or a trend; it had become a nasty habit, a lazy fetish, a primal need. If our trip back in time to bury my past didn't kill our Cirrhosis Tour, what would? Where was the promised land now?

I hadn't a clue.

Brian and I didn't talk much during our cross-islands journey to the Manila airport. We were so exhausted we just took the first flight out of town and aimlessly flew anywhere the wind took us, which was to Singapore, our travel hub.

"You know, I want to be *challenged* too," Brian offered once we got on the plane, "but it's never gonna happen if all we do is lounge around tropical islands with cocktails in our hands."

"Valid point," I replied. "What do you say we just crash at Eric's for a few days until we figure out what to do with the rest of our lives?"

"Singapore's an island, right? *We only visit islands*," Brian said, putting on his eye mask, which was starting to show its age.

"That has to change," I said.

"We have to change," Brian said. "Eric know we're coming?"

"He won't mind. He keeps telling us we should spend a few days in the *Lion City*," I said.

"Are there really lions?"

"No, the guy who named Singapore mistook a tiger for a lion . . . the name stuck."

"So, tigers?"

"The local authorities caned the tigers into extinction a long time ago."

"That's not encouraging. What are they gonna do to us, then?"

We got off the plane and roamed around Singapore like two lost alley cats. We followed the signs to all the touristy places like Arab Street and Raffles Place, which is the financial hub where all the skyscrapers reside. Brian insisted we go up and have a drink in a rooftop bar. He ordered us two Singapore slings, which cost more money than our hostel room that night. We checked out Boat and Clarke Quay, which were beautiful waterfront villages with many bars, cafés, and restaurants. Blah, blah, blah.

Since Singapore was a former British trading post before the Japanese kicked them out during World War II, it was no surprise to find shopping was still the thing to do. There were huge shopping malls everywhere. The bus and MRT system were spotless, safe, and efficient. It was a total contrast from the Philippines. "We've gone from the dirty, lawless jungles of the third world to the clean, lawful concrete jungle of Singapore," Brian said. "Total culture shock."

"We'll never be challenged here," I said. "Let's go somewhere, any-where tomorrow."

"Yeah, sure. Tomorrow."

A week later, I'd become my worst nightmare. I was a traveler who had stopped traveling, a seeker who has stopped seeking. My personal renaissance was on hold and it was all Brian's fault.

We had found Utopia and left it behind. Now I was cursing my fate, stuck in the oppressive techno-Shangri-la known as Singapore, an immaculate city/state with great sights, great food, great bars, and lovely women from all over the world. Sounds like the perfect city, right? By any "normal" standards it is, but I'm not exactly normal. You may have heard Singapore has some very draconian laws. The fine for chewing gum is outrageous, and if you get into a fight or get caught stealing, you will certainly be *canned* and perhaps even *caned*.

From my perspective, we were wasting our time here. I wasn't learning anything new. I was getting antsy. I was getting restless.

Brian was getting comfortable. "Call me a capitalist pig, but I kind of like it here," he said one night at dinner.

"You can't be serious. Why?"

"Why can't I be serious? What am I, some kind of clown to you? Do you think I'm funny?"

"*Goodfellas.* Don't change the subject. This place is *nice* as long as you spend money and don't break the law, but what's the fun in that? I thought we made a pact to stay out of first-world countries."

"We did, we did," Brian said, "but we aren't blowing through money here like we did in Australia—and we got a free place to crash, though I have a feeling Eric doesn't exactly want us here. I'm just enjoying digging under the surface of the city, man, aren't you? There's an interesting melting pot of cultures going on here: Chinese, Indian, Malay—it's delicious, I mean, just look at all this great food! Would you rather be feasting on runny rice water?"

"No . . . but I guess I'd rather be backpacking around jungles and not man-pursing around a big, boring city for weeks on end," I said, knowing it would piss Brian off since he was now carrying a man-purse.

"It's a satchel, asshole."

Brian got quiet and stared off into the distance. We walked back to Eric's apartment in silence. Our habitual nightcrawling had ceased without explanation. I suddenly felt claustrophobic, like I was in some bad relationship—but it wasn't Brian icing me out that was smothering me. I wanted to end my relationship with this city. I had forgotten what it was like to be confined by the laws of civilization, and I didn't like it. I was suffocating.

I let my pent-up feelings out in one big, dirty rant on the cleanest street I'd ever seen in my life. "I wanna get the hell outta here and find beauty in the sewers of the world—why don't you?? Don't you want to go somewhere challenging? Somewhere remote? That was the whole point of this trip."

But just like every other time I tried to inspire us to blow this fascist town, Brian shot me down. "Yeah man, no I agree, sounds good. Tomorrow, tomorrow," he mumbled, before shutting the door in my face.

For the past week Brian had been holed up in his room on the phone with Carrie, his ex-girlfriend back home, running up someone's phone bill. Maybe I was jealous of the sex talk I could hear through the door every night, but who was this new Brian and what had he done with the guy I'd been traveling with for five months? I'd never seen this side of him. It was slightly sickening. Did that nameless stripper he held hands with on the bus really break his heart? Had he gotten scared back to American women by the Filipino AIDS crisis? Was he doing the unthinkable—was he finally growing up?? That's supposed to be my job, *not his*. His job was to push me to new heights of insanity!

Somewhere, my plans for this trip had gone sideways, and it was pissing me off.

Left on my own in a city/state I was growing to despise, I decided to get in shape. I went jogging through the botanical gardens, then over to the hospital where Eric does his research on baboons and monkeys. I wanted to play with his subjects, but since Eric was testing them with sexual arousal drugs, he advised against it.

"They're very mean," he said. "You might get *violated*."

"Can you blame them?" I asked. "Do they at least get to masturbate?"

"No one can prevent a primate from doing that."

After work, I cornered Eric and made him listen to me complain about Singapore's collective tight ass while Brian stayed locked in his room. "Dude, this town . . . Am I right?" I said while splayed on his sofa with a beer in hand.

Eric glared at me over the kitchen bar; I could tell we had already overstayed our welcome, but he was too nice to kick us out. All he could muster was, "Stop calling me 'dude.'"

"Duuuuude—this *town* . . . I mean, when you're Beat at heart like me"—Eric rolled his eyes—"and someone throws down the gauntlet with a bunch of stupid laws, it's just a matter of time before you wanna cross into some serious illegal wrongdoing. Know what I mean?"

"Not exactly . . . but *okay*, Rob. What do you want to do—knock over a liquor store or raid a nearby village? Will that make you feel better?"

"Yes . . . no . . . I don't know. I just—"

"You know what you are? *You're a rebel without a cause.*" Then he left me stewing in front of the television.

"Your humor escapes me, dude!" I yelled.

"Stop calling me 'dude!'" Eric yelled before slamming his bedroom door. I looked at the two closed bedroom doors. "What am I, a freakin' leper?"

The next day I started to rebel like a petulant teen on holiday. They "don't like scofflaws around here," Eric kept warning me, but what does that really mean? Naturally I considered this to be a challenge to my iconoclastic nature. I wanted to find out how far I could push it before I ended up in cuffs. This is what happens when you mix boredom, loneliness, and alcohol. Was I turning into the old Brian?

Wandering the streets alone, I went "Rebel Yell" on the world. I dared to spit a piece of Trident gum out on one of the immaculate streets. "Thwuup!" I strutted away like a Black Panther, then I stopped and looked around to see if anyone noticed. No one cared so I littered some more and waited for the local SWAT team to come swooping in. Nothing. So I peed in an alley . . . Nope. I had to step up my game.

I committed my first felony the following night. I was with Eric, my reluctant new wingman, who after a few drinks had agreed to fill Brian's shoes. We'd been hanging out at the Elvis Room with a few KLM flight attendants. I wanted to take them back to Eric's apartment, but they had to catch an early flight to Kuala Lumpur the next day. So by three in the morning, Eric and I were drunk, randy, and alone, roaming the streets like that wild pack of dogs that nearly ate Brian and I in the Philippines.

We came upon an interesting looking eight-foot totem pole that was decorating the entrance of a storefront. Full of pent-up testosterone, I started to climb it. "I'm gonna summit!" I crawled up the wooden pole like a spider monkey. I used the carved faces as footholds.

Eric, the Boy Scout who was not the type to rock any boat, properly panicked. "Get down before we get arrested!" He peeked into the closed store and saw no security guard. When he came back I was straddling the top of the pole. "They'll take me in as your accomplice!"

"What are you, a man or a mouse? Laws are made to be broken!"

I began to rock the totem pole back and forth. Eric gave the pole a big shove to jar me loose, but the entire pole tipped over and crashed to the ground with me nearly under it. "You almost crushed me," I moaned.

Eric was jumping around like one of his primates. "Time to go! Get up, get *up*!"

I stared into the eyes of one of the totem faces, "Hey, this guy kinda looks like Brian."

Eric stopped jumping and looked at the face. "It does, kinda."

"Have'ta show him." I tried to lift the totem pole off the ground. "This thing's heavy. Grab the other end."

"Why don't you take a picture like everybody else?"

"This thing is mine!"

"If they catch us, we'll spend the *rest of our lives in jail.*"

"That sounds like a dare, kemosabe. Either you help me, or I'm telling your girlfriend you're cheating on her with that sexy intern!"

"That's absurd! I'm not . . ."

I stared at him.

Eric sighed. "You're a disgusting human being," he said, and picked up the other end of the pole.

This caper was not a smart thing to do on any level. The totem pole weighed about two hundred pounds. Eric complained as we hauled it back home and jammed it into the elevator of his high-rise building. No one saw us, we hoped.

We were exhausted by the time we got it inside his tiny apartment. "This should be your Christmas —forever," I said, collapsing on the floor.

"I don't celebrate Christmas, you idiot . . . I'm going to regret this. You will too."

"I regret nothing." I banged on Brian's closed door, "Rakow, wake up! You have to see this! I got you a Christmas present!" I shook his door handle; it was locked. Was he even in there? I grabbed a beer from the fridge and sat on the sofa to admire our new toy. "How great would it be if it's some rare relic. We'd get the death penalty!"

"Um, yeah . . . hilarious. I'm going to bed." Eric left me on the sofa admiring my crime. "And *you* will get the death penalty, not me, after I turn state's witness on your dumb ass . . ."

His words rang in my head as I went to sleep that night on the sofa. I did not have sweet dreams. Jack visited me again. I won't give you the details because I can't remember any. All I remember was Dad was not amused.

When I woke the next day, I did some research and found I had committed a major felony in one of the least forgiving countries in the world. Our big wooden statue was going to get us caned with extreme prejudice. Brian finally emerged from his room around noon. All he said was, "That doesn't look like me." Then he went back into his room with a bowl of cereal and shut the door.

I started to panic. I didn't want to go to jail. *Jesus, what was I thinking?* I had to get rid of the evidence so that night I planned a reverse caper to make it all right. I strong-armed Eric into helping me carry it back to the storefront where we found it. Miraculously, it went off without a hitch.

"Find another wingman, Rob. My outlaw days are over!" Eric said as we speed-walked away.

Eric wasn't kidding. He wanted me out of his apartment, and rightly so. I was backsliding, and this time I couldn't blame it on Brian. With no bad influence around I had become one myself. I apologized. "I'm sorry, you're right . . . This was completely idiotic. I need to go. I'm not learning anything new here. I'm actually forgetting some shit. It's time for me to leave before I get myself into real trouble."

We shook hands. "I accept your apology. And yes, you are an idiot."

I decided to get back on the trail the following day, with or without Brian. While Eric tested experimental sex drugs on monkeys, I planned my next adventure to Malaysia, due north.

I had forty-eight hours until my train left, so I spent the time trying to get back into shape by running through the Botanical Gardens. I had to get more passport pages, so I jogged by the US Embassy and picked some up. My lungs were exploding more than usual. I had atrophied more than I thought.

This fueled me with rage so I went down to the courts and played tennis manically for the next day with some of Eric's doctor friends. I was trying to cleanse my body of all the vice-related toxins it had acquired on the road. But it wasn't working. I was not "acing anyone's deuce," so I redirected my anger to Brian. Every time I smashed a volley I imagined I was beaning tennis balls off his face.

Subconsciously I must have known something was afoot because when I came back to Eric's I found a note from Brian that read:

See you in Thailand?
– B.

The bastard ditched me to meet up with Carrie. I knew it. I vaguely remembered Carrie; she was crazy hot and crazy persuasive. "It'll never last." I crumpled his note and threw it on the kitchen floor.

Eric came into the kitchen. "So now you're littering?"

"Brian left."

"Yeah, I know."

"I thought we left America to *escape* our shallow, cheating, money-grubbing girlfriends??"

"Guess that was only you," Eric said. "He left while you were getting your ass kicked at tennis. Carrie bought a ticket. She's still in love with him."

"Who could love Brian?" I whined. "He's the *definition of unlovable.*"

"I dunno man . . . Who could love *you*?"

"Guess I lost my wingman."

"Filling in as your wingman for one night, I think that position may go unfilled for a while." I asked Eric where they were shacking up, but he didn't know. All he knew was, "Copious amounts of shagging would be involved."

I pretended not to care. "Hope she doesn't mind monkey herpes."

Eric gave me a courtesy laugh. "So . . . when are *you* leaving?"

I wandered the streets of Singapore alone that night. I went back on my promise and bought a small bottle of Bundaberg Rum, which I justified as a money-saving tactic. In my short time here I found the nightlife to be good but expensive. I found the Elvis Room again, where people were dancing on the tables. Most of the locals only go out on the weekends since they're too busy working hard at "living the American dream" during the week. Lucky for me, it was Saturday night.

I spent the night drinking with a bunch of stewardesses from Amsterdam. After the bar closed, we walked around town and polished off the rest of the Bundaberg. I howled at the moon . . . At one point, I was so drunk I thought I saw Jack's ghost following me in the fog like I was living some Shakespearean play. I remember asking one of the flight attendants if they saw him too—but she just laughed at me, then *poof,* Jack was gone.

Was it a hallucination, or a residual effect of another Bundaberg blackout? I told myself it must have been the Bundaberg. Must have been that.

The next morning, I said farewell to Eric and his horny monkeys and caught the famous KTM train (Keretapi Tanah Melayu), Malaysia's national railway service, up the Malaysian peninsula to Kuala Lumpur.

The entire trip took seven hours; I spent most of the time writing in my journal. Observations from the train: The Malaysian peninsula is not an island! It feels like an Asian version of Florida, except there's no Disney World. Instead of swamps, you get jungle as far as the eye can see, until you see the monolithic city of Kuala Lumpur growing large in the distance like the Emerald City in the land of Oz.

Malaysia is really two countries in one. (Three if you count Singapore, which was once part of Malaysia.) The huge space-age cities of Kuala Lumpur and Singapore seemed strangely out of place amid all the primitive jungle villages that surround the two cities. I can't speak for the other half of Malaysia, which is the island of Borneo across the North China Sea, since I didn't see it. (At that point I was trying to wean myself off islands, so I stayed on the mainland.)

When the KTM train arrived in Kuala Lumpur (or KL, as the locals call it), I stepped out into the city hoping to find some filth, and I did—I stepped right into a huge puddle from an unrepaired city street. It was beautiful.

Walking around I got the sense that KL is Singapore's evil twin; a big dirty lawless metropolis in the middle of a tropical third-world country. Maybe KL isn't completely lawless; sixty percent of the population is Muslim, after all, so many of the people are no doubt very devout. But I could tell it had an outlaw dark side lurking out there somewhere. I could smell it. It felt like crimes were being committed all around me.

I was home again.

I checked into the Traveller's Moon Lodge downtown. It was an inexpensive hostel in an expensive city and it showed; the walls were made of cardboard. As I settled in, it felt weird to be alone. Instead of staying lost in a cardboard maze of my own undoing, I went looking for some friends to quiet the demons barking like those stray dogs inside my head.

I met four Norwegian girls at the lodge. They were cute and bubbly and taken with my Americanness. One was named Monica. I liked her immediately. She had kind eyes and an earthiness about her that made me feel good. They wanted to go have some fun, so we went out to eat and had drinks. Monica helped me take my mind off of Brian's betrayal.

When we returned to our hostel, we made our way up to the rooftop deck and saw the full moon hanging over a bunch of backpackers who were all flirting in the night air. "So that's why they call it the Moon Lodge," I said.

"It's very romantic, no?" Monica leaned in for a kiss, which I quickly gave her. Then a guy named Lars ruined the vibe by showing us some huge spiders and scorpions he had as pets, which is not exactly a turn-on to most of the world's female population. Lars told us he was collecting them for a zoo in the Czech Republic. It was fun watching them run around. They were big and hairy and looked deadly, especially to Monica, who didn't seem to enjoy the spider and scorpion show as much as I did.

Monica was busy the next day so I set out to tour Kuala Lumpur on my own like a real adult. It was the rainy season so I saw the city from under my umbrella. Brian and I had been starving ourselves for months, so I followed my nose around town; there were amazing food smells coming from everywhere. With no wingman to lure me into nefarious situations,

I proceeded to eat my way across town. The food in KL was just as diverse and exotic as Singapore; you could find anything you wanted on the cheap.

I started by feasting on a Chinese-Malay cuisine called *nyonya* with all their delicious buffets—then moved on to the many red, green, and yellow curries of India. Then I hit the Malay food aromas and trucks. When I thought I couldn't eat any more, I stuffed myself with Western food; I even found french fries, which were great.

Full-bellied, I walked over to the Petronas Twin Towers, which were the tallest twin towers in the world at that time. They are amazing post-modern spectacles of human engineering—1,483 feet in the air and quite a sight to see, especially considering they're located right in the middle of a tropical jungle.

After my solo day tour, I met back up with Monica and the Norwegian girls. We went to a gay bar, where it was my job to flirt with all the ladyboys and try to score drinks to bring back to the girls. What a job. After a few hours, my beer goggles couldn't tell who was what, so I stuck with Monica, who I knew didn't have a penis.

Later, the girls wanted to dance so we moved over to a hotspot called Jump. We snuck in the back; I had to bribe the doorman to get us in, but it was worth it. We actually stumbled onto something cool. Hundreds of local Malaysians were partying like the end of the world was imminent. We jumped into the madness. I met an attractive girl at the bar named Anna from London and some guy from Austria, who was standing beside her and who appeared to be her boyfriend. We became fast friends—at least Anna and I did.

Our group of five quickly swelled to ten. Monica and I spent the rest of the night dancing with our new friends. I have little recollection of what happened next. All I remember is that Anna's Austrian boyfriend was insulting me in German.

My blackout lifted around seven o'clock in the morning in mid-bite. I was eating breakfast at some restaurant with a bunch of people. All the buttoned up drones were on their way to work. I took in the scene around the table. I was so happy to be back in my own body, I made a heartfelt speech to my new friends: "Wow . . . Here we are, a bunch of lunatics off the grid watching the responsible ones trudge off to their soul-sucking jobs, and we don't have a care in the world . . . I love you guys!"

"He speaks English," my Austrian enemy jabbed.

Everyone laughed. They were mocking me but I didn't care. "So *you do speak English*!" I said to the Austrian.

"I always did, my friend. It was you who were too far gone to understand it." His name was Hans; he wasn't Anna's boyfriend, he was her cousin.

"Amazing what you learn when your blood alcohol level dips." I extended my hand and we introduced ourselves. "Sorry, Hans." He was my enemy no more. I finally let myself be happy again. My brooding over Brian and Jack had subsided. I was back to living in the moment and enjoying the possibility of the now.

This postparty breakfast with new friends felt like a turning point. I can't explain it other than to say it was one of those ephemeral moments that is a big part of what traveling is all about. I mentioned this before, but it's what you remember the most—not the places or the museums or the bars. What sticks with you is meeting new friends from different cultures. It's the only way a California boy like me could get a glimpse into how other cultures view the world.

"You stupid Americans are so optimistic about life," Anna said. "It's rather charming."

"And maddening," Monica said.

This exchange sums up what I've learned over and over again during my travels: Most Europeans love Americans, but they also hate us too. "I feel the same way," I said. "But isn't it why you love us?"

"No!" the table said emphatically, then they threw their napkins at me.

This is the Kuala Lumpur breakfast I still remember like it was yesterday. Just like riding out the rainstorm in Dede's hut while sipping milk and honey tea in Australia, or tripping on mushrooms under the shooting stars in Bali, or drumming in the rain forest with Brian and a bunch of hippies. These traveling moments are pure gold.

After breakfast, we hopped in a taxi to go back to the hostel. Malaysian taxis were cheap but the drivers always seem to be running some scam. Their best one, which is common in Asia and would be taken to the highest level in India, is when they drive around in large circles until you start seeing the same building over and over and finally give up and pay to get out of the cab.

This happened to us on the way back to the Lodge. "Let us ouuuuuut!!!" I yelled after seeing the same turnaround three times. The driver slammed on his brakes and demanded money. Monica and the Norwegians piled out of the taxi while I negotiated the bill down, which is tricky. If you are ever in this situation, try to be firm without offending their honor and you will (probably) avoid jail or an international incident. (Probably.)

Back at the Moon Lodge, we all shared a bottle of rum on the roof that wasn't Bundaberg. We surprised some of the hostel residents who were just getting up for their morning coffee, so we called it a night. We all hugged and said our goodbyes. Even Hans hugged me. We all promised to stay in touch. I knew we wouldn't.

When I returned to my room, I must've missed Brian because something inspired me to call him from the pay phone in the hall. I dialed the number he left. I was surprised he answered.

"Rob! What are you doing up so early?"

"I haven't gone to bed."

"Are you in a Turkish prison?"

"No, we haven't been there yet. I'm in Kuala Lumpur! You deep into your brunette?"

"I'm knuckle deep . . . I'm still in Singapore."

"Am I ever going to see you again, or should I hire a ladyboy to be my wingman?"

"That's entirely up to you, man." He dropped into a whisper. "*I've been trying to break up with her for days, but the nonstop sexcapades have kept me from having the talk. Gymnasts, dude. . . .*"

"Just leave a note on her pillow, tell her you've gone to meet your gay lover, and that nine of ten Philippine doctors agree she should be checked for monkey herpes."

"*This is why Carrie hates you,*" he was still whispering.

"You think I care what she thinks? Seriously, don't let this Cabriolet-driving Yoko screw up our trip. That's why we left America—to flee from these American bitch-goddesses. Remember?"

"*Yes!* But she's not my Yoko . . . she's more like my Cher."

"Same difference."

"It's just . . . *Our naughty bits have a lot of catching up to do. You understand, right brother?*"

"I guess . . . *brother.* Just don't leave me hanging or I *will* stab you in the eyeballs with a Swiss Army knife when we get home."

"Big talker. I need to go have more goodbye sex. Meet me in Koh Samui, Thailand, in three days. Can you swing it?"

"Another island?"

"I hear good things!"

"I'll be there."

And just like that, the Fun & Funner World Tour was back on.

The next morning, I took the train to Butterworth where I hopped a ferry to Georgetown, the oldest town in Malaysia. I checked into the Plaza Hostel for about eight dollars. I met two more backpacker gals from the Netherlands who offered to tour me around Fort Cornwallis, the Khoo Kongsi Temple and the Kapitan Keling Mosque. My new Dutch tour guides had been there for a few days, so they knew their way around.

We wandered through the maze of narrow lanes and streets, visiting all the Chinese and Indian temples and the little shops with their fortune tellers, all the while the skyscrapers in downtown Georgetown loomed over our heads. This was another city with two personalities (one modern, the other ancient). Its historic section is heavily influenced by China with lots of tumbledown shops and colonial architecture.

When we returned to the hostel that night, a couple of backpackers I didn't know approached me.

"You're on the fourth floor, right?"

"Yeah, why?"

"Your room was ransacked. Heard it was some guys from Nigeria . . . Thought you should know."

I burst into my room ready to rumble, but they had cleared out. They only made off with a small amount I had in my pack. Thankfully, I always travel with most everything on me. The thieves never found my real stash, which I hide so well I've been known to forget about it. A few times, my expert stashing skills resulted in me having to reverse course to retrieve my hidden valuables. I slept with one eye open that night.

I woke up the next morning without a hangover for the first time in a few days. I spent a few hours reading in bed naked, and lo-and-behold the thieves had the gall to try and break in again. This time I was there and busted them. "Aha!" I yelled and jumped up ready to pounce. "So we meet again, my Nigerian nemesis!" I chased the two guys out of the room and down the hall. I think my nudity scared them off. It certainly surprised my neighbors, who all got a good look at my bare ass.

The double attempted robberies were a sign; it was time to go. I was sick of slumming it in big cities anyway, so I got up early and left for Thailand the next morning. I was excited to be reuniting with Brian, but I was even more motivated by the thought of tantalizing Thailand—she was drawing me close to her exotic bosom. I had heard she was an awesome mistress. You don't want to marry Thailand, but you definitely want to take her for a spin—for the sights, the sand, the sex appeal, and the scuba diving.

I traveled north by bus, bus, bus, train, bus, then ferried over to Koh Samui, a Thai island off the east coast of the Kra Isthmus. "Island living," I said to another backpacker on the ferry that didn't speak English. "You just can't beat it." The backpacker just looked at me blankly, then we struck up a conversation anyway.

If you're traveling alone, you'll find it very easy to make friends in Thailand.

I walked through town and saw backpackers everywhere, camping on quiet parts of the beach among the palms and coconut trees. I decided to rent a bungalow on the beach for eight dollars a night. Koh Samui has been a hot spot in tourism forever, and for good reason. It has amazing international cuisine, luxury spas, and—more important for young backpackers—beach parties that last for days, especially on the island to the north, Ko Pha Ngan, where they have the famous "Full Moon" parties.

After a long day of travel, I collapsed in bed, exhausted. I hoped there wouldn't be any thieves lurking in the night trying to steal my money. I slept naked, just in case.

The next morning I did the unthinkable. I broke out my new Speedo. I never wear one back home, but I wanted to fit in with all the other travelers and work on my tan. I slipped it on and strutted down Chaweng Beach and laid out with all the other locals and white-skinned foreigners. I felt ridiculous but didn't care—until I met a couple of sexy girls named Carly and Buffy, who were from Canada. They weren't your typical polite, pale-skinned Canadians; they were tan, wildly untethered, and didn't look like they had worn toques in years.

They could tell I was uncomfortable in my Speedo and paranoid about my ridiculous tan lines, but they didn't say anything. We talked for hours while my pasty upper thighs melted under the sweltering sun. I should have taken cover but I couldn't stop staring at their shapely bodies. "Umm . . . is this your first time wearing a Speedo?" Carly finally asked, knowing damn well it was.

"How can you tell??"

They said they "weren't shy" ; they had been "stripping for the last two years in Japan." Then they busted out laughing, like they had just told the best inside joke in the world. They turned out to be super nice. They said they were happy not to have some perverted Japanese businessman drooling over them.

"I'm just a nice California boy slobbering over you!" I could feel my skin sizzling but I couldn't get up; I was talking to the hottest girls I had seen in a while.

We made plans to meet up later and they took off. I spent the rest of the day under an umbrella, putting salve on my thighs and reading *For Whom the Bell Tolls*.

Without Brian, I'd been writing in my journal and cranking through books; my last two were *A Tale of Two Cities* and *Zen and the Art of Motorcycle Maintenance*. I try not to read garbage. I figure if I'm ultimately unable to curb all my debauched urges, at least I can improve my mind while I'm killing it, right?

I woke up the next day in complete agony. My thighs were stuck to the sheets; I had second degree burns. I cursed my Speedo experiment and hobbled around town looking for more aloe vera like I had two prosthetic legs. I ate breakfast at a restaurant called The Wait, then found a spot in a shaded area on the beach to sprawl out with ice on my thighs. I ordered beer after beer trying to ease my pain. I never wore another Speedo again.

That night I foolishly decided to go out and have some fun. The nightclubs in Thailand didn't open until eleven-thirty, so I hung out at the go-go bars until they did. While drinking alone, I noticed I had developed a habit of flirting with the ladyboys who were dancing. Not sure if Brian would approve of my new proclivity; actually, I knew he wouldn't but these ladymen were deceptively hot. I had to keep telling myself, *I only like girls . . . I only like girls.'*

The next day my sunburn had improved, so I called up Carly and Buffy and I went out to cleanse myself of my ladyboy habit. I made the mistake of starting off our dinner with seven beers, then the girls started in with the sex talk.

"So, are you a boobs, legs, or ass man?" Buffy asked.

"Actually, I'm a vagina man."

"Of course you are!" they shouted and showed me they weren't wearing any underwear, which inspired me to order a round of shots for the table.

After dinner, Buffy wanted to go crazy at the clubs, so we rode our three mopeds around town. I kept the shots coming; my hormones were running wild. In the back of my mind I knew if I got too wasted I might end up in a shallow grave or missing a kidney since I didn't have Brian as my wingman, but who cares—I had two strippers as escorts. What could possibly go wrong?

A lot. Around midnight, I started to feel sicker than normal. My Bukowski-esque tolerance was failing me; the club was spinning. I felt like someone had kicked me in the face with a steel-toed jackboot. What the hell was happening? My chance to score with Buffy and Carly was slipping through my fingers. The last thing I remember was fading to black under a strobe light from hell. . . .

The next thing I knew, I was in a bed. It was daytime. Was I still alive?

I crawled to the bathroom to throw up. I looked at a clock, it was five in the evening. "What day is it?" My head was pounding; I was so dehydrated I almost couldn't walk to get water. I limped around outside looking for an oasis, I was sure I got roofied. Who did this to me?? Maybe Carly and Buffy had some dirty plan to do naughty things to me? That was probably wishful thinking. More likely it was some club guys that didn't like my cock-blockage and wanted me gone so they could feast on the girls' ample stripper flesh.

After finding sweet salvation in the form of a gallon of bottled water, I went back to my room and passed out again. When I woke, I realized I'd been down for two days.

That night, I made yet another resolution and this one I was going to keep, goddammit. I wrote it in my journal:

1. No more blacking out, this time I'm serious!
2. No more loud, crazy, hot strippers from Canada.
3. And no more roofies.

That was actually three resolutions. . . .

I kept a low profile after my roofie night. I got out of town and took a moped ride around the island, checking out all the villages and waterfalls. I noticed that besides the nonstop party, which takes most of the headlines around here, if you are a discerning traveler looking for something more spiritual to do in Koh Samui, you'll find many secret Buddhist temples hidden in the narrow back alleys of the city.

I visited one of these tiny temples to pray for my soul, if I still had one. I reflected on what I wanted to do with the rest of the trip and my life. The memories of my shattered life back home crept into my consciousness for the first time in months. I remembered I needed to call Jody, my assistant back home, and let her know I was still alive. She no doubt despised me for leaving her jobless in a pile of rubble from my burned-down life.

I had let a bunch of loyal employees go in my fire sale, but she was the one I most regretted. God, I never even told her goodbye. I'm a bad boyfriend and a bad boss. And a bad friend. Friend—friend . . . wait. That's when it hit me—what day was it? Brian never showed up! Where the hell is he? That bastard! Or maybe I never showed up since I slept for two days. Who was at fault here?

Confused, I found a pay phone and started dialing numbers. How could he ditch me again? Maybe he's dead? Maybe he's married? Maybe he's the one who slipped me the roofie? I called Brian's forwarding number, but got a busy signal. Then I called home and found out Brian was not dead or married.

He was waiting for me in Bangkok. "Bangkok?"

"Yes, Bangkok." Mom said he called her to tell me to "meet him at the Grand Palace tomorrow." Tomorrow??

Would he even be in Bangkok? I had to find out.

There was nothing keeping me in Koh Samui but blackened memories of sunburns, roofies, and carnal pleasures that could have been, so I hopped a boat to Bangkok the next day and said goodbye to Koh Samui. I ran into the strippers again. "You girls—I vaguely remember you." When I stopped to talk they told me they were headed back to Tokyo.

"Vince Neil's sleeping with our roommate!" Carly said. "We want in on that action!" When I brought up our night together, Buffy assured me they had not roofied me and all was literally forgotten.

"That's funny, I remember nothing too."

"Sometimes it's better that way," Carly said. Once I heard they were Mötley Crüe groupies, the whole roofie thing made more sense. They could have gotten roofied and didn't even notice.

I arrived in Bangkok at sundown.

What would the fun capital of Southeast Asia have in store for me? The Book says in Bangkok anything worth doing is "fun," which I found to be true. Everything here can be done with a sense of *sà·nùk*

Some new friends I met in Indonesia—we bought some pot to go back to the hostel and wake up Brian to smoke (it turned out to be just parsley).

During the second month of our journey, we rented and camped with this Toyota on Fraser's Island (the world's largest sand island), in Australia.

Brian and I camel back-riding in Australia, with another backpacker friend in the background.

Brian and I cross-dressed and went out in Surfer's Paradise, Australia, for a hostel party—the prize if you won was all the free beer you could drink!

Angkor Wat in Cambodia.

After shaving my head bald in Bangkok, right before we went to Vietnam.

Wearing rice hats with a backpacker buddy in Vietnam.

Mamma Hahn and I on her booze cruise of the Vietnam coast, where she painted my head.

Hiking the Annapurna Trail in Nepal. I had worn some new boots that wore my heel down to the bone and I had to tape up flip flops to go over the glaciers and finish the hike.

In Tibet, spinning the prayer wheels at the Potala Palace, home of the ousted Dalai Lama.

Children watching us hike by in the Annapurna mountains in Nepal.

Kids borrowing my book while in the 3rd class train compartment going across India.

The Taj Mahal.

Brian and I were walking the backstreets in Dehli, India, and ran into this Hindi Sadhu and some cobra charmers.

Brian and a Sadhu in Varanasi, the most sacred place in India.

("fun" in Thai). But fun here can get out of control fast. Often no words are needed to complete even the most bizarre transactions, especially on Khaosan Road, which is where I went first.

Khaosan Road is the most happening street in the world for back-packers. It's a half-mile long road in the middle of Bangkok packed with a zillion shady hostels, shady travel agencies, and shady bars and dive restaurants. All the backpackers from around Asia start here, end here, meet here, or converge here. Just walking the street is a crazy experience; you can literally get anything in the world, from a bazooka to any drug on the planet to a monkey waiter. "Street life" is what Bangkok is all about. It's what I'd come to crave in all these Asian mega-cities but never truly found—except here. I was at home among the freaks.

I loved the living, breathing urban contradiction of experience that is Bangkok—just the opposite of Singapore, which felt sterile and rigid to me. You can get lost in the streets here and never be heard from again. Many people have. You'll see bizarre polarities everywhere: megamalls jutting out of ancient villages, Buddhist temples neighboring sleazy sex clubs, food carts in the shadows of high-rise restaurants where the wealthy drink their martinis. I never ventured into a skyscraper to dine with the millionaires, but I did walk over to the very impressive Grand Palace hotel to meet Brian, per his instructions.

Walking in, I thought, *this place is way too nice for us. Who had he robbed to afford it? Was he bringing Carrie along?* I tried to look present-able. I felt nervous like I was reuniting with an old lover, but we'd only been apart for two weeks.

I spotted him at the bar alone sipping a Mai Tai. "The poon-hound returns!" I yelled. Brian was glowing—he looked like he'd just had sex for two weeks straight.

He just laughed. "Where's all the white women at??"

"*Blazing Saddles*. Where's Carrie?"

"On a plane back to California with a urinary tract infection."

"So, you're not getting married?"

"Nah . . . but I really do love her. I mean, how many go-go girls can we go through before it all becomes a neverending blur of meaningless fluid exchanges? I want something real, don't you?"

"Real is in the eye of the beholder," I said. "What am I seeing now. Are you for real? I haven't seen this guy in a month."

"Let's live that question for a bit," he said. "C'mon, let's get outta here. This place is too rich for our peasant blood."

We went bar hopping in Patpong, the super shady district of Bangkok, where we drank a bottle of whiskey just like the old days. Things were going great. Was the old Brian really back? After catching up on all the craziness that had gone on in our lives, I decided he was. "You really are back! I guess I won't stab you with my Swiss Army knife after all."

"You don't even own a knife," Brian said.

Then just like that he was gone again. After we polished off the whiskey, Brian got up to leave. It was some unreasonably reasonable hour.

"Where you going, man?"

Brian had never done this before in his life. He explained he "was tired and needed to recharge my penis." When I protested, he said, "Think of this as a role reversal: For once you're the crazy partier and I'm the sensible one with the girlfriend. Have fun! Don't get monkey herpes!"

This, of course, pissed me off, but I stayed out for a nice blackout evening by myself just to spite him.

The next morning I saw how crazy I had become.

I had yet another tremendous hangover, which made what I'm about to tell you seem like a sickening dream. I knew I was alive because I had to urinate, so I dragged myself to the bathroom. As I peed and swayed, I glanced at myself in the mirror and did a double take at what I saw. Half my head was shaved bald. The other half still had the long Tarzan hair I'd cherished for years. I nearly pissed all over the floor.

"I've been scalped."

Why would someone shave half my head? Was it the Nigerians? The strippers with their roofies? An angry ladyboy I flirted with too hard? I rubbed my half bald half and the memory of last night came rushing back in a horrendous blur. After Brian left, I met these two really drunk girls. They said I was cute but my long hair had to go. They were Army brats who only liked military boys. They wanted to cut my hair themselves but I refused. Being drunk and without a wingman, I let them drag me to a Bangkok barber at three o'clock in the morning. That's all I remember.

When Brian dragged out of bed and saw me, he started laughing. "Let me guess: You got your ass kicked by a bunch of Marines last night??"

"Pretty sure I did this on purpose."

"Thought you were done blacking out?"

"I did too. I even wrote it in my journal."

"Some girls did this to you. Didn't they?"

"No! Yes . . . kinda."

I was a strange sight for sure—half Tarzan, half Travis Bickle.

Brian just stood there with his toothbrush. "I stand in wonderment to your insanity." He had known me forever and I've always had long hair. "Charles Manson would be proud."

"I must have panicked and run out before the barber was finished."

"You did it for sex, which never happened, *right?*"

"I don't know why I did it."

Maybe I did it to show Brian I wasn't the crazy one. Maybe I did it to show him I was still the conservative kid from Cupertino who would get a buzz cut to prove it. Whatever the reason, my half-ass attempt at looking normal only proved his point.

I was now the crazy one.

After a lunch of chicken and rice and a few beers, Brian convinced me to go back to the same barbershop and cut the rest off. I argued with the barber about payment. "But I already paid you for a full haircut last night!" The guy hadn't forgotten my insane countenance; he just nodded and shaved the rest off.

It was a liberating experience being bald after having long hair for so many years. When I walked out of the barbershop, I smiled at Brian, who was reading. "Now I don't even need to shower! Half the time I only do it to get the grease out. I'm free!"

Brian just smiled and shook his head. "You're the king of your own world."

We spent our last afternoon in Bangkok walking around Khaosan Road, shopping for supplies. I bought some music, a shirt, and a cap for my bald head. Brian bought condoms, lots of them. Either he was preparing to dive back into the dangerous loins of the stray go-go dancer experience, or he was reinvigorated with love and didn't want to give Carrie anything a shot of penicillin wouldn't cure. I didn't ask.

We left Bangkok the next day and took a bus ride south to Pattaya on the eastern coast. Pattaya is one of the sex capitals of the world; the entire town was built to serve American servicemen on R&R during the Vietnam War. But we didn't come for the sex—at least I didn't. We came here to enjoy the beach for a day or so before we left for our next stop: Vietnam. But looking at all the condoms Brian bought in Bangkok, I wasn't sure of his intentions anymore.

"This place makes Bangkok's red-light district look like Disneyland," Brian said in awe as we walked past all the go-go bars, sex clubs, and massage parlors.

"Good thing you bought all those condoms," I smiled.

"I just need to protect myself just in case."

"You never got tested, did you?"

"No."

"Did you tell Carrie she may have a venereal disease?"

"You of all people can't lecture me about responsible drinking," he said, slapping my bald head.

"Fair enough . . . *Fair enough.*"

During the day, Pattaya is not quite as sex-driven as it is at night. Sadly, the beaches were not very nice; they were crowded and full of partiers by mid-afternoon, jet skis were flying around full of Chinese tourists on vacation. A million open-air bars were going off and it was only three o'clock.

"It's like Groundhog Day; everywhere we go we find the same insane orgy of excess," Brian said. "No way we're escaping this 'City of Sin' unscathed."

Brian was right . . . but we had no idea how strange of a trip it was going to be.

The first sign of trouble was when we saw the American aircraft carrier USS *Independence* arrive in town. Five thousand seaman were streaming off the boat looking for trouble. "Half those dudes will be in the brig by the end of the night," I said.

"Great. They'll take the attention off us," Brian said.

We checked in at the Diana Inn for ten dollars a night. Our room had a TV, a refrigerator, and our own bathroom. It was pretty nice for the price, and we also got a swimming pool—but it was so hot in Pattaya my head was in constant danger of third degree burns, so I couldn't lay out for very long.

That night, we sat on our balcony and watched the party in the street below. Everything was back to normal and all seemed right in the world again. We decided to avoid all the sex bars and watched *Trainspotting* at a restaurant.

Were we finally growing up?

Not by a long shot. The next night it got ugly, oily, and very, very dirty.

It all began innocently enough. Brian and I decided to walk to another beach since the one by our hotel was ridiculously dirty. After about two hours of trekking through back roads, we never found anything worthwhile, so we gave up and decided to rehydrate at this little bar in the middle of the jungle. The tiny bar was hopping, which was strange. Servicemen were everywhere. Brian and I even recognized a few of the Navy guys.

"Didn't we party with you dudes last month in Singapore?"

"You're that crazy guy and that hippie! See you finally got a proper haircut."

We started drinking and it all went downhill from there. We eventually rampaged back to Pattaya's go-go bars. We were going deep quick and had been drinking for about five hours when I convinced Brian to give all of us "servicemen" a show.

Brian, back in old form, took the bait. He hopped up on the bar and started dancing with all the bikini girls. The Navy guys booed. I was too busy to notice since a stripper dancing above me kept pouring candle wax on my head. After a few minutes my entire head was covered in a wax helmet. Meanwhile, the Navy guys kept booing since Brian didn't have a female body and couldn't dance for shit. I knew this kind of foolishness was illegal in the States, but had no idea it would be frowned upon in Thailand where I thought anything went. It didn't.

After a few minutes a gang of Thai police officers rushed in and dragged Brian out into the street, screaming and half-clothed. The Navy guys cheered his ousting. The Thai police saw that I was snapping photos of them dragging Brian out, so they grabbed me too. Brian kept yelling, "You're making a huge mistake!" as they cuffed him while I just yelled gibberish. The police tried to confiscate my camera, but for some reason I wouldn't let them have it. A struggle ensued; I started to swing my camera at them like a fool while Brian cheered my rebellion like an even bigger fool.

"He's an award-winning photojournalist for *National Geographic*! He shoots elephants!"

Thank God I shaved my head because I yelled for a nearby Navy police officer to save our ass. It's their job to make sure the Navy guys don't get in trouble in the ports of call, and when they do, the Navy police arrest them and take them back to the ship.

I was hoping this would happen to us—and it did. The Navy swooped in and the Thai police were forced to hand us over. I stopped resisting arrest and complied. Brian yelled, "Thank God for the cavalry! I'm falsely accused of disturbing a sex show!"

It took a few minutes for the Navy police to haggle for our lives. Watching the negotiation, all I could say was, "I love America." A Navy cop got in my face. "Can it before I shut your yapper for you!" I shut my yapper. Still, I had to smile—who wouldn't? We weren't going to Thai jail.

We were both smiling when the Navy police cuffed us. I told them, "You just saved us from a long, excruciating imprisonment."

"Shutaaap!" the big one yelled then banged my head into Brian's like two coconuts. I could tell they were tempted to throw us in the ocean so they didn't have to file a report, but being law-abiding seamen, they took us to the pier and onto the aircraft carrier for processing.

After our sobering walk, Brian politely informed the Navy police they "really should release us."

"Another peep outta you and—"

"But sirs, really, your commanding officer won't be too pleased to find you're falsely imprisoning two innocent American civilians."

"Nice try. Prove it."

We handed them our passports, which we luckily had on us. The Navy cops did a thorough check to make sure we weren't trying to go AWOL, then after a few minutes of heated debate, they had to let us go.

There were five thousand crazy Americans hanging out in Pattaya, and they had just arrested the only two they couldn't take in. When they unshackled us, they knocked our heads together one final time. "Stay outta trouble, you knuckleheads! If we see you around here again—"

"Don't worry sirs, you won't. We're going to Vietnam."

They gave us one last skeptical look. We walked away, whistling. We turned a corner and looked at each other in shock. "How did we get outta that one?" Brian wailed. We were so happy we weren't going to jail we skipped all the way down the pier. Shaken up, we skipped right past the strip of go-go bars we got arrested in, wisely deciding not to tempt fate and go back in.

But our troubles weren't destined to end there. The next incident occurred when we walked straight into a street that was obviously the gay section of town. It was easy to spot since there were dozens of neon penises and signs flashing all sort of gay slogans and slurs. We should have just turned around and gone home, but I had to push it. I turned to Brian and said with a big, devious smile, "Let's check one out—why not!"

"Why not?? How addicted are you to trannies?"

"They're called ladyboys, and it's the perfect place to lay low."

"It's the perfect place to get a scorching case of herpes."

"We need to get off the streets. What better hideout than this?"

We argued for a few minutes but I held firm. I mentioned our pact to "see everything for the experience. You need to keep an open mind, even in dire situations like these. Trust me."

Brian shook his head and let me drag him in. "I'm traveling with Boy George."

Onward we plunged into our first go-go boys bar escapade. "Don't make me do this, man. I can smell the musky coconut oil from here."

Brian and I slipped into the bar. It was dark—too dark. Then stage lights came on and music started blaring. When our eyes focused on the action at hand, the scene was sheer horror.

I whispered to Brian, "This is no ladyboy bar, dude . . . This is a man-on-boy *sex club*." A red neon sign behind the stage flashed BOYS BOYS BOYS, which summed up our predicament.

Brian wheeled around to flee but ten boys in tight Speedos surrounded us. "Oh, hi fellas. We seem to be in the wrong place here," he said.

They yelled in broken English, "No sailor, you home! You home with daddy!"

"You're daddy?? You're teenagers!" I laughed.

The strippers gyrated around us, circling their new prey. Brian and I were so freaked out we let the gang of strippers back us into a corner where sat down at a table. Brian looked at me and whispered, "I hate you."

A waiter came over and we ordered two beers; boy, did we need them. The ten strippers hopped back on the stage and started dancing in Speedos with numbers attached to them so we didn't get them confused.

There was only one other patron in the club—an old, fat German man sitting in the corner flagrantly French-kissing two boys on his lap. The German was clothed but it wasn't a pretty sight. I tried to lighten the conversation. "Remember the time you wanted to become a male stripper? How is this different?"

Brian shot back: "At Chippendale's a man strips in front of women. It was nothing like *this!*"

I egged him on. "You're so homophobic. These guys dance way better than you. Admit it!"

"I'm closing my eyes." Brian shut his eyes and started humming to himself.

There we were, waiting for our beers, watching ten boys dance for us. There was no escape, I had to look at them. Either that or stare at the dirty German.

Every time a dancing boy came over and tried to sit in my lap, I turned to Brian and said, "Sorry, I'm with him. We're lovers! We're in the Navy!" I asked one of the dancing boys how many Navy guys came in. "Don't worry, you can tell us. We're officers doing a survey on gays in the service." The conversation was highly entertaining but Brian was getting extremely uncomfortable.

Our beers finally came. I was hoping more alcohol would calm him down but it wasn't happening. Brian bolted up and went hurtling out of the club, leaving me with two beers, ten boys, and a gay German with his pants around his ankles. As soon as Brian dashed out, the ten dancing boys pulled down their Speedos and started pleasuring themselves to show me their hard-ons. Seeing I was the only one left in the audience, they hopped off the stage and jerked their way across the floor to me.

Now, I'm confident in my sexuality, but even I was getting uncomfortable. But being on a strict budget, I told myself there was no way in hell I was going to leave two full beers on the table so I started drinking them both at once, which felt strange since I now had two bottles in my mouth while surrounded by a litany of boners a few feet from my face.

The scene was getting out of hand. I had nowhere to turn and didn't want to deal with the boys who were trying to sit on my lap. So after chugging my beers, I got up and tried to exit. To my pleasant surprise, all the boys who had just been jerking off stopped whacking to shake my hand goodbye and told me to "come back soon!" The boys were very gracious.

When I finally escaped the club, Brian was waiting. He laid into me. "What the hell is your problem, *rice queen*!? I know you want to experience new things, but we're wanted by the authorities and you stop to watch a boner fest?"

"Technically, we're not wanted . . . and I had no idea that was gonna happen."

"You dragged me into the most flaming gay bar since Liberace's Slipper!"

"That's funny you remember that. I woulda been outta there sooner if you hadn't left your full beer for me to finish!"

"Well, I hope someone finished you off!"

"They did! I mean, no . . . Who do you think I am?!"

"I'm really starting to question your sanity. I don't know if I want to continue this trip with you. You've lost it!"

"C'mon, those were nice boys—if you overlook their raging boners. You've just lost your sense of adventure."

"I can't talk to you anymore. Go back into the circle jerk; I won't stop you!"

"The only circle jerk I'm enjoying tonight is my own!"

I reminded Brian that we were still kind of fleeing from two police forces and needed to keep a lower profile lest we get arrested for real this time. We quieted down and escaped down a side street. After a few minutes, we came across a baby elephant.

I looked at Brian. "Getaway pachyderm? It's a miracle! C'mon, hop on."

"You must *want* to go to jail tonight."

I looked at Brian. "No I don't."

I gave the elephant's *mahout* (keeper) a few baht (Thai money) and he let me hop on.

"We're not stealing it. We're renting it."

Brian looked at me. Then he looked at the elephant. I thought he was going to leave me in Thailand and take the next flight home, but he didn't.

Instead, he hopped on the little fella.

Brian sighed, "Okay . . . let's go."

We rode the elephant back to our room in silence.

Brian wasn't talking to me the next day thanks to last night's tomdickery.

We packed up our stuff and left for our next destination in silence. I didn't mind; I had a horrible hangover anyway so I left him alone and chatted up a funny surfer bloke from Sweden on the bus out of town. We swapped stories and laughed all the way back to Bangkok.

After visiting a travel agent to get our visas, we jumped the next plane to Hanoi, which was just next door.

"Ever gonna speak to me again?" I asked on our short flight over.

"Just don't drag me to anymore gay clubs from now on," he said with his eye mask on.

"Do lesbian bars count?"

"Don't make me punch you."

"I hear Vietnam has some cool lesbian bars. There's one run by an old Vietnam vet who never left . . . I heard she's hot."

"Bet she looks like Colonel Kurtz."

"C'mon, don't be negative."

"You're crazy, man."

"I take that as a compliment coming from you." Then I used his old line on him, "C'mon, have a drink . . . have a drink." Brian lifted his eye mask up, grabbed the cocktail from my hand, and drank it down. He handed me the empty glass. "Needed that. Can't wait to see what happens next!"

"Gentlemen, start your boners . . . Just kidding."

"Stop," he said, slipping his eye mask back down.

After a month lost in the miserable woods of Singapore, Malaysia, and Thailand, I was a happy traveler again. Who knew what tomorrow would bring, but my friendship with Brian was back on. My personal renaissance was back on. It may sound insane, but there was hope again that if we could survive all this madness, we could come out the other side with our souls intact. I couldn't wait to see what happened next.

Life was weird . . . but good again.

6

Cambodian Zen

WHAT HAPPENS WHEN TWO BURNT-OUT backpackers barely on speaking terms parachute into so-called enemy territory with no clue of what's awaiting them below? What happens when we willingly remove our safety net of wine and women that we clung to for the past five months? Would we burn up during reentry into the straight world? Brian and I were about to find out.

We were rolling the dice and dropping anchor in a former enemy state where we couldn't commit felonies or screw around, a place where the government could send us straight to hell in a bamboo handbasket for anything resembling our past behavior. Why gamble with our lives? We were young and naive and wanted to test the boundaries. We wanted to be challenged; we wanted to be uncomfortable. Island-hopping had nearly killed us, so how bad could Vietnam really be?

Vietnam was a scary place to us growing up. We were born in the Watergate era, so we'd heard all the horror stories about the war from relatives, from teachers, and from movies and television. Now that we were grown, we wanted to see what the country was really like. I had a feeling it would be nothing like I imagined, and I was right.

When we landed in the former communist nation of Vietnam, the borders had just opened to American citizens. Brian admitted he was a tad apprehensive of the lingering effects of the war. "I'm not saying it's going to happen, but we may want to prepare for a hostage crisis," he said as we de-boarded the plane at the Hanoi airport.

"What, why? They kicked *our* ass. What beef could they possibly have with *us*?"

"I dunno . . . maybe because we killed a shitload of their people."

"*I* didn't kill anyone."

Brian looked at my shaved head. "You look like you did."

"*Relax,* man. I'm sure it's water under the bridge."

"But dude, what happens to bridges in war movies?"

"What?"

"They blow up! All I'm saying is, if we get up to any monkey business like stealing statues or starting any barroom brawls with gay strippers, we may find ourselves hanging from our toenails in a bamboo pen."

"How many times do I have to apologize? That was the *old* me—I'm maturing."

"Your body may be a man, but your soul is still a boy." Brian was starting to sound like some of the Zen philosophers he was reading.

"Can't believe you're lecturing me on decorum," I said.

"Believe it."

"Just calm down," I said. "You've seen *Platoon* way too many times."

I promised Brian I would not go crazy in Vietnam. We'd done enough partying in the preceding countries to last a few lifetimes, and I was serious about growing up. I wanted to continue the personal renaissance I'd been talking so much about. Hell, I wanted to start it for real this time, before it was too late.

But could I change—can anyone? Did I even want to anymore? I knew I wasn't the person I left behind in America, but that DNA was still stuck to me. It always will be. *I am a stupid American*! I can't change that unless I get a brain transplant or go back to grad school or defect to Cuba.

"Maybe we should go to North Korea next?" I had to throw it out there.

"Um, let's see if we survive this first," Brian shot back.

I will say at this point, even though Brian had become a buttoned-up pain in my ass, I respected him for finally showing some maturity. After his romantic Singapore sojourn, he seemed to be more Zen about life and less about living on the razor's edge of indecency. He actually seemed to be growing, which was a frightening proposition. That was *my* goal. What was I doing wrong?

Our fears of bamboo incarceration were quelled when we finally arrived at customs. As soon as the customs official found out we were Americans, he got excited and wanted to teach us Vietnamese right there. "See, they love us here," I whispered to Brian as we smiled and pretended to understand what the hell he was saying.

We walked over to a currency exchange and turned in our Thai baht for some Vietnamese money (dong), then we shared a taxi to our hotel with this big English guy named Scott (I called him Scotty), who would end up traveling with us for weeks. After roughing it in hostels for months, we decided to splurge and get a nice room at the Trang An Hotel for ten dollars a night that had functional air conditioning and a private bathroom.

Once we settled in, we were ready to experience Hanoi—the city of bicycles, mopeds, scooters, and rickshaws. Touring around on rented bicycles, we noticed the city still had quite a bit of French influence. We saw lots of French colonial architecture and found the baguette was the bread of choice in town. All this finally made sense when the Book reminded me that Hanoi was the capital of French Indochina for the first half of the twentieth century.

What we as Americans remember, of course, is what happened after the French left. Hanoi "turned to the dark side" and became the capital of communist North Vietnam from 1954 to 1976. Then, after "Charlie" kicked the crap out of our fathers during the war, Hanoi became capital of reunified Vietnam in 1976, which is where we stand today.

Brian and I vowed not to bring up any of these sordid facts to anyone here, which paid off because, despite being in former commie country, everywhere we went the people were extremely friendly—the exact opposite of what we imagined.

"See, anytime you assume anything in life, you're gonna be as wrong as the dong," I said.

Brian wasn't convinced. "The night is still young."

Speaking of the wrongness of the local dong, after spending a few hours in Vietnam, we quickly learned the real currency over here is the US Yankee dollar. The exchange rate definitely benefited us to trade back to the dollar and not convert to the dong—so we did.

I wouldn't describe our first day in Hanoi as "fun" per se, but it was interesting. The first thing you notice is it's an extremely congested and perplexing city. I have never seen so many bicycles and mopeds in my life—they had overwhelmed the city like ten million ants on a mountain of sugar. The only cars in town were taxis; it was like some third world New York except for the nightlife, which still seemed to be run by the old communist regime.

To say there wasn't much to do in Hanoi at night was an understatement. It was barely open for business, so we tried out a few places we heard of (Tin Tin's and Apocalypse) and had a few beers. They were good bars, supposedly, but you wouldn't know by its patronage. We were literally the only human beings in any bar, which was surreal.

"Did somebody drop an H-bomb in here?" I said.

"This is like partying in Chernobyl!" Brian shouted to the empty bar.

"Tourism here is definitely in the nascent stage," I said. "Let's cut out."

Being the great Marco Polo travelers that we were, we decided to go for an aimless Hanoi walkabout. First we stumbled onto a water puppet show. Brian tripped over the puppeteer and had to apologize and sit down and watch the show to make up for his stupidity. The show was in Vietnamese, so we didn't understand anything other than it took place in a temple, but we politely sat through it.

Brian whispered, "This is not long-lasting stimulus."

"No kidding. It's a freaking puppet show."

"I'm already templed out. Let's fly out tonight."

"What, to another party island? We haven't even visited one temple yet."

"I'm projecting into the future."

After the puppet show, we tipped the puppeteer for the effort and kept wandering the streets. Downtown Hanoi was pleasant at night with lots of kids running around staring at us. They all wanted to sell us postcards and maps but we politely declined. "They're looking at us like aliens. What are we doing here?" Brian looked uncomfortable, this was a good start.

"Guess I'm looking for a spiritual clue," I mused.

"A clue to what? I totally agree with shutting down the Cirrhosis Tour, but we may be barking up the wrong tree if you're looking for answers here."

"Just wait for it . . . Maybe the universe will meet us halfway."

It's funny how life works. The moment I asked the universe for help, we had our first moment of Zen. This five-year-old boy approached Brian saying nothing. He just took Brian's hand and walked with him as I trailed behind and took pictures. They walked up a hill that led to a small market, then Brian and the boy went in and Brian came out holding a chocolate bar. I quietly watched Brian split the chocolate bar with the boy. It was an amazing scene of simple human connection.

The universe was listening.

After that, the boy followed us for what seemed like miles. I began to wonder if his mother was missing him. How would he find his way home? After a while, Brian looked back. "Where'd my sidekick go?"

"It's way past his bedtime. That was pretty cool, though."

"Where the hell are we?" Brian stopped walking.

"Vietnam," I said.

"No, literally where are we?"

"Err . . . Asia?" Brian and I recognized nothing.

I put my arm around his shoulder. "We've just broken one of the cardinal rules of backpacking: always know how to get home."

"Way to go, Magellan. I blame you," Brian said. He never had any sense of direction.

Our compass was off in Vietnam because there weren't any of the ubiquitous American franchise signs littered about that we had become so accustomed to seeing in other countries. When we hopped in a

Vietnamese taxi, we couldn't tell our cabbie our hotel was 2 blocks down from the 7-Eleven; there were no 7-Elevens, all we saw was a blur of Vietnamese letters everywhere.

Brian asked, "Dude, what's the name of our hotel?"

"Uh, something *house*?" I drew a blank.

"We're both useless." Brian went to work on the cabbie using his charades skills to somehow mime us back to civilization. When we finally got back to our hotel, one of the backpackers in the lobby told us the first American ambassador had just arrived last week and the first American Embassy was set to open tomorrow on the grand exalted leader Ho Chi Minh's birthday.

"The times they are a changin', man," the backpacker said. "What a time to be alive."

"You said it."

"There's gonna be a killer party tomorrow," he added, which in Hanoi meant there was going to be a somber group procession past the corpse of Ho Chi Minh that everyone was ordered to attend.

I smiled. "We should crash."

Brian yawned. "That sounds like, something."

I eventually talked Brian into visiting the Ho Chi Minh Mausoleum with the rest of the populace to pay our respects.

"It's your funeral, brother," Brian added before turning out the lights.

I couldn't sleep, wondering how we would be received tomorrow. Since we were some of the first Yanks let back into the country since the war, who knew how the mourners would treat an American with a shaved head who shows up to celebrate their dead commandant. We were going to find out.

The next morning was the big day. We needed to get in the mood so we found the only Mexican bar in Hanoi to lube up.

"If we're going to celebrate a dead enemy of the state, we need to be as *un*-sober as possible." Brian didn't need to convince me. We were drying out but not going cold turkey. We proceeded to get as rowdy as you can day-drinking in an empty bar in a former communist country.

It didn't take long for the Vietnam jokes along with margaritas and pints of 333, the local beer of choice, to pour out fast and furious.

Even after a few drinks, something still felt off about Vietnam to Brian. He kept wondering aloud, "Is all this kindness a ruse?" We kept drinking until we forgot the question.

By mid-afternoon, if any bartender in the country spoke English we would've been arrested for public indecency, but no one noticed we were spouting obscenities. I looked at Brian. "It took us twenty-four hours to revert back to our original offensive nature. Luckily, no one cares!"

Brian just laughed, "Is this growth?"

"No!" I shouted and finished my beer. "C'mon, let's go see the dead guy."

We walked down to the ceremony, unsure if we were unwelcome intruders. If Jack the patriot were still alive, he would have frowned on our participation in this event, but our excuse was it was old news.

"This is crazy, this is crazy," Brian said.

"Don't sweat it. That was our fathers' war, not ours," I said.

They rolled out Ho Chi Minh's embalmed body and proffered it to about ten thousand Vietnamese. Suddenly all the boozy joy we felt disappeared. We witnessed how much these people admired their leader, who had won the war for them. We tried downplaying our American-ness and acted serious standing in the line that slowly snaked past the body. Brian did lean in to kiss his glass tomb but I pulled him back before the guards swept him away.

Other than that, the entire event was eerily quiet and serene. What was odd was we truly felt a part of it. I didn't feel any connection with Ho, just with the emotions of the people. I realized I was worried for nothing. No one cared that we were Americans. No one even noticed. For the first time on the trip, it wasn't about us . . . Maybe we were starting to learn something after all.

Our first trip out of Hanoi was to the Perfume Pagoda, a sprawling complex of Buddhist temples and shrines nestled into the limestone of the Huong Tich Mountains. The Perfume Pagoda is a sacred place to many

Buddhists because legend has it that Guanyin, the Bodhisattva deity of mercy and compassion, once stayed at the Huong Tich Pagoda (one of the Perfume Pagodas) in order to help save human souls.

Brian was excited about checking out the temple. "Our souls need saving." We hired two brawny oarswomen to row us up the Day River to the spot. When we got there, a crew of kids materialized to "volunteer" to carry small coolers of water and Cokes up the mountainside to the Trong Pagoda, which was hidden in one of the large caves at the top.

Little did we know, the kids had an angle. Tourism was new to North Vietnam at the time, so the people didn't quite know how to react to travelers, but they were learning fast. These kids with the coolers were gouging us like real capitalists—charging us three times the rate for a Coke in Vietnam—smart little businessmen. We paid up but I knew their game. They even kept us on the right track. Sometimes Brian and I like to get lost and see what occurs but not today; these little troopers were keeping us on the straight up and up.

It took a lot of hiking through the beautiful, verdant mountainside, plush green vegetation, and rice paddies to get to the Pagoda, but it was well worth it. When we entered the Trong Pagoda grotto, we ventured into a huge, hidden cave, which was damp and billowed white fog from the burning incense. Inside the cave was a temple that was surrounded by imposing stalactites that hung from above.

We paid homage to Guanyin, then the kids met us outside with a fresh Coca-Cola and led us down another hundred steps to the base of the cave and another candlelit temple. While we traversed the path, I noticed the absolute splendor of the scene before us. The rice fields were lush and green and neverending.

I looked at Brian. "Are we in former communist Utopia?"

"My idea of heaven has no ethos," Brian said.

After our tour, the nearby Lonely Planet café offered us a beer "and a pleasant meal to finish off our afternoon"—at least that's what the sign on the wall read. "Guess their new vacation industry is trying to rip off any English tourist verbiage they can," I said, pointing to the sign.

"Wouldn't you?" Brian replied.

The next day, we booked a trip to Ha Long Bay in the north. Our tour started with a five-hour cramped minibus ride on terrible dirt roads. We bounced up and down like two kangaroos on springs. Brian looked at me while we were getting battered: "Thiiiis issss a commmmmical amounnnnt of bummmmmmps, duuuudddddddde." What do you expect for a two-day all-inclusive trip with transportation, food/drinks, and boat for twenty-two dollars?

During the bus ride, we stopped to watch the locals harvesting rice in the green rice paddies. It was moving to watch people working the same agrarian job their entire lives, doing something that had been going on for a millennium. It gave us a moment to reflect on our own modern existence while drinking overpriced Cokes, which were everywhere.

"What a tranquil sight . . . really connects you with the past," I said.

Brian was less moved. All he said was, "Coke is clearly the first American company to conquer Vietnam."

Our tour bus was also a transport company so the rest of the ride was spent stopping for relatives of the passengers and drivers. When we finally arrived, we took in the view of Ha Long Bay, a beautiful area off the Vietnamese coast. We marveled at the limestone rock islands jutting out in the bay; they looked totally uninhabitable unless you were a barnacle or seagull.

We bought a ticket to tour the islands and headed out on a fifty-foot boat with some other tourists. Our guide was a smallish Vietnamese man who was clearly gay; we liked him. We traveled out to the solo monuments; the guide told us there were sixteen hundred rocks with many caves to explore. The boat stopped so we could take a dip and explore the caves around the canyon of monuments. We swam into a cave with large stalactites that was totally amazing, then we explored a few more caves and swam into a big one that had a large circular tide pool with facades rising to the heavens. We were surrounded by large walls of limestone jetting out of the water. It felt like we'd found a secret lagoon.

"Where the mermaids at?" Brian asked, treading water.

Our guide swam up behind us and replied in a slightly creepy watery whisper, "Only mermen here, mistah."

During our swim, I started talking to the guide whose name turned out to be Ty. He told me his thoughts on Americans: We were "dangerous" because he'd read about Hell's Gate, whatever that was. He also said, "London was crazy because they had werewolves there." After a few minutes, I realized he based all his feelings from a lifetime of reading Vietnamese newspapers and watching American movies. When we were finished, we swam back to the boat against the current and headed back to land.

The next day we took the five-hour bumpy bus from hell back to Hanoi, getting out to "water the rice paddies" every hour or so. We met a few gals from England, who we chatted up the rest of the ride. I took a liking to Emily, who was tall and stood out from the others.

When we arrived back in Hanoi, we went out to dinner with the English ladies, then walked around Hoan Kiem Lake in the center of Old Town, attempting to flirt with them—to no avail. Brian and I went home alone that night.

The next morning, Brian "Templed-Out" Rakow got up early and decided to incorporate exercise into our neverending temple tour. He said he was going to "get his tourism in by going for a temple jog," and it worked. He came back invigorated like he had seen the face of God—and maybe he had. "Dude! The people here are amazing. Their smiles are all different! Some are large, some are small, some sideways, some upside down, some toothless but *they're everywhere* like they come from different parts of the soul. I had another moment of Zen!"

"That's great! You had an epiphany, man! Guess what? I've got a date with a bodyguard tonight!"

Brian just looked at me.

"A female bodyguard."

"Right."

Brian stayed in that night to read about Buddhism (he was getting into Alan Watts, the Buddhist philosopher) while I went out with Emily from London, who was a professional bodyguard back home. She was tall and good-looking. When you've been on the road for five months, she was an absolute ten, regardless of whether she shaved her armpits or legs.

After dinner, we went back to our hotel slightly tipsy, and started playing cards in her room. These were no ordinary cards; they were Vivid cards we brought from California that had graphic sexual images on them. Brian and I had been whipping them out in party scenarios with girls. They were definitely an icebreaker . . . but not with Emily. I never saw her again after that night.

The next day, Brian and I hopped the train for Hue, a town in the middle of Vietnam. Since it was a fifteen-hour journey, I decided to buy a hard berth and stretch out. Scott, our ubiquitous traveling companion from London, bought one as well since he was a giant. So we went in on a little room that had six tiny berths.

Turned out, our sleeping companions were three adults and six young children who shared the four berths below us while Scott and I managed to jam into the two top berths. Brian, the poor slob, was stuck sleeping in a seat. He suddenly couldn't afford a sleeping birth. He said he was running low on money. (I suspect he blew too much dough on his lady friend.) Of course I felt bad for him but didn't have the money to start paying his way, so he got a crick in his neck and cursed my name the entire trip. Making matters worse for him was everything in Vietnam seemed to be made for smaller people. Every chair was the size of American baby seats—literally ten inches off the ground.

I awoke in the early morning needing to pee; the train was still chugging toward our destination. I tried not to wake the entire household getting down from my top bunk. I didn't want to step on the kids sleeping below so I ended up grinding my butt into the ceiling fan, which woke everyone up. The kids laughed hysterically.

When I found the bathroom, it was just a closet with a hole in the floor so I peed on the train tracks speeding by wondering what the scene would be if I had eaten a heavy dinner last night. There was no toilet paper to be found.

After the long journey to Hue, we finally got off the train and checked into the Thai Binh hotel, which was nice for five dollars a night. Scott and I walked around town to The Citadel, an old dynasty fort with moats, then ventured down to the local market where we scared the crap out of a baby who had never seen white people before.

Brian was already bored by Vietnam, so he started spending more nights in bed reading while I started spending more time with Scott, who I quickly found out had odd historical fascinations, one of them being the Vietnam War and the other being coins.

After finding a random bar to drink warm beer in, we were starving so we stumbled into a restaurant where a midget named "Mr. Coin" tried to sell us some old coins. Scott, the coin freak, perked up.

I ended up buying one dong coin for two thousand dong and left scratching my head.

On our way to our hotel, a deaf mute tried selling us some tours, which we declined. We followed the train tracks back to our hostel, but since I remembered the bathroom on the train was just a hole in the floor we made sure not to walk on the tracks like we did as kids did back home.

In the morning, I dove into the unspoken unpleasantness of the unspeakable War.

Scott and I toured the Demilitarized Zone (DMZ), where we saw the damage we inflicted here from the Vietnam War. It was highly educational but not pleasant. I was the only American on the tour except for this scruffy old US vet who spent the entire time yelling at everyone. His only act of grace was he bought some old spoons from a local who said they were relics from the War. Then he pissed in a water bottle in front of a couple of ladies and walked around with the yellow bottle the rest of the tour. I can't imagine how a trip to the DMZ would be for someone who actually served in "the shit," as they used to call it.

We visited the shell of a blown-up church appropriately dubbed "Skeleton Church," then the bridge where North and South Vietnam were divided. Next we went into the Vinh Moc war tunnels, where we crawled underground for miles. There were three layers of tunnels: the first was for the soldiers, the second for families, and the third for ammunition—that was thirty meters deep. During the US carpet bombing, the people were safe here. We were told there were ten babies born in the tunnels during the war.

Afterward, we went to some famous battlefields where the land was forever barren because of all of the napalm that was dropped by our warplanes. There were craters as far as the eye can see. It was a humbling experience.

I wish Brian had joined us, but he couldn't take the reality of the situation. When I left him at the hotel in his underwear, he said, "My karma can't handle the DMZ. I'm staying above all those past atrocities, man, keeping my head in the clouds and soul in the garden of the Buddha." He was really getting Zen with this trip.

After our day tour, we all had dinner as part of the package, I had frog and goat. I liked the goat. I tried to order "bird wrapped in a blanket," but they were out of it "for the year."

I got home late from the military tour—I could hear the Doors's song "The End" on full blast as I approached our room. When I entered, I found Brian drunk, reenacting the Martin Sheen karate scene from *Apocalypse Now* in front of our mirror, still in his underwear. I just let him do his thing. He appeared to be covered in some kind of guava fruit and totally out of his gourd. Had he reached enlightenment? I'm not one to judge.

We took off early the next morning to Hoi An. On our way, we drove past China Beach, a famous playground for US servicemen during the war. We checked in to the Vinh Hing hotel where the service was great, again for five dollars per night.

There was a beautiful restaurant next door where you can sit outside and have a great meal while watching the action. A gang of little boys swarmed us, trying to sell us postcards. When "junior capitalists in training" attack, the best thing to do is buy a postcard from the first one, then prominently display it on your table so when the others come up you just point to your postcard. This seems to be a time-saving trick with touts anywhere in the world.

It took one hour for my shrimp pizza to finally arrive. It turned out to be fried bread with carrots—no shrimp. In the middle of the meal, Brian said to the boy who was demanding some of our pizza, "Where is the shrimp?" The boy said, "No have shrimp, just carrot." At this point we'd learned to take what we can get and like it. We used to give servers hell back in the States but now we ate whatever they served us with gratitude.

The next day we continued our journey south on Highway 1 that ran the length of Vietnam. It was an arduous fifteen-hour ride to Nha Trang. When we finally arrived, we were happy to find that it was a nice little beach town with lots of other travelers.

I immediately hired a cyclo driver to go find me coffee. He had a family with three children and drove his bicycle all day so I promised I'd give him a dollar tip, which was unusually large over here. We started talking about the war and he started crying when he told me how his dad died in it. I felt bad being an American here for the first time. I gave him a hug. Maybe I wouldn't have been as sympathetic to his tears if I were hearing his story twenty years ago, but time heals all wounds, I guess, and watching him cry in my arms, I could see both sides of the war. The fighting was done by young men who were just following orders. There was no real hate between the participants. I said goodbye to my friend and left him with a two-dollar tip.

That night we bought some pot and a packet of Vietnamese cigarettes and hired a guy to meticulously take out all the tobacco and put in marijuana. We were now able to hang out anywhere and smoke "cigarettes," even though the smell was obvious. The locals didn't seem to care. We partied on strong beer and our cigarettes and passed out at six o'clock in the evening. When we woke up at midnight with our first Vietnamese hangovers, we realized if we were going to smoke the rest of our cigarettes we needed to pace ourselves.

The next day we found out why all the backpackers were hanging around Nha Trang. The most popular thing to do in Vietnam that isn't temple- or war-related is to go on Mama Hahn's boat trip, which is famous around Asia and written up in the Book. The first time we heard of Mama Hahn was in Australia, where some travelers were raving about her booze cruise.

Somehow we had forgotten about her until now. But now that we knew, we couldn't go on without her. For seven dollars, Mama takes thirty travelers on a day tour around some of the islands, with a boatload of terrible wine and crappy pot. We were in. We had stayed sober long enough.

We bought our tickets and boarded her boat to drink while heading out to the islands. We met some European backpackers, which was a welcome sight. When we got out to the islands, we all took a well-lubricated dip—including Mama Hahn, who was sampling plenty of her own product. We bobbed in the water and Mama kept passing out drinks, smokes, and fruit from her floatie.

There we were, thirty travelers floating in the ocean with smiles on our faces talking to each other in languages no one else understood. After a while another boat pulled up to watch all us weirdos Brian, now fully tanked, jumped from Mama's boat onto the stranger's boat while it was moving, then cannonballed off the stranger's boat right in Mama Hahn's face, wilting her smoke. Mama was naturally pissed, so we had to play nice the rest of the tour or she said we'd have to swim back to shore.

When we finally staggered home, we somehow found the liquid energy to pop into a bamboo beach bar called The Sailing Club with Mama Hahn's gang of traveling miscreants. We took over the bar, smoking dope and shooting pool. I had so much fun I raced home at five in the morning on a cyclo to get some rest so I could do Mama Hahn's again the next day—a feat she said had never been done before. She said if I did this, she would let me go for free, saving seven dollars. The gauntlet had been thrown.

Of course, I overslept the next morning and totally missed it. Scott and I stumbled down to breakfast around three in the afternoon. Afterwards we found our way back down to The Sailing Club to feed our throbbing heads with more food—this time an Australian pizza. It was the best I'd eaten in six months. In these countries you stick to what you like. Even in my blurred state of consciousness, I knew I would be back.

Scott and I went back to our rooms to rest. I found Brian passed out on the floor; he hadn't moved in over twelve hours. I poked him with a walking stick to make sure he hadn't died choking on his own vomit. He yelled, "Get that pool cue out of my ass!" then started snoring again.

Brian finally came to around ten o'clock at night and we all decided to ramble back down to The Sailing Club. I was still in the throes of the "Hahnover" and stuck around just long enough to get a few free beers from the San Miguel drinkathon they were having.

On my way back to the hotel, I ran into a couple of missionaries who were preaching about how horrible backpackers were. They took one look at me and started in on their diatribe.

"You're irresponsible, all of you! If you kids get killed or kidnapped, how do you think your families would feel?"

I responded to them as politely as I could. "Everyone from America should move here cause it's safer!"

The missionary wife didn't like my line of reasoning. She started shaking with anger, so I knew I better stop talking and move along or I'd end up telling them how I really felt about their destructive impact on the world, and they definitely didn't want to hear that.

The next day, after twelve hours of sleep, Scott and I did Mama Hahn's again and it was the same shenanigans. This time, Mama took us to a fishing village where we rowed little boats around the harbor while she painted our faces and my bald head. Later, we went to shore and explored the villages. The kids must have thought we were aliens with our painted faces because they all ran when they saw us.

The next morning we jumped a bus to Dalat. It took us eight hours to get to the mountainous village but we didn't care; the camaraderie with all the other backpackers on the bus—some we'd been traveling with since Hanoi—was great. When we arrived in town, we all went to dinner; I had grilled deer, Brian had goat, and Scotty had roasted pigeon but the pigeon was the size of a mouse. Our server told us how lucky we were, "the government just recently started allowing restaurants."

"No wonder," Scotty said, picking at the bones of his tiny meal. Later we went up to an artsy hotel called Hang Nga House. It was an exotic place to have a drink with rooms inside of trees and caves—a very unique find.

The following day, Scotty, Brian, and I jumped on a bus for Saigon—though it's best to call it Ho Chi Minh City since the north renamed it when they took it over in 1975. We met some more girls from England on the bus and decided to get a room with them at the Le Le Hotel on Pham Ngu Lao Road in the 1st District, which is Vietnam's version of the Khaosan Road. The place was swarming with backpackers. Our room had three beds and was nice for our low standards. Later, we all went out to the 333 Bar and smoked way too many funny cigarettes, then spent the rest of the night discussing the concept of "utopia" in our room with Scott and the girls. Does it exist? Did it ever? Could it ever again?

"Those old chestnuts again," Brian said when the subject was brought up for the thousandth time on the trip. No one ever had any answers other than arguing what the concept of utopia actually meant to them. It seemed to be an infinitely malleable abstraction that looked and felt different to everyone. Nevertheless, it was great late-night party conversation for stoned people who wanted to "get deep" because it always led to the concept of heaven and whether that fable exists, which always got us into some kind of rousing argument. But it was a revealing topic that I always encouraged. I mean it's better than talking about movies or television, which is what most Americans love to yak on about.

The next afternoon, Brian and Scott ran off with some other girls that were not our roommates, so I decided to get into the Zen mood by reading more of *Zen and the Art of Motorcycle Maintenance*. Brian and I had been trying to read difficult literature on the trip, but I definitely met my match with this book. Just then I looked out of my open door and saw three girls and a guy walking by. Wanting a distraction from the book, I invited them in. It didn't take long until I broke out the marijuana cigarettes and my wisdom nirvana moment disappeared in a cloud of laughter and smoke.

The next morning we drove to the famous Mekong Delta where we took two boat rides. We saw floating markets, swimming snakes, and met lots of amazing rustic river people. We spent the night in one of the riverfront villages where we learned how to make straw hats and rice wine. Brian enjoyed the rice wine making while I made a straw hat to cover my head.

When we arrived back in Saigon Ho Chi Minh City from our three-day journey, we went for a nice dinner at a place called the Sinh Café. I was starving and ordered grilled squid, which they brought out and let me grill at the table myself. I'm not an expert chef with the little clay grill, so I must have undercooked it because I got a hellacious case of food poisoning.

I was on my back or on the toilet for the next two days, unable to eat or drink anything. Food poisoning is like drowning in your own defecation; it is the third concentric circle of hell. I wouldn't wish it upon my worst enemy.

I really thought I was going to die and, to make matters worse, Brian comes home and tells me he saw Monica, my Norwegian girlfriend from Malaysia, out on the town. "God, I would love to see her." I moaned in between dry heaves.

"You can't see her—look at you. You're an unholy mess." Brian the Zen bastard handed me a towel and laughed at my sad state of affairs.

"Never grill your own squid in Saigon . . .Ugh," I growled. "Don't tell Monica I'm here . . . I'm wretched." I made Brian promise not to tell her that I couldn't sit up without soiling myself. I went to bed thinking about her smile; she was so much fun.

Two days later, I had lost three pounds and was weak but finally on the mend. I had spent so much time sleeping that I was awake when Brian tomcatted in at dawn (again). He took one look at me and said, "Has anyone ever told you that you look like a POW?" then he laughed like a hyena.

"I see you've been having a grand old time with my Norway girls."

"When the cat's away . . ."

"I want to punch you in the face right now." I opened my eyes and saw him standing over my bed gloating.

"Don't worry, I covered for you. I told Monica you were wallowing in your own excrement," he said with an evil laugh.

I sat up. "You're no Buddhist; you're an asshole! I need food!"

I had to get up. I had to get out. I was literally sick of this wonderful country.

At noon, we checked out and went to the bus station; it was time to say goodbye to Saigon and Scotty, who loved coins. He was going back home and we were on our way to Cambodia. I gave him my expensive dong coin to add to his collection.

"You'll appreciate this more than me," I said and gave the big lug a hug. Scotty looked touched. We promised to look him up the next time we were in England, but we knew we'd never see him again. Such is life on the road.

After Scotty's bus left for the airport, our supposed bus to Cambodia ended up dropping Brian and I off at some weird intersection that had no border crossing. We were so confused that we had to talk some moped riders into taking us the rest of the way to Moc Bai, the border between Cambodia and Vietnam.

Moc Bai turned out to be a remote speck in the middle of the jungle. We were the only people within a mile of the border post, which was just a tiny shack. Inside, we found a border guard sitting behind a desk. We stood in front of him with smiles on our faces for about ten minutes in complete silence.

The guard wouldn't even look at us, even though we were the only ones in his office. So we just stood there trying to get his attention, which became a comedy routine. Brian would make funny faces at him, but this border guard was a master at his craft.

Eventually, we walked to a corner to confer, which was only four feet away from the guy. Brian leaned into me and whispered, "I think this guy wants a little palm grease."

"What?"

"*Grease the wheels, dude.*"

"Huh?"

"The border guard wants a *kickback* to let us in."

"I'm not giving him a bribe. You do it."

"Why me?"

"Why *me*??"

"*You've got more money.*"

"*So, what is this, New Orleans? I'm not in the mood.*"

"*Neither am I.*"

"Let's call his bluff," I said. So we walked back up and just stared at him. He still wouldn't look at us; he just sat there, eating what appeared to be barbecued grasshoppers and writing in a notebook. I'm pretty sure he was just pretending to be working. Brian kept saying "ahem" loudly, but the guy didn't feel like letting us in. Everyone in Saigon had told us not to cross the border here—we never asked why. Now we knew.

We waited around for an hour, then told the guy to piss off (with our body language) and left defeated. Outside, I looked around and got an idea. "Let's just cut through the jungle into Cambodia. How will they ever know?"

"That's the best idea you've had all day." Brian was game. "But if we get caught I'm telling our captors it was your idea."

We pretended to walk back down the road then we veered right and tromped about a half mile through the jungle toward Cambodia. We had no idea what we were doing.

Eventually we came upon a dirt road.

"Are we even in Cambodia?" Brian looked at the sun, which was of no use since it was a cloudy day and he was terrible with directions.

"I have no idea . . . We're lost."

We started walking down the road until we saw an old four-door car from the 1970s coming our way. "Let's hitch into town!" I held out my thumb, and so did Brian. The car approached. Brian started to get cold feet.

"What if this guy is going into Vietnam?"

"Then we'll just walk the other way. Relax. We're being *Beat* here!"

"Look what happened to the Beats," Brian said.

We kept our thumbs out and magically the car stopped in front of us. The guy behind the wheel just stared at us. "You going to Phnom

Pehn?" I asked, hoping the guy would at least understand our destination. I got a closer look. He was a small and extremely sweaty Asian dude with a handrolled cigarette burning down between his lips. I looked at Brian. "Is he Vietnamese or Cambodian?"

"*I have no idea,*" Brian said then he leaned into the passenger side window and held out some money. "We'll pay!"

Those were the magic words. The guy motioned for us to get in the back seat.

On our way into Phnom Pehn, our driver finally piped up, and in English, which surprised us. He asked if he could pick up two other guys on the way. We said "sure" so he stopped at a gas station where we saw two Asian guys waiting for him. Our driver hopped out to talk to the guys; Brian and I scooted over to let them sit beside us.

We heard the trunk pop; we looked back and noticed the two guys were getting in the trunk. When the driver got back in the car, I asked him, "We aren't going to jail if they get caught, are we?"

"We're no Cambodian coyotes, sir," Brian said.

The driver just laughed and put the pedal to the metal.

We sped through the countryside, still unsure what country we were in. All I knew was it was extremely rural and had lots of potholes. After some driving, we came to a checkpoint. Were we still in Vietnam?

"Dude." I pointed to the checkpoint sign. Brian nodded. We were headed to the right country. We proceeded to enter Cambodia by running the gauntlet through, not one, but ten roadblocks, sweating bullets the whole way.

One of the border guards approached our car. Brian whispered out of the side of his mouth, "Our passports aren't stamped and we have some random dudes in the trunk."

"Cool as a cucumber," I said through a plastered on smile. "And deny everything."

The border guard took one look inside our car, noticed we were Americans and kept walking. They started hassling the Cambodians in the cars around us instead.

"Do they think they're leftover Khmer Rouge?"

We watched in amazement while the border guards let us go, again and again, through ten checkpoints. Every time we made eye contact with one of them, all we got were smiles.

"There's that smile again." Brian nudged me. "They're beautiful aren't they?"

All the smiling border guards never asked to see our passports and never checked our trunk. They just waved us in. I looked at Brian. "No kickbacks here."

Brian had a perma-grin plastered on his face. He said, "I was thinking, we should to go Nepal after India. I want to see the holy land."

"All those quiet Buddhist nights in the hotel room have turned you into a hippie, haven't they?" Brian just kept smiling with his eyes closed. He seemed truly content in the moment and in his own skin.

After the guards let us into Cambodia, it was a beautiful scenic ride to Phnom Penh, the capital city. Rice paddies flew past us in neverending succession, all the while Brian kept smiling. I said, "You've got sunbeams shooting out of your mouth. Your smile is giving me a contact high. Pretty soon you'll be farting flowers."

"Deal with it," he said in his kindest voice. His smile was infectious; I started smiling too. Brian said he was "in the middle of some kind of spiritual metamorphosis." He said he'd "been having private epiphanies" without me.

We cruised through the Cambodian countryside with the windows down. I felt truly Beat for the first time on the trip. When I began our journey, I thought experience was going to be the key to happiness, but maybe it was a state of nirvana I was looking for. Basking in Brian's newfound state of Zen, it felt like I was getting enlightened by proxy—by simply smiling.

Brian pointed out the window. "I learned it from watching them." I looked out the window and saw two women picking rice turn to smile at us right as we zoomed by.

"Whoa," I said. "On cue."

Maybe we had found heaven after all.

The moment we arrived in Phnom Penh, we ran out to eat and exchange our currency. The Cambodian capital was beautiful at sunset; it looked and felt like a big, rundown city and we loved it. That evening, we checked into the Capital Hotel, then went back out to see the town, being careful not to cause too much trouble since everyone we met kept saying this place was dangerous.

But we found no danger, only kindness and those smiles everywhere.

The Cambodian women had some of the most beautiful faces in Asia. We saw them selling baguettes everywhere, like in Vietnam. Crickets were also for sale all over the place (to eat, not keep as pets like in Japan, where they're sacred), but I haven't tried one yet and probably never will just in case they are sacred little creatures.

Brian agreed. "Eating one of those is bad karma."

When we got back to our hotel, we were exhausted but happy. Maybe we were finally having the personal renaissance I had been searching for? I didn't care if Brian was touched by it first. I could feel it, too, and it was better than any drug you could find on earth.

Is this what true happiness feels like?

Of course, as is life, my state of nirvana could not last forever.

Traveling to a bunch of countries can have weird side effects: like not knowing what the money is called, having five different currencies in your pocket, and being unaware of what's illegal (like in Singapore)— though I don't think much is illegal in Cambodia.

But one of the stranger side effects is "*location amnesia*." It started happening our first night in Cambodia when I woke in the middle of the night and had no idea what country I was in. "Dude, where are we??" I was in a cold sweat.

Brian sat up in bed, mumbled, "You are a lotus flower in the garden of the Buddha," then flopped back down snoring. Brian reminded me we were becoming Buddhist, but that didn't help. I was scared and confused; where the hell am I?? I got up and threw some water on my face and still had no idea where in the world I was, so I spent the next hour counting off the countries we had visited, starting from home until I got it right.

I went back to sleep happy again.

The next morning we were refreshed and ready to check out something amazing. We took a five-hour boat trip to Angkor Wat, one of the seven man-made wonders on earth. It's famous for being the largest religious monument in the world. It was first designed as a Hindu temple complex back in the twelfth century where people worshipped Vishnu, but the place went Buddhist at some point since its creation eight hundred years ago. We had to check it out.

We traveled up a huge river system on a fifty-foot boat to our destination at Siem Reap, where a hotel owner near the ruins greeted us. He came all the way out to the boat in hopes of getting our business, yelling, "Three-dollar night, both of you!" We jumped at the offer.

After we checked in, we rented two mopeds (and drivers) and took off to see the amazing monuments. We were tempted to rent a Cambodian military helicopter for fifty dollars, but we kept to our fiscal restraint.

Riding around on mopeds with our drivers zipping in and out of ancient ruins was incredible. The Angkor Wat temple was otherworldly, like some pharaoh spent ten lifetimes building it. We learned Buddhist monks had been caring for it since the 1400s, and it showed. It's an architectural masterpiece.

Brian was as serious as I'd seen him since the last time he had to appear in court. "The profile of this building looks like a lotus bud, and look—some of these passages were designed to fit elephants."

One of our moped guides told us Angkor Wat was a stone replica of the universe and "an earthly model of the cosmic world." While we walked around the "universe," the guide pointed to the central tower, which he said symbolizes Meru, the mythical mountain that's located at the center of the universe.

"The outer wall corresponds to the mountains at the edge of the world, and the surrounding moat represents the oceans and beyond," he explained.

Brian soaked it in as only he could. "Gnarly."

We left the massive complex to explore the many ruins that were spread out in the jungle. Nature had reclaimed much of the stone facades. We drove through the jungle surrounded by hundreds of ancient trees that had slowly swallowed the stone structures over the centuries.

The place was so inaccessible that there were literally no other travelers around us much of the time, which was awesome. It was a full immersion experience that was life changing.

That night we stayed at the Naga Guesthouse and spent the next day touring the Angkor ruins again. We even drove out to the countryside and watched the Cambodians work in the rice fields—it was a serene pastoral scene that made us feel that groovy high that I'd been getting a taste of ever since we entered Cambodia.

Later we went out to eat dinner in Angkor and discovered all the restaurants offer marijuana on the tables (like they offer bread in America), so we started smoking again—we had run out of our funny cigarettes in Vietnam.

At night, a bunch of the locals kept warning us that Cambodia was still a dangerous place—with *The Killing Fields* and all—which went down in the late 1970s when the Khmer Rouge killed two million people. It didn't seem dangerous now, but the stories they told were horrifying.

"I'm feeling the stark reality of humanity's dark side," Brian said once we learned the atrocities the past regime committed on these beautiful people.

After smoking some of the complementary weed at a local restaurant, I got the hare-brained idea to buy a cobra and sneak it back into the US where I planned to sell it to pay for my trip. "A baby cobra would fetch a high price back in the states."

"What, are you a freaking zookeeper now?" Brian said.

"No, but when I was a teenager I smuggled the world's largest snake, a baby reticulated python, down my pants from the Philippines and sold it for a pretty penny back in California. My dad didn't even get mad."

"You realize you're insane."

"Yeah, I caught it in the jungle. This old villager led me to a whole nest of 'em. I kept it in my bathroom sink until my flight out."

"I hope you tipped your cleaning lady."

"All you have to do is put it in a breathable sock and stuff it down your pants. "

"How did you keep it from biting off your dick?"

"He had tiny teeth. He was just a baby and didn't make much of a bulge."

"It's not like you have anything down there anyway."

"Let's go wrangle us some 'pant cobras'!"

"Okay," Brian said, "but don't say that in mixed company."

I asked around and found out where I could procure a cobra, but I needed a baby, which was limiting my options. Turns out there were no baby cobra orphanages in Cambodia.

After spending way too much time on the hunt, Brian said, "Is this really the way you want to live your life—as a snake smuggler?" Brian had a point. It wouldn't be until a month later that I actually came close to buying one (you can find anything in India, but that's another story).

One hot Cambodian night, we decided not to smoke so much pot so we could stay awake long enough to finally check out the local clubs. When we asked one of the locals where the good clubs were, he told us about one but with a warning: "Don't bring any bombs or guns, or you have to give them to the guard before you go in."

"Awesome." Brian was into the lawlessness of the land. "A terrorist club."

"Oh, we've gotta see this!" I was pumped.

We hopped on our moped and cruised to the club, which always excited the village children; they loved to chase us down the street and wave at us until their arms got tired. It was great to feel love in a land that love had seemingly forgotten until recently.

"I'll remember their smiles, man! Their smiles!" Brian was driving the moped, smiling and waving at the kids like a kid himself.

I yelled at the kids, "The tide's turning, kids! Pol Pot's dead and your future is bright! Be cool, stay in school!"

When we got to "Club Terror" it was closed down due to a recent bombing, but we didn't mind. It was time for us to say goodbye to Cambodia.

We went back to the hotel and slept like babies, then departed Siem Reap on a five-hour boat ride back to Phnom Pehn. Like earlier, we could have hired an Army helicopter to jettison us for fifty dollars, but the pilot told us if there was a conflict "they would have to divert."

Brian laughed at the proposition, "Divert? Are you saying we might have to shoot people from a helicopter?"

The pilot stared at Brian with a "maybe" look in his eye.

We opted to travel by sea and stay out of any guerilla warfare–type situation. On the five-hour boat ride out, a Cambodian gunboat stopped us armed with torpedoes. It was quite intimidating, but the only thing that attacked us on the ride back to Phnom Penh was the sun. It felt way more intense than at the equator. My hair was thankfully growing out, and I'd made myself a straw hat so my scalp didn't melt.

The next four days were a blur of travel. Our schedule had us hopping around four countries in four days: Monday, Cambodia; Tuesday, Vietnam; Wednesday, Singapore; and Thursday we were on our way to India. We completed half of our travel gauntlet then stopped over in Saigon and spent the night at the Le Le hotel again in what appeared to be their "love room" this time. We laughed at the amorously decorated room with all the love oils and amenities on hand. I asked Brian, "Are they trying to tell us something?" He just smiled.

When I unpacked my bag, I found a surprise. "I'm an international drug smuggler!" I whipped out a joint I'd forgotten about. "This little baggie was with us the whole time from Vietnam to Cambodia and back again. And you didn't think I could smuggle a cobra in my pants. . . ."

"You're like the Pablo Escobar of village idiots," he said.

"One might ask why I'd smuggle pot into two countries that basically gave it away at every restaurant."

Brian grabbed the baggie. "Don't ask questions. Let's get enlightened." He lit up the joint and we both sat on the circular bed and got high in the love room. It was one more moment of Zen in a faraway land that had finally showed us two crazy Americans that our personal renaissance had to start from within, with one single act of kindness.

You want to get enlightened? Start with a smile.

7

India Is Burning

We left Cambodia riding high on a wave of spiritual nirvana. All was momentarily right in the world as we trekked toward India, a mysterious country that would do its best to pull us down from our high perch and into the flaming pits of "eternal samsara" called *reality*.

It would be an understatement to say India is no place for the faint of heart. If you're a tourist looking for a relaxing vacation paradise, look somewhere else. The India experience is more like a rugged leap of faith into a sometimes beautiful, oftentimes surreal landscape, full of a billion hopelessly impoverished people who are all living on top of each other waiting to be reincarnated into a better world. If you are up for the challenge, by all means check it out. Just come prepared to stare death in the face.

Brian wanted to visit India because it was "the birthplace of the world's greatest religions." After obsessing over Buddhism, he was getting into Hinduism because it's the one religion that's based on devotion to a *personal God*.

"So essentially, what Veda Vyasa is saying is, 'We are *our own* gods.'" He looked at me and smiled. "This is my kind of religion, Rob."

He'd been reading *The Bhagavad Gita* during the entire flight from Singapore. I felt like he was internalizing the philosophy, but had no idea what we were getting into by immersing ourselves in India's culture.

"This isn't going to be a cake walk, you know," I told him. "Prepare yourself." I know he heard me but he didn't say a word.

After reading a few hours, he put on his sleep mask. As he drifted off he mumbled, "No moment of Zen can last . . ." which was a half-asleep non sequitur that bothered me for several reasons. I shot back, "I hope you're not giving up on nirvana *already*." But I knew he was right. Nothing good lasts forever. That's the bittersweet duality of our universe. Ask a wise man, he'll tell you that "life isn't as sweet without the sour." Ask a physicist, he'll say, "from order comes chaos." But damned if I wasn't going to try and keep my state of nirvana going, no matter how much Brian tried to ruin it by bringing up my sordid past.

"Do you think we should head home after India?" Brian asked. "Be honest: what are we really accomplishing here?" He started mentioning the dreaded R-word during our layover in Dhaka, Bangladesh. *Reality* was something I'd been avoiding for months.

"What are we accomplishing?" I said with a fair amount of sarcasm. "We're seeing the world outside the prism of our American eyes, following our bliss, looking for Utopia. Need I go on?"

"But, are we growing? Or running? I hate to bring up reality—"

"Then stop talking."

"—But the reality is they're gonna be looking for you back in—"

"They? Dude."

"You could go to prison."

"You're jumping to conclusions, and I'm way too sober for this line of questioning."

I led us into the airport bar and ordered two "doubles" to try and forget the truth of my own reality, but the bartender had no idea what I was talking about. Turns out doubles are an American thing so we ordered two Jack and Cokes and two shots of Jack and mixed it in ourselves.

After a few drinks, I finally admitted to Brian, "Yes, I'm probably wanted by the 'tax police' and definitely penniless if I ever decide to return home. But remember young grasshopper, there is no such thing as 'debtors' prison' in the United States. Do you see me worried?"

"I dunno, you keep your cards close to your vest, man."

"My denial has good intentions, buddy. I'm just trying to keep our state of nirvana going."

"I know, it's just—"

"Why drag us back into reality now? I'm not ready to give up on our dream. Are you??"

"What were we dreaming of finding here, again?" he asked.

"We were dreaming of finding *ourselves*."

"That's exactly my point. I haven't found me yet." Brian explained he'd been "taking inventory" after coming down from his spiritual high and wasn't sure what he'd really learned from this travel experience. He also confessed California was on his mind and he didn't know what his future held. "Our trip is almost over and if I'm concerned about what awaits us back home, then you sure as hell must be."

"It's always in the back of my mind, man."

We spent the next two hours having a heart-to-heart where we boiled our situation down to its essence: Should we go home and face the music, or become permanent expats living on the proverbial lam? Start a new life in a new country.

Brian said he was running low on funds and was leaning toward cutting it short and going home. "I vote we keep going," I said. "We still have sixteen weeks left on our ticket."

"I don't think I can last that long."

"Is this because of what's-her-name?"

"No! We broke up again. I just . . . feel lost." Brian looked out the window at the planes landing on the runway.

I tried to cheer him up. "Who doesn't? This is life, there is no perfect solution. If we go home, we're screwed, if we don't, we're two men without a country. I mean, at this point, I'm a hundred percent sure that I'm not sure! Aren't you?"

"I'm not sure of anything."

"So let's keep living the question, man. Don't give up on us now. We'll be fine!"

Our deep discussion almost caused us to miss our connection to India. When we realized the time, we took off running and were the last ones to board the plane. "See?" I said as we collapsed in our seats. "It's meant to be."

"Is it 'meant to be' that you're gonna loan me the money to pay for the rest of this trip?" Brian smiled sheepishly.

"Umm . . . let's pray on it."

We flew on to Varanasi, India, the holiest of the seven sacred cities according to Hindu culture. After spending a few days there, we agreed it's the craziest city in the world—maybe the universe.

We were still discussing our uncertain future as we exited the small Varanasi airport under brown clouds of an overcast day. We went looking for transportation and ran into a swarm of the most extreme touts in all of Asia. "These guys take it to a different level!" Brian yelled while being swarmed by beggars coming at us from all directions like ants on two wounded grasshoppers.

I will give it to them—these Indian touts were very creative in their attempts to relieve us of our money. They asked us for religious donations; they offered to take us on boat rides; they tried to sell us pot, jewels, or their children; and some wanted to give us massages, which was cool (a bit creepy). But creepier still was what happened when we didn't bite.

After saying "no thanks" a hundred times, they turned on us. The pack of rejected beggars started hurling undecipherable curses in our general direction—the only phrase I could understand was "stupid Americans!"

I said to Brian, "Their smiles have turned to rage. *Run!*" Brian and I started gently pushing through the crowd; after a few minutes we escaped to higher ground, where we caught a ten-cent bus into Varanasi.

On the bus, we watched two Indian men having an argument; maybe they were just talking, but every time one would say something, the other man would refute him then step across the isle to spit over the head of the other man, out an open window. "Interesting custom," Brian remarked as he watched the show.

Later, the bus mysteriously stopped for twenty minutes with no explanation. It started to rain. With the engine off, it gave us time to people-watch. I looked at Brian. "I don't speak Hindi, but isn't this bus full of a lot of people yelling and spitting?" We looked around and the entire bus seemed to be in one giant argument.

"Very astute observation," he said.

We finally got off the bus outside of Varanasi, "the Holy City of India," and went looking for a ride into town. We found a kind-looking rickshaw driver who was sitting under a tree to stay dry and hired him to peddle us into Old Town, where our hotel was supposed to be.

Of course, we picked a driver who was either directionally challenged or a master manipulator—or both. "I would say this kid is either half-blind or not the brightest kid in the traffic jam," Brian remarked. The guy got us lost down a myriad of narrow, cobbled streets that were dark, dirty, and totally packed with people who all seemed to be looking at us like we were aliens from another planet.

He peddled us to the wrong Yogi Lodge, then down and around, inside and out all the congested streets that were as wide as a small walk-in closet back in the States. When it was clear our rickshaw driver was taking us for a "ride," we leapt out to fend for ourselves and immediately landed ankle-deep in cow shit.

We both made the mistake of wearing flip-flops, so the wet dung wedged between our toes and caked our feet. Grossed out by all the waste on the ground, Brian the clean freak couldn't take it anymore so he went looking for a water source to clean off his feet. He soon realized there were no clean water sources here. He tried to wash his flip-flops off in a filthy puddle. He looked up at me: "I'm trying to clean shit off with shit water in an acid rainstorm!"

"Just give it up, man! Let's find our hotel before I pass out from hunger."

We were out of our element, being pushed around by dozens of sacred cows road-hogging the tight city lanes. Cows rule here; it's illegal under Hindu law to mess with them, so we let them by anytime they got too close. A few of the beasts tried to gore me when I entered their personal zone; some even flipped shit on my shorts when I bumped into them while sidestepping the dung landmines that were everywhere.

"These cows are way cockier than the ones back home," I said to Brian.

"Top of the food chain, man," Brian said.

We kept slogging through the crazy traffic jam. I said, "Who knew we'd have to circumvent garbage, shit, and cows to find our bed for the night?" Brian just smiled. "It's just like living at the Phi Delta house!"

Thankfully, we met two young boys who helped us find the right Yogi Lodge. They told us the rickshaw driver (called "*wallahs*") "probably" got confused because there were "many, many Yogi Lodges in Varanasi"—but they knew where ours was. We would later find out there were three Yogi Lodges in Varanasi.

After some trekking we found ours, hidden down a dark alley that was literally three-feet wide. We had to take a hairpin turn up some stairs, past a humped cow, then over some wet cement where we tight-roped across a six-inch plank before we arrived at our hidden lodge.

We thanked the boys; Brian gave them some chocolate. He'd started tipping everyone who helped us with chocolate since Vietnam.

We dragged into the hotel, Brian looked at me and said, "Does the Book mention this place is hidden behind a sacred cow taking a sacred shit on a not-so-sacred street?"

"That's clever. Maybe we should write our own book?" I said.

"I don't write, only doggie-paddle," Brian said.

We checked into our Yogi Lodge for one dollar and forty cents a night each person (or 50 rupees). The second we paid for our room, the power went out in the hotel. *Bzzzzz.* Darkness. Our smiling bearded front desk guy quickly lit a candle. I asked him if we could get a discount since we now have no power and he said, "We don't bargain with Americans."

We found our room in the dark then went down to the candlelit dining room to eat. The food was really good, which was a surprise since the Book says you have to worry about eating anything that is prepared this close to the Ganges River. "We'll see if we die of food poisoning tomorrow," Brian said.

"Just kill me now," I said. "I can't take another bad squid experience."

After dinner, we ventured out into the dimly lit streets of Varanasi. Vendors were everywhere selling silk, pot, jewelry, soft drinks, and anything else you could possibly want. Brian exchanged some US dollars into rupees at a silk vendor stand. We watched the silk vendor try to sell his wares to a lady tourist by burning the edges of a scarf to prove it was real. "Real silk. For the lady, two hundred rupees," but the lady tourist was not interested. After a long day of travel, we were too tired to buy anything so we turned in early.

We awoke the next morning refreshed and ready to unlock the mysteries of India. Brian started the day brimming with excitement. "Jerry Garcia's ashes were spread here, man. Let's go smoke some grass and get in a drum session by the river!" Brian whipped out his small drum he bought in Australia and started playing it terribly.

The first thing we did was what everyone does when they get to Varanasi—we walked up and down the many ghats (or steps) that led down to the sacred Ganges River.

I read aloud from the Book while we walked the ghats. "The Book says Varanasi was founded in the twelfth century BC and is a most auspicious place to die. Everyone from India makes pilgrimages here because, according to Hindu scripture, this is where one should die for a beneficial rebirth."

"Will you put the Book down already? Let's get crazy." Brian said he was ready to take a dip in the holy water, but I wasn't sure if "the germophobe" knew what he'd be getting into, hygienically.

He'd already seen the sea of feces running through every street, but was he ready for all the dead bodies? I'd read about how seriously the Hindus take this sacred river but it was bizarre—even to me who was prepared for it—to see them shitting and pissing all over the place.

After getting a good look around, Brian finally said, "Soo, they're bathing, defecating, and peeing in same river of holiness that others are washing their clothes in?" He frowned. "I'll hold off on the swim."

"That's not the worst part . . ." I said, pointing to a dead cow floating by, followed by a succession of half-charred human bodies. He stared at the floaters going by. I could see the bliss leave Brian's face. "There are corpses . . . on parade."

He sighed and put down his drum. "There will be no drumming today, but if we die here, which is a distinct possibility, I hope to Shiva we aren't reincarnated as a pile of rancid cow dung."

Our first day on the Ganges, we witnessed death ceremonies going on everywhere. Up and down the West Bank, Indians worshipped and bathed all day and night on the steps.

"Everyone here seems to be waiting to die," Brian observed as we sat on one of the ghats and watched more bodies being carried out in colorful robes for burning.

We watched them build the funeral pyres and I found out why some are larger than others: the higher the woodpile, the wealthier the man. A larger woodpile makes a stronger fire, which means the rich man's body would probably be burned into ash. As for the poor man with the small woodpile? His body may not even get all that warm . . . Nevertheless, they all end up in the same place: thrown into the Ganges.

While the death rituals played out around us, packs of stray dogs would run up and tear at the flesh of the bodies while they were being barbequed. Goats and cows were surrounding the area, crapping everywhere. Brian was exasperated by it all.

"I guess if we have to go we should just pinch a loaf in the river?"

I said, "Just pop a squat downstream from the kids, okay?"

Brian whipped out some hash he found stashed in his pack. "Lookie here what I found—hallelujah!" We needed to get stoned to tolerate the death show, so we did.

Now mildly sedated, we sat back and watched some destitute man who was chipping in and helping throw the dead bodies in the river after they'd been charred on the spit. Another guy was in charge of keeping the dogs that were scavenging flesh away from the corpses.

We lost our reasoning ability in a marijuana fog. I said, "This is a perfect picture of total chaos."

Brian added, "With bonfires roasting people as the centerpiece . . . Someone should really tip those guys." Brian pointed to the guy who was shooing away the scavenging dogs. "I'm going to give him some chocolate."

I would find out later that Brian had been handing out these little squares of hash chocolate to everyone who was "nice" to him.

We kept wandering around the riverbank and eventually met two gals from London who offered to take us out for some *bhang lassis*. We didn't know what a *bhang lassi* was, and they weren't telling. Brian said, "I wanna bang, I'm *in*."

They said, "It's a mystery date then! We'll go for bhang lassis and dinner at the Shanti Lodge!" They said it was their favorite rooftop restaurant in town because it overlooked the burning ghats. The English girls were a lot of fun and a welcome distraction from all the death going on. They told us how they'd been traveling around India for a month and loved India's spiritual side.

Brian told them we had just bought a "chillum," which was a trippy looking pipe to smoke our hash in. So we broke it out and the four of us got stoned in the street. No one cared.

We walked around and could tell the girls were more desensitized to the madness of our surroundings than we were. The filthy streets, rampaging cows, and procession of corpses didn't seem to bother them anymore. What did still bother them, they said, was the poverty, which was (and still is) outrageously bad in all of India.

"Children are walking around with gangrene on their limbs or stumps, poor wretches," the blonde girl said.

"The sad part is," I said, "most of these people could probably be cured with a simple dose of Western medicine."

"If only they could afford it," she said.

"Don't worry, lads, you'll get used to the squalor," said the other girl, who was so high she laughed at our serious conversation and coughed a puff of residual smoke out that must have been trapped in there for God knows how long.

I said, "Is that residual hash smoke, or the remnants of some Indian corpse you just breathed in?"

She smiled. "Both. How did you guys smuggle that hash in from Cambodia?"

Brian took another hit. "We haven't been checked by customs in *months*," then he blew smoke all over us.

We roamed around looking for the Shanti Lodge in a "jolly good haze," as one of the girls put it. We stumbled onto a government-run drugstore where they sold all kinds of crazy pharmaceuticals, and ran into one of our backpacker friends, Andy, who offered to buy some opium for us.

"This will take it up a notch for you Yanks," he said as he handed us the narcotic.

"Why don't they have these government stores in America??" Brian gave Andy some cash. "You really can buy anything here." Brian stuffed the opium in his pocket and looked at his pipe. "A chillum won't work with this; we need to buy an opium pipe." He explained that opium pipes were long and thin and very different from chillum pipes.

"Dude, you've never smoked opium," I laughed.

Brian said, "I saw it on TV."

We never did buy an opium pipe. We were too high to take it up any other notches.

We didn't need more drugs; what we needed was food. We finally found it at the restaurant the girls were looking for. "There it is," one of the girls said as she pointed to the Shanti Lodge roof. "Let's go get high as the sky."

"I love these girls!" Brian shouted. He put his arm around the really stoned crazy one like he might be ready to move on from Carrie, which I fully approved of.

We climbed what felt like ten stories to the roof of the Shanti Lodge. We sat down and took in the view of the Ganges. Then we ordered a table full of food and four *bhang lassis*, which they promptly brought out first.

"Indian milkshakes?" I asked, the girls just smiled. "It's their specialty. Just drink." and so we did. Brian loved not knowing what was in it "See you guys in nirvana!"

It took ten minutes before we realized how extraordinary these beverages were; they were super-potent marijuana milkshakes the likes of which we had never seen. We downed the first one fast—too fast—while enjoying our conversation with the gals who were talking a mile a minute, giving us tips on how to backpack "properly" through India. After a while, I didn't hear a word they said.

At some point, the girls decided to order another. I looked at Brian, who was clearly in bad shape. "This restaurant's revolving too fast around the sun." He was giggling like a stoned schoolboy.

I laughed. "Dude, what are you talking about, it's night time!"

Brian was smart enough not to order another one, but being the brazen man I am, I yelled, "Another round!" There was no way I was going to let these two little English girls out-bang me. . . . This was a huge mistake.

I finished my second "bhanger" (as we now called them) and was able to hold a conversation for a while. Then I lost all sense of reality. I started laughing uncontrollably at the girls, who were regaling us with some absurd tale about a "crazy man driving a bus" who was trying to kill them.

I was laughing so hard and spinning so badly I had to look away. When I turned my head, the trip got worse. I saw everyone on the balcony staring at us, or I thought they were.

I saw one of the girls lean over to Brian and say, "Has he gone bloody bonkers?" Then I heard someone say (in slow motion), "I'm wondering if there really is an emergency room in this towwwwn."

I stopped laughing and the table fell silent. I started seeing double then I left my body. I looked at Brian as I floated into space. I was hovering over the table. His eyes were tiny red slits. "Dude, grab my leg," I whispered, "I'm too light."

I wasn't sure if I'd actually spoken that out loud until Brian replied, "Too light? You're huuuuge!" Brian was no use. I gazed down on my body sitting at the table, frozen in time. I couldn't believe what was happening.

I flew away, high above the rooftop restaurant and felt the warm, night air blowing my shirt. Everyone on the roof was staring at my body while my soul kept floating up into the cosmos. I tried to concentrate on getting back into my body but I couldn't .

Then, terror struck. Would I ever come back to earth? Am I going to keep floating up to heaven? Or hell? I could hear myself say, "Is this howwww Jerry Garcia went ouuuuut?"

After what felt like hours of having this crazy out of body experience, my three confused dinner companions decided to get the check. When it came, they pushed the bill toward me (or my body) and told me to split up the rupees we all owed.

This must have been a sick joke by Brian. I wasn't even back in my body, and he knew it. I couldn't talk much less count; I was terrified. My body just sat there and didn't move. A few minutes passed before Brian pulled the bill back, tallied it up, and paid for me (since I wasn't moving). They all got up and walked to the staircase and all the way down the long stairs to the dirty streets below to do some "bull dodging," as one of the girls called it.

I was alone at the table. I couldn't stay in my chair a second longer but I also couldn't walk, so I slowly got on my hands and knees and crawled through the restaurant full of people who all stopped eating to stare.

I got to the long, steep stairway. I looked back and every eye in the restaurant was on me. I knew there would be no walking, so I crawled down the stairs to escape. I cursed Brian for leaving me to the wolves. Once I got down the stairs, I motioned to Brian that I was going to kill him. But he just turned around and stared at me. He couldn't talk either.

I don't know how long it took but I finally managed to stand up and ramble through the tight alley. Every cow that got in my face was a horrific nightmare; I think the beasts could sense my madness; it felt like they were all trying to gore me so I kept bobbing and weaving.

I tried to look past the stock show, but all I could see was shit and dead people. We kept walking for what seemed like hours, days even—jumping over goats, sidestepping speeding motorcycles, leaping over dead bodies, yelling at touts, and everything else someone on the highest caliber acid trip could imagine.

Where was I? Where were these insane people leading me on this most troubled night?

We ended up back at the worst place a tripping person would want to be—the burning ghats, where we watched bodies burn and dogs try to eat them for the rest of the night. This was my own personal hell. I don't believe in God per se, but I felt like he was punishing me. I told Brian, "This is crazy . . . I've never felt this insane in my life," but I could barely register a whisper.

I motioned to Brian to get me back to the Yogi Lodge as soon as possible. His face was morphing into some Neanderthal. He told me,

"You're juuuust trippinnn', maaaan." At some point we left and Brian, the Neanderthal beast, led me back to our hotel room where I crashed into bed and held on to both sides to try and stabilize my brain. Brian yelled, "I can't believe they serve those *bhangers* to children!"

"Everything is moving!" I cried.

Brian, who was holding onto his bed too, said, "Hold on for dear life! If we let go we'll be sucked into hell!"

When the roller coaster ride briefly subsided, I felt an immense pain in my bladder. I must have guzzled four bottles of water to wash down the *bhang lassis*. I had to pee like a racehorse, but I couldn't walk. Somehow I managed to crawl to the shared bathroom in the hall and pee for about twenty minutes.

Good times? I'm not so sure.

I woke the next day around six o'clock in the evening and staggered down to the hostel communal room where I ran into the two English girls, which was slightly awkward because I had no idea what the hell I said to them the night before. Clearly I had been an idiot because they were just staring at me. I meandered over and said, "Oh . . . hi."

"Oh my God, are you okay?" They said they were extremely concerned for my safety and were "upset" about how I behaved the night before. I played it cool. "Girls, that wasn't *me*, that was my stoned twin brother, who is now seeking treatment at a nearby facility." They laughed nervously. After a while they realized I was fairly normal when I wasn't having an out of body experience.

That night, the girls used their feminine wiles to tempt Brian and me into round two of utter madness. We went to the Shanti Lodge again to have more *bhangers*. We were gluttons for punishment and obviously deranged since we agreed to repeat last night's atrocity.

The possibility of a little coitus will make a man do some crazy things in life.

At least I was much smarter about my bhanger intake this time and only had three-fourths of one, which only resulted in constant fits of laughter. Every time I turned away laughing, Brian checked in on me. "You okay??" I laughed. "I'm thinking about my mom dying horribly! It's the only thought that can make me stop laughing!"

After dinner, we foolishly stumbled back down to the burning ghats next door, where they had five people simultaneously roasting on the same fire. "I only had one bhanger and I'm still tripping, hard," I told Brian, who was way higher than I was for some reason.

"I shouldn't have smoked that hash after dinner," he said as we stretched out to watch the show, again.

Watching five people burn as a menagerie of cows, goats, and dogs walked past us was horrifying. Brian said, "The Fourth of July in hell must be just like this." He sat up and pointed, "Look, dudes are drying their wet clothes over the bonfires. That guy just lit his smoke off a burning corpse. Satan is orchestrating all this. I don't want to die Rob, I'm not ready, I'm Catholic!"

I shushed him, "Calm down, you're freaking out the . . . girls. . . ." We looked around. We were alone. The English girls had skedaddled due to our insane highness long ago.

"Where did the girls go?" I asked Brian. He just looked at me.

"What *girls?*"

"Were there ever girls?" I asked.

"What *are girls?*" he asked.

"I need to rest, man," I said. "Someone sane tell me *where the hell we are?*!" The fear was coming back.

"I think we're part of a video game that God and the Devil are playing," Brian said. "And the Devil's winning."

Brian's surreal answers were not helping so I tried to take charge: "We need fresh air. C'mon, get up!" I tried to stand Brian up, but I immediately fell over on a dog that appeared to be gnawing on a charred hand.

Brian was dying. "I need water . . . help me, God."

I screamed, "Stop talking about God, you're freaking me out! I need to go home."

"*Now* you want to go home!?" Brian yelled, laughing uncontrollably again.

"Reality's hard to avoid when death's shitting all over you," I said, which was probably the most salient thought I'd had since I entered this maniacal country. "Just take me to the hotel."

We got to our feet and tried walking, but we were so high we couldn't make it down the dark stairs without crawling. "This must be how the cows feel," I moaned.

Brian tried to carry me to the only light source in the darkness, which was, of course, more burning funeral pyres. "Crawl toward the light!" Brian shouted, then fell over in a spinning heap of madness. "Whatever you do, don't drink the water. . . ."

And that's all I remember. I have no idea how we got back to our room. A pack of wild dogs could have dragged us back.

The next morning, Brian and I woke with the worst weed hangovers of our lives, smelling like roasted dead Indian corpses.

"I feel terrible. . . . Who the hell is sleeping in my bed?" I held up a Barbie doll that was inexplicably under my sheets. "My first lover in ages."

Brian didn't open his eyes. "We found her in a gutter on the way home. You said you wanted to marry her. You were out of your mind last night."

"She's so beautiful."

"She's a filthy, dirty girl. Just your type," Brian said.

I looked at Barbie's dirty blonde hair, tattered dress, and filthy ashen features. She'd been through hell, just like us.

"Wish I was back home in bed with a California girl who loved me," I said.

"You have no home. No bed. And no girl," Brian said.

"God, I hate you."

Brian, Barbie, and I lay in our beds for hours talking about women and staring at the fan going round and round.

We finally dragged ourselves into the sunlight and caught a train out of this madness to Lucknow—on our way to Agra to see the Taj Mahal. We took our little girlfriend with us. She would stay with us the rest of the trip.

After our train pulled into Lucknow, the state capital of Uttar Pradesh, we spent the rest of the afternoon walking around to clear our heads. It didn't work. We toured the Bara Imambara, a beautiful complex built by Shia Muslims. The only comment Brian made the entire tour was, "Bara means big."

"Really? That's all you got?"

"That's all I got." Brian said his brain cells were Silly Putty after the last two days. I knew the feeling. "Feels like I have a blanket of *bhang lassi* fog draped over my head."

With Brian checked out mentally, I went to the Book to try and get some real information on my surroundings. I learned the Bara Imambara is a shrine built for mourning the death of some guy named Imam Husayn ibn Ali, who died at the battle of Karbala in 680. That was all I could read. I had to put the Book away; it was hurting what brain I had left.

We spent our only evening in Lucknow watching a Muslim demonstration at one of the crazy downtown markets, which was complete chaos with everyone running around. In the middle of the maelstrom, thousands of cows were standing around shitting and staring into the void.

"I've noticed the cows are the only calm ones in India," Brian said.

"They should be. What do they have to worry about?"

We spent the rest of the night at the train station waiting for our train to Agra. It was late but we were still recovering so we were happy to just take in the scene. When the beggars approached us, we recoiled at first but these guys were very nice, helpful even; the total opposite of the touts who accosted us by the airport.

We finally caught our night train to Agra. We decided to upgrade to a first class cabin, which was twice the price but only about four dollars for the long haul across India to the Taj Mahal. We quickly fell asleep in our wooden bunks to finally purge our souls of the *bhang lassi* experiment, for good.

We woke at ten o'clock the next morning. I looked at my watch and realized we'd missed our stop. "Dude, wake up, we overslept!" I roused Brian, who sat up with his sleep mask on. "Mom, is that you?" We got up and grabbed our stuff and went looking for the conductor, who told us we missed our stop. "You oversleep, very bad," then he laughed at us for missing our stop by four hours.

We blamed our night of fitful slumber on all the rowdy kids who were playing near our bunks until all hours. At one point during the night, I sat up and yelled, "Where are these kids' mothers??" But I got no response, just more laughter. I remember Brian (in his sleep mask) trying to shoo them away like they were raccoons that invaded our campsite. At some point they passed out. Maybe they were high on *bhang lassis*.

We hopped off the train at the next stop, which landed us in the middle of nowhere in a tiny Indian village where the people gawked at us like they'd never seen a white person before, which they probably hadn't. The village children all came running up to us and just stared. Brian smiled and handed out all the chocolate he had left in his pack. "This is just like *Indiana Jones and the Temple of Doom*," Brian said. "*Chilled Monkey brains.*"

"Never saw it."

"You never saw *Temple of Doom*? What kind of adventurer are you?"

"I played soccer."

We spent the day in the village train depot watching everyone watching us. We enjoyed being off the beaten path of anything touristy. No touts were in sight. This was the real India and we liked it.

Our third class train finally arrived four hours later. The ride back was quite an experience; everyone onboard had to share their seats with at least two other people. On the ride, we taught some kids English; Brian even taught them some pickup lines, which he told them "will come in very useful when you hit puberty." Of course the kids had no idea what he was saying, but they knew what the lines were for: sex is a universal language.

After the five-hour ride back, we finally chugged into Agra for the second time, but this time we got off. We found a rickshaw *wallah* who knew where he was going to peddle us a few kilometers northeast into the city where we checked into the Kamel Guesthouse and passed out from exhaustion.

The next day we ventured out into the *chowks* (or marketplaces) in the bright sweltering town of Agra, which is a tourist mecca because of its crown jewel—the Taj Mahal, whose very name has become a cliché for opulent architecture around the world. Agra was once part of the Mughal Empire and its legacy can be still be felt everywhere in the form of all the ancient tombs, forts, and mausoleums that were open for tourists to visit.

After touring the *chowks*, we set off to see the mighty Taj. As we approached we could see it overlooking the holy Yamuna River from a large bend. We got closer and ran into more touts, vendors, and rickshaw *wallahs* lining the paths around the Taj. None of these guys were angry, though—more like annoying, but we kept our sense of humor while politely turning them down.

The moment we entered the grounds of the Taj Mahal, also known as the "Crown of Palaces," we were in awe of its majesty. The morning sun was warming it up like a huge glowing marble. We had to wear our sunglasses to gaze at the brightness of its exterior.

It was about a hundred and twenty degrees outside. Every hour or so, we found a shaded area inside or in one of the opulent gardens to reflect and recover from the heat.

We learned the Taj was built starting in the 1630s by a lovestruck emperor named Shah Jahan who ruled during the Mughal Empire. The legend goes, he was so grief stricken after his wife, a Persian princess, died during childbirth, that he set out to build her the greatest mausoleum in the world. It was an amazing tribute to the woman he loved.

"Do you think you could ever love someone so much?" I asked Brian.

"I want to say yes, but I don't know. Maybe I have a black heart."

"What about what's-her-name?"

"Barbie?"

"No, Carrie."

"Never called her back."

"Maybe you're right, then."

After our day tour of the Taj, we ran into a pack of ill-tempered cows on the way back to our hotel. I could tell they were up to no good. When I walked past a few of them, I sensed they were watching me from their peripheral vision. I'd heard if they saw movement they'd swing their heads at you, which doesn't give you much time to react if you're sharing a tight alleyway with them.

We tried sneaking past the herd; Brian went first. It was a tight squeeze but we had almost gotten past the procession when one swung its head and got me in the hip. "Aggggh!" I cried out. "I'm gored, call 911. Call anyone!"

I was bleeding all over myself. Brian was quick to react; he helped me escape the bovine traffic jam and found us a nook with some steps where we could sit down to examine my bleeding hip.

"Our first bull-on-man injury of the trip. Does it hurt?"

"Yes, it bloody hurts!"

"This could get infected with all the filth," Brian said just as a cow walking by nearly shit on our heads.

"Yeah, no shit . . . no pun intended." I was in intense pain. I glared at all the cows walking by while we tried to stop the bleeding by applying pressure. "I've never wanted a burger more than I do right now!" The herd of cows *mooed*.

Brian helped me limp back to the Kamel Guesthouse where the electricity was out for the night so I wasn't able to examine my injury in the mirror. Also, we had no first aid kit so I washed my puncture wound as best I could, then sat on my bed to drink beer and smoke hash with Brian.

"This is not a good black and blue night!" I moaned.

"Stop screaming. We got enough hot air in here already," Brian said.

With no electricity, our fan—which we paid extra to get—was useless. It was a hellish hundred and ten degrees in our room, so I just lay there in pain staring at the unmoving fan blades. I tried to use telekinesis to make the fan blades move. It didn't work, so I sweated profusely into my sheets until I finally drifted off to sleep.

I woke at the crack of dawn with my hip hurting so bad I had to immediately smoke more hash to ease the pain. I considered smoking the opium we'd bought back in Varanasi, but Brian said he lost it during our *bhang lassi* bender.

"Maybe a stray dog ran off with it."

"That bastard mutt probably died a painless death," I moaned.

After I smoked enough hash to think straight, I manned up and we caught a bus to Jaipur, the "Pink City," which is the capital of Rajasthan, India's largest state, which borders Pakistan. It was our first venture north into the "Land of Kings" where the Great Indian Desert resides. Jaipur is a rare bird because it's one of the few ancient cities that has a modern feel—the streets are not a succession of crazy winding alleys, they were actually paved. It was a pleasant surprise that there were some amenities for us to enjoy.

I limped around like a crippled beggar to the Jewelers Market and then the Hawa Mahal palace, which is a unique piece of architecture. They call it the "Palace of the Winds" because it's just a high-screen facade made out of red and pink sandstone. It was built specifically for the women of the royal household so they could watch the street festivities while remaining unseen by the masses.

Outside the Hawa Mahal, touts accosted us every chance they had; they walked beside us begging, demanding, and trying to con us out of money. They had ingenious schemes: Some put a guilt trip on you if you didn't give in to their scams. Others tried to force you into committing to their scam, or they threatened to call the cops on you. But the worst were the touts who, if you ignored them, started yelling, "What, you hate Indians?" which will get your attention real quick, especially when you're surrounded by hundreds of locals who begin staring at you like you're some kind of racist—you'll pay anything to shut the guy up.

During our tour, we walked up to two guys playing with some king cobras out in front of their house. They were nice enough to let us play with them. They showed us how to make the cobras dance. Brian was excited to be a snake charmer! I asked them if they had any baby cobras for sale—no luck.

Our last night in Jaipur, we saw an Indian movie from Bollywood. The movie was a funny mix of dancing, fighting, and singing. Of course, we had no idea what was happening since there were no subtitles and we didn't speak Hindi. When intermission came, we thought it was over and left. "Did we just walk out at halftime?" I was confused since we were leaving while others were coming back inside.

"Oh well," Brian said. "We know how it turns out. The male hero saves the day in every Bollywood movie."

"Just like back home," I said.

The next day, my hip was healing nicely, "No gangrene for you!" Brian said, "Let's keep moving." We continued our slog across India by taking a bus to Pushkar, a quaint little mountain village nestled into the hillside around a beautiful lake surrounded by ghats. We checked into the Pushkar Palace Hotel, which had a really laid back atmosphere. Pushkar is a beautiful place to relax; we could finally take a break from the constant chaos of the other villages. The only downside was there was no meat or alcohol served anywhere in town.

"They're starving us with sobriety . . . not a good combo." Brian was not happy and neither was I; we'd both lost a ton of weight on the trip so far. We'd also been forced to give up our workout regime months ago and were now in pure survival mode. We walked around Pushkar with our stomachs grumbling. We found a restaurant that served *bhang lassi*. I looked at Brian. "Dear God, do we dare?"

"Oh, *we dare*." Brian walked in and ordered two. We gulped them in moderation and prayed they weren't going to creep up and send us into the stratosphere. Thankfully these were lower-grade *bhangers* that just gave us a nice buzz.

After our liquid lunch, we wandered around the village, appropriately stoned. There were all the typical street vendors and cobra charmers lining the dirt paths leading around the lake. Several snake vendors tried to sell me their full-grown cobras, but they were too big to smuggle in my pants.

At some point, I got the bright idea of getting my hand henna tattooed (it was either that or my head), so I found a lady tattoo artist who had a tent next to a snake charmer that had six cobras dancing nearby. "Free entertainment," I said and pointed at the snake dance party. Brian was burnt out on snakes so he sat down to read a book.

While the henna artist worked her magic on my hand, I couldn't help but notice this Indian mother nearby who was squeezing her milky nipple stream into one of her babies' mouth. The exposed breast must have triggered something carnal in Brian because he looked up in time to witness the milk stream, then said, "That kid must have sharp teeth," and went back to reading.

It seemed like every woman in the village had at least three or four babies on their hips, with no husbands anywhere to be found. "Where were all the dads?" I said. "Doing 'man's' work?'"

Brian never looked up from his book, he just said, "You mean touting?"

Later, with my hand freshly adorned with a crazy henna tattoo, we walked back to our hotel where we came upon a blind woman who had lost her nose in a fire. She was standing outside the hotel singing like an angel, yet she seemed invisible to the people rushing by. Even Brian, who was lost in his own thoughts, brushed right past her into the hotel but she stopped me in my tracks.

She would sing a song then talk to herself, then sing another song. I couldn't look away; she had this glowing aura that was like this spotlight from heaven shining down. It was hard to miss, yet everyone but me was missing it.

She also stood out from the rest of the street people because she was not begging. While all these able-bodied men were asking for money, this disfigured songbird wasn't taking tips. She didn't even have a tip jar.

I asked around and learned that she lived on the street. No one seemed to know her name or her story. I wanted to help her so I went into the restaurant next door and ordered an Indian pizza. When I returned outside to give her the pizza and some money, she had vanished.

I went up to our room with her pizza and dropped it in front of Brian, who was doing yoga in his underwear. "You got pizza."

"Yeah, I was going to give it to this blind woman with no nose but she disappeared without a trace."

"Noseless women will do that," Brian said.

At night, going to sleep, I couldn't stop thinking about that woman. Why was she stuck in my head? Was she real, or just another *bhang lassi* hallucination? It felt like some force was compelling me to find her the next day, wherever she was. Maybe she was one of those true Beat angels I'd been looking for my entire life.

The next morning, I got up early and went outside to find my street angel and there she was again, singing her heart out, all by her lonesome. When I approached her and gave her some money, she grabbed my hand and thanked me profusely. Even though she was blind, she had these piercing green eyes that seemed so truthful and sincere.

I wanted to say something to her but I didn't speak Hindi, so I ran into the hotel and asked an older Indian woman if she would be "nice enough to be my translator so I can talk to the homeless woman outside? I need to speak with her."

The Indian woman agreed and followed me out. I bought us all some food and the three of us sat down on a long bench. I asked the blind woman about herself. She said her name was Gita, and she had no home. I told her she had a beautiful name. Gita said her name meant "song" in Hindi. When she said her name, I remembered Brian had been reading *The Bhagavad Gita* all trip.

I asked Gita why she was on the street. Where was her family? She told me she had not seen her family in years. Her father had kicked her out of the home when she was young, and she had not been home since. She said she did not want pity—she was very happy singing and was thankful that I liked her song.

While she spoke, she seemed so serene and at peace in her own skin. It was amazing to meet someone who had been given this lot in life who was still so full of positive energy. I'd never felt anything like her spirit before; it gave me chills to be in her presence.

I held Gita's hand for a long time as we talked. When I said goodbye, I thanked her for talking to me, placed some more money in her palm, closed it, and kissed the top of her hand. I thought I may have been a bit too brazen kissing her hand, but she didn't seem to mind and I didn't care. She was beautiful.

I walked back into the hotel with the Indian woman who had been translating our talk. She looked at me and said, "Gita is an angel of the streets. In suffering, she sings." I told her the same thought had been echoing through my head since I first laid eyes on her. "Remember how good you have it, young man," the older lady said to me, then she pointed to all the people outside, "There are many others who are not as fortunate."

This interaction woke something inside of me. I guess you could call it a deep compassion for those less fortunate than myself. I went back into our room and Brian was still sleeping. I wrote the story down in my journal, just as I'm retelling it to you right now.

Later that day, I went back outside and gave Gita some more money and she was overcome with joy again. Brian was watching the entire thing this time, semi-perplexed. "You have a crush on this girl?"

"She speaks to me without words," I said. "She's an angel of the streets. I want her to be okay."

"This is not like a baby cobra, Rob. You can't smuggle her back in your pants." Brian searched his pack for chocolate to give Gita, but he had given it all away. "Did you give her some money?" he asked.

"Yeah. I want to rent her a place to live," I said.

"You're homeless yourself," he laughed. "Maybe you should move in together. She would be a very appreciative lover."

"Will you shut up? I'm serious."

I knew it was impossible to rent Gita a home, but I truly felt for this woman and admired her. She moved me to the point of epiphany, or *satori*, or whatever you want to call it.

"No, seriously," Brian said, "that was a very selfless act. See, you're growing your dharma. I can appreciate that."

I turned to Brian. "What do we really have to complain about in this world, man? Gita's soul is still full of joy after everything life has dealt her. What the hell is our problem?"

Brian was getting it. "This is a lesson for both of us. We *are* blessed— we don't have any *real* problems."

"Never forget how this feels. What we're feeling is truth, Brian. Truth!"

"If you say so, my 'dharma bum,'" Brian smiled and put his arm around me. "Maybe we were fated to be here after all . . . Now let's go get some *bhangers*."

The next day, it was time to leave Gita behind. I went to her spot but she was gone. On the bus out of town something occurred to me. "I may never find my baby king cobra," I said to Brian, "but I think we learned something about life here."

"You would've been bitten on your balls and died a painful death over the Pacific if you had found what you *thought* you were looking for," he said.

"Bitten by a stewardess, right?" I shot back.

"Keep dreamin', brother," he said.

Our next stop was Jodhpur where we spent the day with this crazy rickshaw *wallah* who used his horn incessantly while peddling us around town. He asked us where we wanted to go and we said, "Anywhere." So he took us on a ride in which we visited another palace and yet another intimidating-looking fort, this one overlooking the city. "They're all beginning to look the same," I said to Brian, who was sleeping in the rickshaw.

It was clearly time for us to go. India had been exotically fantastic (and freakishly challenging), but the adventure was wearing us down. My weight had gone from 185 to 145. "Jesus, I lost forty pounds," I said while weighing myself on a livestock scale at an outdoor market.

"You look like you've been vacationing in a POW camp," Brian said. "You should eat more. Here, have some chocolate. It's from my emergency stash." He threw me a square of hash.

During our ride back to our hotel, I asked Brian, "So, have you thought about our future?"

"Yep. I'm not ready to stop dreaming yet. I'm no quitter. What country should we invade next?"

"There are many stops on the road to spiritual enlightenment, but I have an idea." I pointed to a map in the Book. "Are you thinking what I'm thinking?"

Brian looked at the page and smiled. "You know the answer to that question."

We decided if we were ever going to find our bliss on this trip before returning to Western civilization, we may as well look for it at the top of the world. "I can't think of a better place to find our Utopia than the epicenter of Buddhist nirvana," I said.

Brian started smiling that Zen smile again, "I like the way you think."

We had our rickshaw *wallah* drive us to the travel office, where we booked an airline ticket to Mumbai for the next morning. The following day we were going to Tibet.

Brian and I were dreaming of becoming Buddhist monks when we walked out of the travel office. "In Nepal, we will look into the eyes of God," I said to Brian. "Utopia awaits . . . this could be the place."

He said, "It has to be."

The next morning, we caught a rickety-looking Indian Airlines flight (which looked like the aeronautical equivalent of a flying rickshaw) to Mumbai. It was a tense flight but we made it without crashing.

We got a ride to our hotel. Our first impression was awe. We were overwhelmed by the sheer size of the big Indian city. It was madder and bigger than anything we had seen so far. We took it all in—the street people, the cars, the congestion, the crazy pollution—even the garbage. "Severe poverty plus grand architecture," I said. "The sweet and the sour, all in one."

The largest city in India and eighth largest in the world, for centuries Mumbai was renamed Bombay by the English imperialists, but as soon as the Brits left the natives changed the name back. "Don't call this place Bombay, it's like calling America 'The Colonies,'" I said to Brian, who nodded while looking out at the city going by.

We got a room at the Hotel Prosser's and spent our only night in Mumbai checking out the bar scene. We hadn't seen many bars in India so our tolerance was at an all-time low. It didn't take us long to get blooming drunk at this place called Café Mondegar, where we conquered their specialty drink called the "Royal Challenge." Or maybe it conquered us.

With our bellies full of liquor, we walked around the Colaba area, where Brian noticed these guys chewing some tobacco. He said it "looked interesting" so he asked if one of the guys would make him up a chew. The guy obliged with a smile.

Brian thanked him and we walked away. But after ten seconds of chewing, he got dizzy and started swaying, "This is stronger than any beer I've ever had," he said, before throwing up the chew and the Royal Challenge in the middle of the street (without breaking stride).

We could hear the tobacco guys laughing at Brian for being a novice, but he was a good sport about it. "Thank you for almost killing me, sir—thank you!" he said as he waved back at them. When I heard him say, "almost killing me," a cold chill came down my spine.

I realized I had made a horrible mistake.

"Oh shit!" I ran off down the street like a madman. Brian just stood there looking at me in his puddle of puke, then he began running after me, screaming, "What have you done!? What have you done!?"

We both sprinted past the "'Gateway to India,'" which looked just like a miniature Arc de Triumph, across the Colaba district and all the way back to Café Mondegar where I ran into the bar like an insane lunatic screaming. In my drunkenness, I had left my pack with all our passports, money, and tickets in the bar.

Luckily, my pack was still sitting right where I left it. *Pheewwwww!* "Oh my God. I think *I'm* gonna throw up!" All the patrons who were drinking their Royal Challenges laughed at me, then applauded as I raised my pack above my head like I had just won the Cricket World Cup.

When I staggered out of the bar with my pack around my shoulder, Brian was standing outside wheezing for air and shaking his head, "You almost ruined us, dude."

"I know! But it's all here—even Barbie! Thank you, Vishnu! Thank you God, thank you for everything!"

"You were born with a lucky horseshoe up your ass."

We decided to quit while we were ahead and went back to Hotel Prosser's to get some sleep before our flight the next evening.

Our last afternoon in Mumbai, we took Barbie to see an American movie. Everyone thought we were insane for having a doll sitting on the armrest between us but we were giddy as school children to see anything from Hollywood; it had been months since we had any connection with our homeland. The movie was a ridiculously unrealistic tale about a large predatory snake, but we loved it.

After the movie, while Brian packed back at the hotel, I walked over to the Gateway to India to try and buy a baby cobra one last time. I knew if I actually found one I would have to head home immediately since I didn't want to backpack around Tibet with a baby cobra in my pack. But all the cobras the snake charmers were selling were too big, so we jumped on our flight to Nepal.

On the plane to Kathmandu, we reflected on our time in India. I told Brian I thought it was worth slogging through all the garbage and corpses to meet beautiful angels like Gita and learn something about life that we could never learn back in California. Brian philosophized, "That's the way of the universe, man . . . Nirvana is like a fleeting orgasm—gotta catch it when you can. Reality is the other shit you have to slog through to find the real truth."

"Real truth?" I asked.

"The eternal samsara of the universe: birth, suffering, death, rebirth. That's life."

"So you're saying life is not supposed to be one big orgasm? If I weren't a more mature man, this could be depressing news."

"Smile, brother . . . here," Brian handed me the airplane menu from the seat. "Have a *bhang lassi* . . . I saw the pilot order two before we took off."

8

A High Nepalese Adventure

I AWOKE TO TURBULENCE AND THE SOUND of a ticking clock. There was no bomb on the plane; it was coming from inside my head. Time, which had been our most valuable commodity, was slowly slipping away. I could feel it. I was running out of a dream I didn't want to end.

Ever since Cambodia, Brian and I were finally on some kind of sideways path to enlightenment, but still, the "R-word" was unavoidable. So far nothing tangible or earthbound had been resolved on this trip. Nothing had come from "all this running," as Brian had put it back at the Bangladesh airport. And the *reality* was, we were nine months into our journey and our future was still hanging in the balance. I didn't want to admit it, but the uncertainty of it all was making me sick.

The crazy dream that started this whole trip was to escape the vapid clutches of America and become "Beat" like Jack Kerouac on a global level. Now, after kicking around the world for nearly a year, my worst nightmare was ending up "beaten" like Kerouac's muse Neal Cassidy, who died at fifty chasing a train in Mexico that had long passed him by—penniless, destitute, and forgotten. I wanted more out of life than just adventure. I wanted to accomplish something lasting, something real, something true. The problem was I didn't know what that *something* was. Not yet.

With life more uncertain than ever, what better time for an agnostic kid from Cupertino to go "knock-knock-knocking on heaven's door" and gaze into the eyes of whatever God is? Right after that thought crossed my mind, Brian stirred from his sleep-mask slumber and mumbled, "What if we find God and I have nothing to say?"

He was listening to my thoughts again.

I thought for a minute. "The scarier question is . . . what if *he* has nothing to say?"

"Not sure the Almighty One speaks English."

I tried to lighten the mood. "A wise man once said, 'If a fool looks directly into the eyes of God, it will burn his eyes.'" I pretended to give Brian an eye poke like one of the Three Stooges. "So, no pressure."

He pulled off his sleep mask, "I need to go to confession."

"I have a confession for you. I feel like I'm having a semi-panic attack right now. I feel the Sword of Damocles dangling over me," I said.

"Relax. With great privilege comes great responsibility. You knew that going in."

"I know, it's just . . . I'm the one that feels lost now."

"So the tables are turned, eh? Now you're feeling it. My advice is to remember our mantra: Live—"

"—*the question*, yeah I know."

Just then the captain came on and told us to look out the window at the Himalayas. Hypnotized by the stunning view, I admitted to Brian that I "couldn't stop thinking about my songbird."

"Elena?"

"Hell no. She couldn't sing—Gita."

I thought he was going to laugh but he didn't. "It may sound insane, but I've been thinking about that beautiful bus angel that held my hand on the way to Angeles."

"The hooker with a heart of gold."

"The *go-go girl* with the heart of—"

"Right. Why are we even talking about women—we should be thinking about ourselves."

"Because that's what we do. Women and happiness are intertwined."

"We are inferior creatures. What a fine pair we'd be, returning home with two foreign wives: mine a noseless Indian beggar and yours an underaged Filipino hooker."

"*Go-go girl.* That would be beautiful . . . a double wedding—think it'd stick?"

"Husbands never stick around for long. It's our primal nature to pollenate many flowers."

Brian laughed. "What a gross reduction of the human spirit!"

"Love is a false reality. It never lasts."

"Such a nihilist . . . Think you'll ever marry?"

"You asking me to marry you?"

"A woman, dude," Brian sighed. "I'd like to give myself to someone completely one day. Is it crazy if I went back to the PI to track her down?"

"*Yes.* You'd never find her, trust me."

Brian thought for a while, "Maybe the only reason we like these girls is because we don't know them."

"I talked to Gita through a translator."

"But if we got to know them, we'd probably be totally turned off."

"Who's trying to burst whose bubble here?"

"They're just dream girls. They're whoever we want them to be. That's why we like them . . . They're pure."

"Your girl was definitely *not* pure. And I would never marry Gita. I just hope she has a good life."

"Maybe we don't want women to talk? Maybe we should marry mutes?"

"Hot mutes."

Brian thought for a moment. "This conversation proves we have a long way to go until we reach any sort of enlightenment."

"That is why we're headed . . . there." I pointed out the window to the majestic view as we flew over Mt. Everest. "Our Yoda awaits."

Brian said, "You know the only thing better than flying over the world's highest peak is doing it absurdly high."

"You still have some?" I asked. Brian pulled some hash out of his pack and showed it to me. "Ate some before my nap."

"Share. It'll help stop my panic attacks and propel me onward and upward during our high Nepalese adventure."

We toasted our plastic water cups. "To a life-altering experience."

After flying high over the Himalayans, we landed in Kathmandu on an even higher plane of consciousness.

"Nepal is home to eight of the ten highest peaks in the world," I said to Brian while we exited the plane. He just looked at me smiling like a Cheshire cat. "We're way higher than that, man . . . *way higher.*"

We were in no condition to handle the utter chaos at the airport. We should have been used to this by now, but we weren't. There seemed to be five thousand touts outside the customs area. When we walked into the cold mountain air, they all attacked us; their weapon of choice was verbal assault. "Taxi here! Taxi here!"

They were running the typical scams, claiming we'd get free rides as long as we used their guesthouse. In the madness, we found a savior coincidentally named Darma. He was a short, fit Nepalese guy who was touting but wasn't trying to screw us. He offered us a "free ride," which we quickly took to get out of the scrum.

A short ride later we arrived at the Dolpo Guest House where Darma negotiated for us. He got us a two-bedroom with a balcony overlooking the mountains for eight dollars. We were probably getting screwed, but we figured we couldn't negotiate much lower and Darma deserved a cut. I mean, he even scored us more hash.

Darma arranged it so within an hour of landing we were happily smoking Nepalese hash on our balcony overlooking the high Himalayas. "Dude. If we found tropical utopia in the Philippines, this is mountain utopia." Brian said, taking in the view.

I felt I was higher than any man should be, yet as high as all men should. "My panic attack is long gone."

"Most excellent. The Himalayas do quench the thirst of the eyes, don't they?" Brian said, then put down the chillum and slumped into his lounge chair. "I'm sufficiently blitzed. Let's ramble."

It took us two more hours to get out of those deck chairs.

We eventually ventured out of the Dolpo Guest House and walked around Kathmandu in the late afternoon. The town had a very peaceful atmosphere, the opposite of chaotic India.

"We've landed in a Buddhist village that's been frozen in time," Brian said.

"This is total 'before Christ' architecture."

By now, we were really stoned, too stoned to do anything other than stumble around, which was too bad because if you're into extreme vacations with a seriously spiritual bent, Kathmandu is the perfect home base for all types of excursions like rafting, hiking, and jungle safaris. We were planning on doing them all once we sobered up. But today we explored the narrow cobblestone streets and alleys of Thamel, Kathmandu's busy tourist center, to check out all the artsy, artisan stores and cool little shops. Vendors were walking around touting anything and everything. It was probably because of all the hash we'd ingested, but there seemed to be amazing merchants everywhere. We stopped to take in all the hawkers selling knives, swords, clothes, and jewelry. Brian couldn't stop smiling. "This is, by far, the best bazaar in the world."

"Heaven's marketplace," I said.

Brian spent the next hour talking to a bead guy about the energy of his beaded yak-leather necklace. "The 108 beads represent 108 manifestations before Buddha's enlightenment," the bead guy said, while adding a matured sandalwood bead to Brian's necklace that "represents the heartbeat of the Buddha."

Brian stopped to buy a Coke and gave it to the bead guy. "You're so American," I said, walking away.

Brian said, "I know, right? He reminded me of what I read last night from Wu Li, 'The textures of a rose petal . . . or a grain of wood.'"

"I have no idea what you're talking about, but I love it," I replied.

"I've made a simple observation about myself," he said. "Not that I can comprehend vast amounts of knowledge at once or that I dream in Technicolor, which I already knew . . . but that I'm fascinated by the old and the rotted, the used and the worn-out. I have a soft spot for relics of the past, Rob."

"Uhh . . . that's cool."

Brian explained that he explored many markets in India over the past few weeks while I was "rhapsodizing over disfigured beggar girls."

"Before we left America, I only shopped at IKEA. Who knew?" he said while taking a deep breath of mountain air. "Maybe I should become an importer."

Our walkabout led us down to Durbar Square, a complex that houses a bunch of palaces, temples, and courtyards. Once home to Nepal's royalty, it dates as far back as the twelfth century. Its coolest feature was the Hanuman Dhoka Palace Complex, which was named in honor of the monkey god Hanuman. There's even a statue of the deity standing at the main entrance, which Brian photographed while admiring its texture.

"Good energy coming off this thing," he said.

That night we went out to eat and had an interesting conversation over dinner. Through the window of the restaurant, Brian saw a boy of ten come up to him and mouth, "You give me food."

Brian shook his head no.

"Do you feel good about refusing him?" I asked.

He sat there for a second just staring at the boy then turned to me, "I want to give, but when do you stop? I gave all my chocolate away in like five minutes. I gave those kids who followed us around for an hour my full bottle of water. I bought that one kid milk who said, 'You buy me milk or give me five rupees, or I get very mad.' Should I help all these kids, or should I be giving food to *that guy*?"

He pointed across the street at an old man with no legs who was pushing himself down the street on a skateboard, using a cane as a row and holding an umbrella between his other arm in the rain, which just started to pour down.

"What's the right way to give back? And to whom?" he asked.

"That's a question we need to meditate on."

After dinner, we checked out the Kathmandu scene. We went to two dive bars, Tom and Jerry's and the Blue Note Jazz Bar, that had great personality, with Christmas lights hanging inside and lots of colorful candles burning. We hung out with more backpackers and got to know some of the Nepalese people.

Brian got himself into a drinking contest with a hardcore hiker girl named Kiki at the Maya Bar who looked and drank just like Karen

Allen from *Raiders of the Lost Ark*, according to Brian. Combine the high elevation with the fact that our alcohol tolerance was no longer at Bukowski level, and Kiki kicked his ass.

He barely downed a twelfth shot of the local moonshine before he keeled over in defeat. "Party's over, said the little girl," he said with a face full of dirt floor. Kiki stood up victorious and the crowd in the bar roared with laughter.

I helped Brian back to our guesthouse. "Too bad you're so wasted, man, I'm pretty sure she was flirting with you." Brian was in no mood for love. All he could say was, "I thought those *bhang lassis* were . . . bad news."

The next day we decided to stay away from the bars and take a plunge into a whitewater rafting adventure. For fifty dollars, we booked a one-day, two-night expedition with Exodus, a local booking company. We took a bus up near the Himalayas through some small villages. The bus was so old it swayed dramatically from side-to-side on the cliff roads. The Norwegian girls on the tour with us screamed the entire time.

We set up camp the first night beside the Bhote Kosi River with Mount Everest as our backdrop. Our Nepalese guides broke out their guitars and we all sang around the fire pit and drank beer. We kept the hash in our bags since we wanted to be sharp for our river ride and were still hungover from our hash and *bhang lassi* bender of the past few weeks.

When it was time for bed, we didn't pitch a tent because we didn't have one. "Let's sleep outside under the stars," I said.

"Well . . . duh," Brian said.

Once everyone was asleep, Brian and I snuck down river to sleep in the rafts, which were more comfortable than the rocky ground. We lay there staring at the moon.

"It doesn't get any better than this," I said.

Brian yawned, "Another priceless romantic moment down, many more to go . . ."

"Too bad I have to spend them with you," I said.

We drifted off to sleep happy. An hour later, we awoke miserable. I thought someone had thrown a bucket of water in my face, but it was raining buckets. Our raft had become a bathtub full of rainwater. We ran back to the campsite and tried to sleep under the school bus, which was a disaster. Torrents of rain came rushing under, drenching us all night. The last thing I remember before I passed out was Brian looking at his feet and saying, "I got two soakers. This sucks."

The following morning, we woke to sweet sunshine. The rafting adventure was still on but since it rained all night (combined with the Himalayan runoff), the river was now up to a Class 5. The guides were having nervous arguments with each other and kept walking down to the river to check the water level. "There appears to be some disagreement among the natives," Brian said.

"The river is too high; this is Class 5 all the way," I said.

Even though we were amateur rafters, we decided to go for it anyway.

The safety course was virtually nonexistent. To put it politely, our guide had "public speaking problems" and barely spoke English, so after our limited instructions we pushed off from our campsite while all the buses took off to meet us down river. Our raft was in the lead (the four girls and us, plus our guide).

We knew we were in trouble after two minutes on the water. Our raft was hauling ass out of control down an angry river, and we weren't even to the rapids yet.

The second we hit our first major rapid, our guide was quickly thrown overboard. Brian reached over and pulled him in. "Dude, you can't leave us to die! Be a leader!" The guy had no idea what Brian was saying. We went careening down the huge rapid with our guide barely hanging on—everyone was screaming, our guide included.

Brian and I were having fun amid all the chaos, until our raft got stuck at the base of the rapid. A torrent of freezing river water rushed down on our heads. All the girls were screaming bloody murder. "Dead on our first rapid—you gotta be kidding!" I shouted. Our guide was going crazy, shouting nonsense.

"*Worst guide ever!*" Brian yelled.

Stuck in the middle of a huge whirlpool there was no way out. Our raft was sinking under the weight of the rushing water. "Nobody panic!

This thing's gonna flip!" I yelled. The moment I said it, it flipped and we were all dumped into the river with the raft on top of us.

Under the raft I heard Brian shout over the girls' screaming, "We're drowning like rats!"

I yelled, "Dive under and out!!" Brian and I dove under the raft like two seals. I got to the surface and took in a huge breath of river water. Sputtering for air, I looked around and saw no Brian, no nobody—just some of our gear floating around.

The current rushed me away. I got into the whitewater position with my knees in front of me, holding my paddle like we were semi-trained to do. My scuba rescue training kicked in; I tried to lodge my paddle between some rocks to try and climb back to help everyone, but the current was too strong. I couldn't fight it so I stopped trying to be a hero and focused on saving myself.

Going down the river solo was fun, except for the getting slammed against the rocks part. After a few minutes, I emerged from the rapids and floated into calmer waters, where I swam to shore. "What a ride!" I yelled, full of adrenaline.

I looked back and saw no one else behind me. "C'mon, Rakow! Whatever you do, don't die!" I was worried about Brian but more worried about the girls. I thought for sure one of them had drowned.

Was this how our trip would end, one of us entombed in a watery grave? We had skirted danger and escaped death many times so far. Had our collective luck run out?

Finally, I saw heads bobbing up in the whitewater. "Please God, don't let those be decapitated." I said.

They weren't. I saw some of the hands waving for rescue. I laughed when I saw Brian emerge giving me the finger. I looked up at Mount Everest. "Thank you, Buddha!"

Once he got into earshot, I heard Brian cursing up a blue streak. "Lawsuit pending! Lawsuit *pending!* Where's that idiot guide!"

Brian made it to shore and we hugged it out.

"We all signed a waiver, dude," I said.

"*That was not legally binding!*"

After a while, the girls struggled ashore, then our guide, who apologized profusely in a language I didn't understand. We counted heads to make sure no one was lost. We were all there, but we were a bloody mess and the girls were hysterical.

When the other bus arrived, the rest of the tour piled out to help us. A few of them told us they'd wisely gotten off the river before going down the first rapid—then watched in horror as we got hammered. The Norwegian girls were so shaken up, they said they quit and stumbled over to the bus to go straight back to Kathmandu. We never saw them again.

After their bus took off, Brian and I looked at our guide and said, "You owe us, let's finish!" He thought we were joking but when he saw we weren't, he said, "Very, very good!" So we all hopped in the raft and finished the trip.

We only flipped two more times.

At the end of the day, while walking back to the bus with Brian, I said, "All in all, near-death experiences like these make you realize where you stand in the grand scheme of things."

"Dust in the wind, man," Brian said. I looked back at the shadow of Mount Everest swallowing us and knew he was right.

We skipped the second night camping and took the bus back into town and checked into the Kathmandu Guest House. Located right in the middle of town on a large parcel, it's a great place to hang with other travelers. If you're ever backpacking in Nepal, you'll probably either stay there or eat in their café.

Brian and I weren't doing much eating. We had developed severe stomach problems because of all the river water we swallowed. We were also fairly beaten up, so we spent a few days recovering on their grassy grounds; it was the perfect cure to what ailed us. We hung out in their lush gardens with this Nepalese guy named Ram who kept begging us to bring him to America. I told him I'd try and get him a visa. Brian said, "Why are you filling this guy with false hope?"

"I don't know. He's a nice guy and I guess I wanna help him keep the dream alive."

"You are a cruel man."

"Sometimes false hope is better than no hope at all."

After recuperating, it was time to pack more adventure into our search for enlightenment. We decided to do the quintessential Nepalese back-packer hike, the Annapurna Trail. While other hikes around here could take months, you can do this one in a few days.

We'd end up on the trail for two weeks.

Brian and I set off on our adventure by taking a bus to Pokhara where our stomach problems returned. The bus driver was flying around the curves like a maniac. We saw two buses that had recently gone off the cliffs, which was alarming since our driver seemed oblivious. When we arrived in Pokhara, we kissed the ground then checked into the Oslo Guesthouse for one dollar a night each.

That night, we looked around the small town and nearby lake. We saw rowboats rowing and people swimming in the warm water, but we didn't take a dip. Instead, we went shopping for supplies and started arguing about our plan of attack. The only thing we agreed on was we didn't want to spend a bunch of money on gear that we would use once then have to either sell or lug around the rest of the trip.

Brian said, "Here's an idea: we don't bring any gear."

"How are we gonna camp or eat or—?"

"We won't camp and we'll eat what the other hikers have lugged up. Get it? We trade our way to the top! It's simple economics."

"You never took economics."

"Just hear me out. We don't bring food, supplies, or gear. Every other hiker on the mountain will have that crap, right? Instead, we pack something truly valuable that's cheap and easy to carry—something that we can trade, that the rest of the campers don't have."

"Are you proposing I risk death and agree to this hare-brained scheme?"

"Yes, I am."

We proceeded with Brian's "trade-our-way-to-the-top" plan. We stocked up on nothing sensible, only easy-to-carry (cheap) vice-related goods that the other hikers would not have:

- eighteen Snickers,
- ten Mars bars,

- five Milky Ways,
- one plastic bottle of Jack Daniels,
- one plastic bottle of Jose Cuervo tequila,
- two packs of smokes,
- three condoms,
- two cans of Pringles potato chips, and
- a bag of weed.

We would trade all this crap for real supplies.

"We'll be the most popular campers on the rock!" Brian exclaimed. I was skeptical, "If we die of hypothermia, I'm going to kill you." He laughed, "If this doesn't work and we die of hypothermia, I'll kill myself!"

With our pack chock full of supplies that will kill you, we met up with a backpacking couple we'd hung out with at the Kathmandu Guesthouse (Peter, Nichole, and Jasper, their baby) and all split a taxi to Phedi where the Annapurna Trail begins. Our first glimpse at the mountain peaks was magical. We all cheered.

"Let's summit!" I shouted. "How hard can it be?!"

"How bad can it get!?" Brian said, with a slight tinge of fear in his voice. Was he having a premonition? Were we about to die? I put the thought out of my mind.

We were slightly naive, foolishly foolhardy, and woefully underequipped as we began our trek into the Himalayas—but we had heart and a half-baked plan. Brian and I started off like gangbusters. The trail was full of backpackers. We noticed a lot of our fellow hikers had camping gear, but not us. We were counting on staying in the teahouses (or guesthouses) that the locals said were on the trail every few hours or so. The other hikers warned us that, since it was the offseason, some of the guesthouses may be closed so "we may have to charm our way into somebody's home, or sleep in a barn."

Brian was game. "Hope there are some farmers' daughters up there."

"*Settle down.* Remember, the eyes of God are on you. Should we get a Sherpa?"

"No way. They're five dollars a day and we packed nothing—what are they going to carry?"

"They keep us from getting lost."

"Lost-*schmost*. I've got this." Brian held up a map of the Annapurna Trail.

While we hiked, when we needed something we would trade our pack full of vice-goods for essentials like food, water, nuts, and toilet paper. So far it was working out as planned. We thought this rotund German hiker named Gunther was going to trade us for our entire pack, but he ended up buying our bottle of tequila and a Mars bar in exchange for two days' worth of bratwurst sandwiches, some fruit, a hunk of cheese, four bottles of water, and six protein bars. "Sweet haul for a bottle of tequila," Brian said, stuffing my pack with our new supply of "real food."

Every once in a while, we noticed some other hikers watching our transactions from afar. We could tell they were looking to score. Later they'd come up to trade us for something. One guy who was hiking with his girlfriend traded us for a condom. When the condom guy left, Brian patted his pack. "I feel like a total drug dealer, and it's awesome."

"This may have been the smartest move you've ever made, Rakow. But save a condom for yourself—there may be a randy farmer's daughter up the mountain for you."

"What I wouldn't give for a mountain angel like what's-her-name," he said wistfully, still waxing on about his nameless bus beauty from the PI.

"Too bad you didn't get her stripper name," I said.

"*Go-go girl* name. Is there a stripper database somewhere I don't know about?"

We entered a valley that led to the most magnificent mountains I'd ever seen. We hiked past rice terraces with sacred cows and babies with runny noses. Even though we'd lost a ton of weight and probably already had cirrhosis and brain damage from all the toxins we'd ingested, Brian and I still *felt* fit. So we went hard all day and passed many other travelers, except for the Sherpas (ages five to seventy) who kicked our ass. Our trek was slower because it was the rainy season and the trail was very slippery.

At one point, Brian slipped and fell. When he got up, I made a shocking discovery. "Don't be alarmed, *but* . . . you've got bloodsucking leeches all over you." I pointed. He looked down and saw three on his arms.

"*Get 'em off.*"

"A really big, hairy one is sucking on the back of your neck."

It took five seconds for Brian to strip down to his underwear. He was making a hilarious scene. "Remember *Stand by Me!*'" I yelled, "Check your underwear!" I was not helping things. A few hikers stopped to laugh, others to gawk. One small Nepalese child walked over and calmly helped him remove them one by one. The kid thought it was a game. When he was leech-free, Brian put his clothes back on and gave the kid a piece of frozen chocolate for the effort.

"You smoke?" He pulled out the pack of cigarettes from his pack and offered it to the kid. The kid declined while gobbling the chocolate. "Bad for lung. *Namaste.*"

After a grueling eight-hour hike, we dragged our wheezing asses into a village called Landruk; our legs, feet, and lungs were frozen and burning at the same time. We checked into a teahouse on the edge of a mountain for fifteen cents a night and collapsed in our tiny beds. I tended to my wounded feet. They had silver dollar-sized blisters on them from the Blundstone work boots I'd bought in Australia but never broke in.

"Dude, you're a mess!" Brian said while he watched me clean my wounds.

"I'm an idiot for hiking in new work boots." Brian was cleaning his leech bites. "You're not looking so good yourself," I said. "We gotta get it in gear, this is only day one."

"I believe now is the perfect time to break out the JD." Brian cracked open the bottle of Jack Daniels. An hour later, we passed out from exhaustion.

On day two we took off like lightning. There aren't many trekkers up in the Annapurna region during the rainy season, so we hiked alone.

It only took us a few hours before we got completely lost. "This is why you get a Sherpa!" I lost it on Brian.

"You're being very un-Zen, Rob," Brian said looking at his map, which was upside down. "It's gonna be fine. C'mon." He put it away and pretended like he knew what he was doing. "Let's just have fun with it." And he kept walking in the wrong direction.

After hiking a steep ascent for nearly two days, we had somehow descended into a marijuana field on the wrong side of the mountain. "This is how people get shot for trespassing," I said. "Keep watch while I go pick some weed."

Brian ran off further into the abyss. I scanned the mountainside for signs of life while Brian stole marijuana. In the distance, I saw someone coming up behind us on another trail. It was a pregnant mother who was hiking her kids up the mountain.

Brian returned out of breath. "*Now* our vice pack is fully loaded."

"Look, there's a lady!" I said. We yelled for help and motioned for her to stop—which she did. We told her we were lost. She said to follow her.

"Thank God for mothers. They've got that nurturing gene." I said, "Any man would've let us die to thin out the pack."

"You're such a Darwinist," Brian replied.

I started chatting with the mother while we hiked. She noticed we had no camping gear so we told her our theory of packing light and relying on the kindness of strangers. She said we were foolish, but she also said she owned a teahouse on the Chamrong side of the mountain where we could stay the night. "You pay to stay."

I looked at Brian. 'Kindness of strangers' . . . That's Tennessee Williams, by the way. And you say I never read."

"You're not illiterate, congratulations. Here, have a protein bar."

Back on the trail, we couldn't keep up with the pregnant mother, either. She left us in the dust with two kids on her back. It was a torturous six-hour uphill battle to Chamrong; I was limping in agony uphill on bloody heels while leeches were attacking Brian again. We were a mess; we had blood all over us when we finally made it.

We clamored to the only "guesthouse" in the village, which was some person's ramshackle home.

"Wonder if this is that mother's place?" We walked up to the front door and saw the same pregnant mother we met hours earlier. She was outside scooping Yak dung with her bare hands. She waved a handful of dung at us and invited us inside. She said they use dung for "cooking."

"Can we order takeout tonight?" Brian asked.

"Think she means they burn it like wood."

"Sure she does."

We paid her sixty cents apiece for one night's stay in a little wooden back room attached to her house. Before dinner, we drank tea in her kitchen and watched her kids run around the house swatting each other with uncooked chicken legs, which we would later have for dinner.

After dinner, I hobbled around the village and bought a pair of flip-flops off a local vendor. They're not ideal footwear for a fifty-mile trek in the Himalayas, but I was done with my boots and the stores had nothing else to offer.

"So, you're going from boots to a pair of cardboard slippers?" Brian was not impressed.

"Beats going barefoot." I showed him my heel, which was worn down to something resembling the bone.

Brian shook his head. "Always be prepared, Rob." I stared at him blankly.

"You were never a Boy Scout, were you?"

"No."

"I can tell."

The third morning on the trail, the mother served us lemon pancakes for breakfast, then we took off full of energy again. We tried to keep pace with the locals and my flip-flops were working better after I cut some toe holes into my long socks and tied plastic bags around my feet to keep them as watertight as I could.

We thought we were making good time until we saw an old Nepalese man blow past us carrying a fifty-pound bag of rice on his head. "The rice head guy is a monster," Brian said puffing for air. We couldn't catch up with him for eight miles. He was amazing. Later, a little Nepalese girl passed us with the customary *namaste* greeting while hiking straight up!

We tried to at least keep up with one of them. Trailing the old rice head and the kid, we heard faint crying coming from the kid's straw backpack; it was a baby. "We just got passed by an old man carrying a bag of rice on his head, a little girl, and a baby!" Brian said.

"I used to be a soccer stud," I moaned.

"Try not to think . . . it saps energy. Focus on improving."

A little later Brian said, "Aren't there supposed to be monkeys and tigers up here? They must be freezing . . . Haven't seen one Yeti yet."

"I've been telling everyone a Yeti ate my hiking boots."

We took a long hike through a rhododendron forest and finally saw a gang of monkeys and they did look cold, but no Yeti yet. We descended to a suspension bridge over the Chomrong Khola and hiked through the villages of Sinuwa, Kuldiha, and Bamboo to the village of Dobhan, where we came upon a shrine that was the sacred home of the deity Panchhi Baraha.

Next to it was a spectacular view of a waterfall. From there on, the trail was a steep incline all the way to the Himalaya Hotel, where we would stay for the night. An hour away from the hotel, we stopped at the Hinku Cave, a popular camping shelter that's a landmark for many mountaineering expeditions. It was a cool place to rest my aching feet and trade our vice pack for more supplies.

After Hinku Cave, we crossed several streams before entering the Annapurna sanctuary. By nightfall, we made it to the Himalaya Hotel where we ate bad pizza and warmed our sweat-soaked clothes by the fire. It was so extremely cold that we had to beg, borrow, and steal extra blankets to sleep with at night.

The next day, we started to notice two blokes from England on the trail who quickly became our comic relief. They didn't look like they belonged here at all. Brian took one look at the overweight one and said, "If we stay at the same guesthouse as that dude, he's buying the whole pack."

We hiked all day then checked into our teahouse for the night. A few hours later, the front door swung open and in dragged those two blokes, completely gassed and about to die. "We need beer!" one of them shouted, then they both laughed and literally collapsed on the floor by the front desk.

Brian looked at me, smiled, and patted his pack. "We're not the sorriest souses on the hill, after all."

We ended up befriending these two maniacs for a few days. They turned out to have great senses of humor. Paul was the unfit, chain-smoking one from London and Ted was a huge guy who was a bit more fit but had no stamina. At night, we'd spend the evening drinking beers and joking around with them. They chain-smoked and cursed incessantly.

Each morning we started off together (after our customary lemon pancakes) and Brian and I would try to get them to hike hard with us. But after a few hundred paces, Ted would start swearing at us, telling us to "piss off" then he'd just lay down panting. Paul was never far behind and would always collapse on top of Ted.

Brian and I just stood there watching them rolling around cussing at us. They smoked even when they were on the ground gasping for air. The juxtaposition of their polluted bodies and the beautiful natural surroundings was hilarious. "Those cigarettes are glued to your gasping blowholes!" Brian cackled and took pictures of their failure. "You both need immediate medical attention!"

After four nights with these characters, we'd developed a good friendship.

While we were hanging out one night, some backpacker who was on the way down the mountain told us a secret. He said there was a MBC base camp up at four thousand meters that had a hostel where you could get a double room or go on the cheap out in the common area for one dollar.

"What's so cool about that?" I asked.

"The funny part is—if you stay in the common area, there is this old Nepalese woman who works there who will come out late at night and try to screw you. No shit."

"No farmer's daughter?" Brian frowned.

"More like the farmer's grandmother. Talking post-menopausal here," the backpacker said. "You gotta check it out."

Despite her purported age, a loose woman on the mountain still interested Brian, but I could tell Ted had a much higher degree of interest. "That's where we're going then!" Ted said, puffing on a cigarette.

Some kind of immoral game was afoot.

Still hiking long days up steep dirt paths. It was a bit slippery wearing flip-flops, but feasible. After rope-crossing two glaciers, we finally reached the legendary MBC base camp and checked in at the infamous Yeti Guest Home. Brian and I weren't interested in getting molested by the old Nepalese women, but we wanted to make sure she wasn't hot, so we hung out at the lodge and after a while out came an old, squat little lady.

"That . . . is no mountain angel, my friend," Brian said. We looked at each other and immediately secured a double room; we had no intention of having sex with this borderline elderly Nepalese woman. When Ted finally made it up, however (chain-smoking slows him down in many ways), he went straight to the lodge area and spread out his sleeping bag! He was a better man than we would ever be.

That night, we all sat around drinking beers and staring at this infamous "mountain cougar." I don't know if I was more horrified at the idea of Ted getting molested by this old Nepalese woman, or by the fact that he was excited about it. We were so tired from hiking all day, Brian and I didn't even have the energy to stick around and watch.

The first thing next morning, we were about to leave but had to see if Ted was still in the grasps of this legendary cougar. When we finally saw him at breakfast, he had this big smile on his face. "So??" We couldn't stop laughing. Ted told us it "was great!" over a double stack of lemon pancakes. How that could be was beyond me . . . Ted went up very high on my admiration list.

We started our trek down later that morning, which was more dangerous this time of year with the glaciers and the rain. If you fell, it meant instant death. We had seen LOST photos of hikers that have never been found at every guesthouse on the mountain.

Hiking back down over iced glaciers in flip-flops was challenging, especially with the thousand-foot drops. Still, we made it in half the time it took us to get up. "Do you see the face of God in these mountains?" I asked Brian while we stopped to take in the view.

"I do," he said, and smiled that Zen smile of his. "God has a snowy white beard," he said, and pointed to a mountain peak, which did look like a bearded man's face.

We were at peace but we missed our buddies Ted and Paul, who we lost on the trek down. "I hope they don't end up on the 'Lost Hiker' billboards," Brian said.

It took us five days but we finally made it down to the Captain's Lodge, where we stayed for fifty cents a night. We actually had a hot shower, which was our first in two weeks. It was orgasmic. That night, we went to bed contented. I would have felt better but I was attacked by a tick and Brian had to cut into my chest and pull the little sucker out.

On our last day, we hiked back down through several villages with cornfields coming out of the mountains and into Pokhara. We finally completed the hike. We had met many beautiful people on the trail and somehow survived by bartering vice goods and relying on the kindness of strangers who let us stay in their teahouses and with their families. It was moving to experience how nice the Nepalese people were to a couple of strangers like us.

We spent two nights at Hotel Oslo in Pokhara recovering our beleaguered bodies, then we took the bus back through the mountains to Kathmandu where we saw two more buses flipped over.

"Not to alarm you, but . . . those weren't here on the way up," Brian rightly noticed.

Back in Kathmandu, we enjoyed two nights back at the Kathmandu Guesthouse, where we prepared for our next adventure: exploring the Royal Chitwan National Park, one of the largest jungle preserves in Asia.

I was nervous about the drive since the locals said the road from Kathmandu to Sauraha was even more dangerous than the drive to

Pokhara. Brian was not afraid. "Someone is watching over us; can't you feel it?" Brian said. "Why stop now?"

"Exactly," I said. "*Why stop now?*"

We left for Sauraha the next day on a bus and arrived in a Jeep. The bus got stuck in a flooded river, so we abandoned it. No one was hurt, which was a blessing. Seven of us backpackers piled out of the back of this little Jeep to check into the Rainforest Guest House, which had elephants on the property. That night, I bonded with one outside my window. He came up to say hello; I fed him two bananas. It was incredible to look into his eyes and wonder what he was thinking.

"He has wise, kind eyes," I remarked to Brian. "You can sense a deep understanding."

"I wouldn't mind being reincarnated as one in my next life," he said.

We checked in and walked around Sauraha, which is a tropical village on the outskirts of the park. The villagers here lead a simple life, raising corn and rice. They were all beautiful and had many children trailing them. The women have pretty dark complexions and slender bodies. "I think I'm in love," I said when a few of the young women walked by us.

"I'd keep your distance, or their fathers will string you up," Brian said, pointing to two frowning elders who were watching us gawk.

Later that evening, we sat around the campfire outside our hostel, talking and smoking some of the pot that we picked in the Annapurna field. We got on the topic of how to delay orgasms. My method was thinking about my grandmother (which was effective), but some of the other guys' ways of doing it around the world were fairly disturbing. One guy from Germany thought of the Holocaust, and the other guy, a Spaniard, thought about the Crucifixion.

Brian explained he never holds his orgasms. "I'd rather die than block my chi, man."

We moved over to the Hotel Wildlife Camp that was inside the park the next morning. Brian and I hired an elephant to take us on an excursion into the jungle. It wasn't the most comfortable ride, but it was energetic and fun. It didn't take long to notice that a giant elephant crashing through the jungle tends to scare off any other animals. We didn't see much except for a rhinoceros, which was exciting but it was only a fleeting view.

The next day, we hired a guide to take us on foot into the jungle in search of tigers, rhinoceros, and whatever else was lurking. We went in quietly this time. I asked our guide what kind of defense we would have if we were attacked; our guide assured us we would be safe, even though he only carried a stick.

"That stick better be an enchanted wizard's staff, or we're screwed," Brian said.

We trekked through tall elephant grass and ran into a bunch of monkeys. Then we met some rhinos. Every time one appeared, we scampered up a nearby tree since rhinos can't see very well and will charge any movement. We'd stay up in the tree for a while until the big fellas waddled away.

The next thing we knew, we stumbled on two fully grown tigers. What an adrenaline rush it was to see them face-to-face. Everyone says to stand your ground, make a lot of noise, and slowly back away—but the reality is you're shitting your pants and it's every man for himself. After freezing for a second, Brian and I panicked and took off running, which was probably the worst thing we could do. Sprinting away, I looked back and saw one of the tigers jogging toward us, but it stopped.

"Must be full!" Brian said in full sprint.

"Keep running!" I shouted.

We ran ahead of our guide all the way back to the village, and didn't stop until we were inside a little store where we bought some beer. Amped up, we told our tale to the villagers. The village elder smiled at our excitement. He told us spotting a tiger is very rare and that we were "blessed to have that experience." We took it as an omen of good things to come.

That night we sat by the campfire and watched the elephants eat fruit from the trees by our guesthouse. "Well, Rakow, we dodged another bullet from the death gun."

"If those tigers were hungry, we'd be so dead right now," Brian said.

"Or our guide would. How many lives do you think we have left?"

"Enough to get us to the promised land," he said. "It's time."

9

Turning Point in Tibet

B RIAN WAS PLAYING mind reader again.
Once the thrill of the chase died down it occurred to me that spiritual nirvana was on the northern horizon, and here we were bragging about getting barely chased by a fat tiger like a couple of wide-eyed tourists when we were so close to doing something *real*. What were we waiting for??

The adventures of the past few weeks had tested our bodies and our spirits, but Brian and I decided over our post-tiger beers to stop screwing around once and for all and test the sanctity of our souls already by visiting Nepal's neighbor, Tibet—once home to the Dalai Lama and still the epicenter of the Buddhist world.

We were coming to the party a few decades late. The Chinese, threatened by the influence the Dalai Lama, govern over a hundred million of his Buddhist countrymen after they forcibly took control of Tibet back in 1959 and committed genocide on a million plus Tibetans who dared to passively protest their invasion. So what we were about to experience is a communist-controlled, watered-down version of Tibet. Still, we had to see "the roof of the world" for ourselves. The Chinese may have taken over their land, but they could not kill the Tibetan spirit.

"It occurs to me that our entire lives have led to this moment," Brian said, eager to start our bus journey north through the clouds into the highest elevated country on earth, a whopping average of sixteen thousand feet. "I have a feeling when we leave Tibet, we'll be changed forever."

Brian had no idea how prophetic his statement would turn out to be.

It took our bus five hours to get to the Nepal–Tibetan border, where we were to begin a steep ascent. Brian and I were on a tour with eight other travelers, which was the only way the Chinese would allow us into "their" country.

Even though we followed protocol, a Chinese border official took one look at our papers and refused to let us in. It took us a few minutes to realize he wanted us to pay a bribe. Every time we told him, "but we already paid for a tour guide," he suddenly stopped understanding English. I have no idea how our Chinese-speaking driver did it, but he somehow argued our way across the border without paying anything— but the Chinese border police didn't just let us go. No, they gave us a quiet, suppressive-looking "guide" (for free) to keep an eye on us.

"They'll only let us in if we have a guide," I whispered.

Brian's eyes narrowed. "It's our duty to make his life a *living hell*."

Our unwanted guide got onboard. We hoped he wouldn't sit next to us and he didn't; he sat by himself in front, never looking back. Brian got a look at him from the back of the bus and whispered, "We're totally ditching that little tyrant . . . just you wait."

That night, we stayed in a small guestroom with the other travelers on the bus; we had no choice, they were herding us into the country in a pack. Our Chinese guide had his own room. We went to the only restaurant in town to eat dinner, which had two dishes on the menu: noodle soup or fried rice. I chose fried rice for eighty cents. Our Chinese guide had noodle soup.

We rose the next morning and had omelets, bread, and milk tea for breakfast, then got back on the bus for the long haul across the Tibetan plateau on a series of sketchy cliff roads. I noticed clusters of tents dotting the landscape. "What are those?" I asked the other travelers. Our Chinese guide said nothing, then a British lady on the bus piped up: "They're nomadic Tibetans, sweetie."

While we stopped to stretch our legs, a few nomads came down from their camps to stare at us. They were rugged-looking people with flat faces; many wore red headbands, which distinguished them from the Chinese. They were very warm and inquisitive.

During one pit stop, an old nomadic man came up to me and gently touched my face. I smiled and let him feel my features. "Is he blind?" I asked Brian.

"Just go with it," Brian said out of the corner of his mouth. So I touched the old man's face back and he gave me a big toothless grin.

Before I got back on the bus, I gave a pretty nomad girl a quarter and her eyes got wide with excitement.

The bus kept driving into the night; the muddy mountain passes were slick with rain. We came across three landslides, which we crossed slowly. Then we ran into a bigger one that stopped us cold. "Wake up. This does not look good." Brian nudged me and said he had a premonition we were going to die out here.

"Relax," I said, "this is just a minor setback. C'mon, let's go stretch our legs."

Brian and I got off the bus and started throwing our 49ers football around while the rest of the passengers stayed warm inside the bus. After a few minutes, the door opened and the British lady staggered off the bus moaning. She threw up a few feet from Brian's shoes. Then another passenger got off the bus to do the same . . . then another . . . then another.

"Altitude sickness," I said to Brian.

"It's gonna be a puke-athon," Brian yelled. We kept tossing the ball around.

We had climbed thousands of feet in a few hours, but we foolishly thought the thin air wouldn't affect us. It didn't take long until we started feeling it, and it wasn't pleasant. Our football tossing slowly stopped, and we both doubled over and started throwing up just like everyone else.

"Okay, I'm done!" I groaned.

"This isn't heaven; this—," Brian started, wiping frozen vomit from his lips.

"Stop saying that!"

We got back on the bus and tried to keep from using too much precious oxygen. "Baby breaths . . . baby breaths," Brian kept repeating.

Our Chinese guide had a long discussion with our driver, then they told us the landslide was too dangerous to cross and we were going to have to spend the night in the bus. Everyone groaned. "This was not in the brochure!" Brian said while putting on every layer of clothes he had in his pack. "Somebody's getting sued if we die on this freaking mountain."

"When did you get so litigious?" I asked.

We'd packed exclusively for tropical weather and didn't have winter jackets, gloves, hats, or shoes, which was obviously a huge oversight. Brian layered on every T-shirt and tank top he had, which did nothing. We asked the others if we could borrow some warmer sweaters (there were four other Americans [all men], one Norwegian, and the British lady onboard). Two of the Americans turned over some clothes begrudgingly. "What kind of moron comes to Tibet without warm clothes?"

Brian said, "Dude, we're from California. We don't even own winter jackets. Here." He pulled out something from his pack. "Have some chocolate as payment."

We fought over two sweaters, one scarf and some gloves. I told our donors, "I promise to give this back louse-free when we get off this mountain . . . I can't speak for him though."

"Don't worry, the crabs froze off a long time ago," Brian said.

We layered up and heard a loud rapping on the bus door. "Could it be? Saved by the commie police?" Brian asked sarcastically.

Our driver opened the door and in stepped three Tibetan nomads from a nearby encampment. They saw we were not moving and wanted to bring us blankets, dry noodles, and a thermos of hot water to help us survive the frigid night. Everyone on the bus thanked them profusely, then they disappeared back into the dark.

"That was some Three Wise Men shit, right there," Cameron, the American who lent me a sweater, said.

"The kindness of strangers," I said to Brian, who went for the thermos of hot water like an Arctic refugee.

We all warmed up a bit after we ate our noodles, then we huddled in our blankets and spent the rest of the night hoping our bus wouldn't slide off the mountain. We watched a candle on the front dashboard burn down for entertainment. We couldn't fall asleep so we filled the silence by talking.

We found out the British lady (Laurie) had led sixteen excursions into Tibet. What was interesting was her other occupation was "past-life regression therapy." She told us she could levitate. Brian asked, "Can you levitate this bus out of here?"

"To do that, I reckon you'd have to believe the way I do, son," she said.

"I guess that's out then . . . Can you tell who I was in a past life?" Brian was baiting her.

"I'd have to regress you, but you look, and frankly sound a bit like a petite Neanderthal in this light," then she cackled like a British hen. The rest of the bus laughed. Brian was not amused, but he did kinda look like a Neanderthal with his scruffy beard and wild hair.

Once our only light source burned down, we were in the pitch black. The wind was howling. It was so dark I couldn't see my hand in front of my face. I spread out across two seats with a couple of packs as my pillow. Brian sprawled out in the back row right behind me.

Everyone tried to sleep while Brian and I talked like kids who were camping in the dark. "Think we're gonna die here?" Brian asked.

"Only if there's another landslide. Or we freeze to death . . . You got enough blankets?"

"No . . . we need to huddle for warmth."

"Don't—"

"Dude, we have to."

Brian got up and moved up to my row and cuddled up behind me. We spooned for dear life. I said, "This isn't weird or anything . . . Just don't spork me in the middle of the night."

"I can't make any promises."

I quoted Steve Martin from *Planes, Trains and Automobiles*: "Those aren't pillows!" We both laughed to cut the awkwardness.

We lay there like two frozen sardines awaiting certain death. I could feel Brian's breath on my neck and it was making me slightly uncomfortable, but I welcomed his additional body heat. After a long bout of quiet, Brian whispered, "If we die . . . think you'll go to heaven?"

"I don't know what heaven is. One thing I know is, we're not getting out of this life that easy," I said. "This is just another test."

"You didn't answer my question."

"I don't know what I believe."

"You believe in anything?"

"I believe in some kind of higher power, whatever you want to call it . . . and I believe in me . . . and you."

"I believe in us too."

"That night I crawled down the stairs on *bhang lassis*, you looked just like a Neanderthal."

Brian yawned. "Your judgment was skewed . . . let's stop talking."

We drifted off to sleep with the rain tinkling lightly against the window.

I awoke to the bus engine revving the next morning. We were still hanging off the side of the cliff in our frozen jalopy. I was thrilled to still be alive.

I sat up and noticed we were not alone. The nomadic Tibetans had come to see us off. "Look . . . they all got up at the crack of dawn to make sure we're okay." I roused Brian, who got up and rubbed his eyes.

Two nomad kids who came down put their gloved hands on our window. We put our hands up to theirs. The kids held onto the bus until we pulled away. Brian stuck his head out of the window and yelled goodbye to them as we drove off.

He pulled his head back inside, "That was beautiful, man. . . . Life is beautiful."

We weren't sure how long our bus would hold out but it got up enough gumption to cross the landslide easily. Brian smiled, saying "Thank you, Buddha" as we crossed over. The British lady was incensed, "Why didn't we do this last night? What changed in a few hours??"

"Perhaps they were afraid to try at night," I said calmly, as I played cards with Cameron (we were betting peanuts and squares of frozen chocolate).

We puttered the jalopy over Lhotse, the fourth tallest mountain in the world. We stopped at a small strip of buildings where we ravenously ate breakfast. When the lady rang up our bill, she used a black abacus.

Our bus slogged onward to Shigatse on the Friendship Highway, a name given by the Chinese government. Brian was getting stir crazy. He kept asking Dawa, our Chinese guide, why it was taking us three days to get to our destination.

"No one ever said *three days*."

Brian got no reply, just a shrug. He got in close to Dawa's ear and said, "If this was New York, you would be fired."

We finally stopped at a guesthouse in Shigatse, the second biggest town in Tibet, where we took our first shower in three days. We had observed Tibetans don't customarily wash; this was seen as a foolish waste of resources, so we hadn't either.

After a dinner of noodles and milk tea, we headed back to the guesthouse to relax. There was a small television in our room. "A TV? Sweet!" Brian said and started flipping channels. "One show playing on every channel? All propaganda, all the time?" We dozed off to the Chinese propaganda with the sound turned down.

Lying in my tiny bed, I thought about how the Dalai Lama had been living in exile all these years. It was surreal to be in the same room as the "conqueror television" when all we were here to do was study Buddhism. That black and white TV made me appreciate the freedom we have in the United States. It may be a corrupt oligarchy of consumerism—but it's not an oppressive fascist regime. (Not yet, at least.)

I fell asleep feeling homesick, dreaming of American women. It had been far too long since I had seen one. . . .

The next morning, our bus tour took us to the Tashihunpo Monastery, one of the largest monasteries in Tibet and home of the Panchen Lamas. Brian meditated while I went into deep personal reflection. We learned the Panchen Lama had been "relocated" to Beijing—unfortunately for him. We spent the day praying on top of the world; it was magical.

"I'm finally getting that Buddhism is not just a religion; it's a way of thinking," I said, interrupting Brian's meditation like it was some kind of revelation.

"That's what I've been saying," Brian said. "Maybe you'll get into it now."

We spent the day at the monastery, then started our descent into Lhasa on the usual muddy tracks. We kept asking Dawa when they were going to build more Friendship Highways for these poor people.

We got no answer.

A few hours after nightfall, our bus decided to finally commit suicide and ran off the road, crashing near the edge of a cliff. "It was just a matter of time!" I yelled. Brian looked out the window. All we saw was darkness. We got off the bus; we were stranded in the middle of nowhere, again. There were no nomads around this time.

Standing on the side of the road, we saw some headlights coming our way. We tried to flag them down, but it was a Chinese Land Cruiser that wouldn't stop. We walked for half a mile to a light we saw in the distance, it was a midway station where a Chinese police officer in another Land Cruiser finally stopped for us.

"Let me take care of this," Brian said then tried to bribe us a ride by offering the dude chocolate. The guy just stared at the Milky Way bar with a communist frown. "Bad for health," he said, which made us laugh.

Our laughter held him up long enough for Dawa to come barreling down the mountain to the midway station. Dawa eventually bribed the guy to give us a ride. Or threatened him. I have no idea how the Chinese negotiate, but it worked.

Late that night, all ten of us (eight travelers, one bus driver, and one guide) finally made it into Lhasa, the capital of Tibet, in the back of a Chinese police Land Cruiser. Don't ask how we all squeezed in there, but when you're desperate, you'll make anything work.

"I've never been happier to be in a patrol vehicle," I said while jammed into the cruiser like a frozen sardine.

Brian replied, "Thought we'd be leaving town in one of these, not entering."

"It's a strange world."

The police cruiser dropped us off at a place called the Snowland Hotel, where we all checked in and collapsed into our beds from exhaustion.

Twelve hours of sleep later, I awoke to Lhasa sunshine. It was a beautiful, clear, and cold day. We walked outside and saw that the famed

Potala Palace, which was the old home of the Dalai Lama, was perched right above our hotel, hanging off a mountain.

"Think we came to the right place . . . That's God's old casa," Brian said.

We were about to take a bus up to the monastery but then we heard the annual horse races at the "fairgrounds" in Gyantse were happening that day. This was a huge event. Tibetans from all over the country were coming to enjoy one crazy weekend at the races.

Should we join the festivities, or get enlightened? "Enlightenment can wait, right?" I convinced Brian to put off the monastery for another day. "But, no tourists are allowed. What about Dawa?"

Brian said he'd take care of it. Ten minutes later he came back and said, "C'mon let's go!" He had somehow convinced Dawa to let us have a day at the races even though the Chinese don't allow foreigners to see Tibetans in celebration of anything.

We walked over to the fairgrounds, and Dawa didn't stop us but he was following close behind. "How did you get Dawa's approval??"

"I gave him some hash chocolate and ten minutes later, he was agreeing to anything," he laughed.

"You just dosed and bribed a Chinese official at the same time!?"

"*That one's* for the Lama," Brian said.

We led our drugged-out Chinese guide down to the entrance of the festivities, then we patted him on the back and told him to go take a nap while we dove into the madness with ten thousand Tibetan villagers who were all drinking homemade barley beer called Chang. Dawa just smiled like Buddha and let us go on in.

"Those chocolates should be called Jedi mind trick," I said.

Brian and I were taking another big risk. We were the only foreigners at the party and couldn't exactly blend in. If the Chinese caught us breaking the law, we knew we could get locked up so we tried to lay as low as possible.

"They may send Dawa to Siberia for letting us come here!" I shouted over the mass of Tibetan humanity.

"Just don't commandeer a horse and we should be okay!" Brian yelled back.

Dawa tried to keep an eye on us, but once we entered the throng of thousands there was no way he could keep up. We wandered through the crowd, playing keep away from the only sober people in sight, the ever-present Communist police.

Our attention turned to the crazy horse race. I'd never seen anything like it. There was no track, the horses would just blow by you a few feet away and the people would cheer. I got so caught up in the race I lost Brian in the crowd.

I had a few beers and befriended a group of Tibetans who invited me to sit with them. We just sat there and stared at each other, then they put a giant vat of beer in front of me and insisted that I drink it. Every time a sip was offered I had to drink or it would be an insult. So I drank and drank and cheered with everyone else when the horses whizzed by. I had no idea what was going on but I didn't care.

Communication with them was nil, but somehow it was working. I became a fast expert at sign language. I spent the next two hours talking subversive shit about the Chinese using facial expressions and makeshift hand gestures with all my new Tibetan friends. My presence was a novelty to them and they treated me extremely well. It was another one of those moments where I felt like a celebrity just for being the only American at the party. They were so embracing and I was so drunk drinking their milky beer, it was a wonderful bonding experience. To thank them, I bought the group some peanuts and cigarettes, which were delicacies around here. This led my group to roar in happiness. Every time they roared, I looked around to make sure the Chinese cops weren't coming for me.

Maybe they had already nabbed Brian, who was officially missing. I didn't care. After five hours of non-stop drinking, I was completely inebriated and had to pee, so some Tibetans walked me to the bathroom, which was a giant open field. I took a piss watching two hundred drunk Tibetans peeing and shitting on top of the world. It was surreal and amazing.

"The biggest port-a-potty on earth," I mumbled to no one. "Brian's gotta see this."

By early evening, the grass field was full of running horses and drunken Tibetans falling all over themselves. I knew I needed to hightail it before

I got locked up so I went looking for Brian, who I found on the other side of the grounds leading a table full of blasted Tibetans in song.

"Dude, you're supposed to be keeping a low profile!" I shouted. Brian didn't hear me, he was overjoyed and completely in the moment. It sounded like he had them singing Billy Joel but I must have been hearing things.

I finally got Brian's attention, "Party's over, we gotta blow . . . *now!*" He got up from the table laughing, but the crowd of revelers kept pulling him back. Eventually we made our escape; we smiled and thanked everyone for their hospitality, and they gave us hugs.

Near the fairgrounds exit, we passed Dawa sitting with an old Tibetan woman who was rubbing his head. They looked very cozy. His greasy black hair was standing on end; he looked happy for the first time.

"Look . . . Dawa's got a lady!"

We laughed like two drunken parrots then stumbled our way back to the hotel, weaving through the village while repeating "*Namaste*, baby" to everyone we passed who were all as drunk as we were. I finally asked Brian, "Were you singing 'Piano Man' with a table full of Tibetans back there?!"

He laughed. "They taught *me* the song!"

We sang "Piano Man" all the way home.

The next day we treated our hangovers with some spiritual medicine. We forced ourselves to get out of bed early so we could tour every temple and monastery in town. It was ambitious, but Brian was on a mission. He even shaved his head to get into character.

"Dude, you're not kidding around," I said when he appeared from the bathroom looking like David Carradine in TV's *Kung Fu*. He dried off his head.

"You shaved your melon looking for sexual pleasure . . . I shaved mine looking for enlightenment."

"Geez, you don't have to make me feel bad about it."

"I do not judge, I only point out that *this* is not a fashion choice."

"Yeah, okay. Out of respect, I won't mock you incessantly."

Our first stop was the Jokhang Temple, a four-story wooden complex with a golden top in the center of town. The ultimate spot for

Buddhist pilgrims, it was founded in 639 during the Tang Dynasty. We stood in the center of its square and saw the entire complex. We followed a row of flickering votive lights that led to the main hall, which housed the oldest shrine in the temple that was over thirteen hundred years old. Above the main entrance hung a dharma wheel flanked by two golden deer. "The dharma wheel represents the unity of all things," Brian pointed out.

While we were admiring the golden bejeweled statue of a twelve-year-old Buddha that sat in the middle of the hall, an old Buddhist monk named Da Shin struck up a conversation with us after he heard us talking about California.

"California, eh? Do you surf?" he stopped to ask.

"I tell all the girls I do, but I'm embarrassed to say not really," I said.

"The Beach Boys, I love them," he laughed. "I see you have shaved your head very recently."

Brian smiled sheepishly, "I think I want to become a monk."

"And I want to be a surfer when I grow up!" he replied and laughed. "Seriously, I suggest you rub Tiger Balm on your head so you don't chafe."

Da Shin introduced himself and we all hit it off, which was great; we had an expert mentor and a guide for the day. Da Shin toured us around the Barkhor that circled the Jokhang. He stopped to talk to all the beggars, touts, and hawkers, calling them "sir" and "madame." Da Shin blessed them all.

"Do you bless all the touts and beggars you see?" Brian asked.

He smiled. "I do not judge. They are, how you say in California, 'making lemonade out of the lemons' that life has given them."

"But many do not work, they beg when they are able-bodied," I said.

"If you walked a day in their shoes, you might find their circumstances to be more complex . . . In this life, the tragedies one endures don't always show on the faces of men."

He began to tell us "the story" we had traveled all the way to Tibet to hear: the story of Siddhartha Gautama, or the Buddha.

"Siddhartha was born in India in 566 BC. He was the only prince in a royal family who married by arrangement at age sixteen. Siddhartha had all of life's earthly pleasures, but he chose to leave his palace in search of spiritual knowledge at age twenty-nine."

"That's my age," Brian interjected with a smile.

"Will you please let him talk?" I said. Da Shin smiled then continued:

"Siddhartha went into the streets to meet his people. He had never seen poverty or sickness before, and it made him very sad. Before he left the palace, no one had told him that humans must die one day. Realizing his ignorance, he began searching for truth. He became a student of yoga under two hermit teachers where he sought enlightenment through deprivation.

"He ate one leaf or nut per day in his search for truth—but became so weak he collapsed in a river and nearly drowned. Near starvation, he looked up and saw a beautiful village girl offering him milk and rice pudding, which he accepted. Her name was Sujata.

"At that moment, he had an epiphany. He realized the road to enlightenment could not be found by severe asceticism—but somewhere between sensual indulgence and deprivation. Somewhere in the middle . . . He called it 'The Middle Way.'"

I said, "So that is why Buddhists believe it's good not to get too high or too low."

"That's right, good. The Middle Way consists of Four Noble Truths. Buddha taught that through the mastery of these four truths, a state of supreme liberation, or nirvana, is possible for any being," Da Shin said. "Nirvana is the perfect peace of mind that's free from ignorance, greed, and hatred."

"We're quite familiar with Nirvana," I said.

"It's not the band, you know," Da Shin said as he laughed. "Though I love Kurt Cobain."

"It's when no personal identity or boundaries of the mind remains," Brian added.

"Yes, you two have been studying!" Da Shin said.

"We don't just surf back in California," I said. Da Shin continued.

"So. When Buddha discovered the Middle Way, he became known as 'the *Enlightened One,*' but he had yet to discover the ultimate truth,

237

so he sat under a Bodhi tree in India to meditate. He vowed not to rise until he had found it. Then, on the forty-ninth day, at the age of thirty-five, Buddha attained full enlightenment . . . He had complete insight into the cause of suffering, and the steps necessary to eliminate it. Buddha spent the rest of his life teaching this wisdom, which are the same lessons that we as monks pass down to future generations. And that, my friends, is Buddhism in, how you say . . . a nutshell?"

"Can I have an application to join the priesthood?" Brian asked.

"Monkhood."

"Sorry, right."

"We don't take applications, but you can join us anytime. And contrary to popular belief, a shaved head is not necessary. We only do it because it is one less thing to attach yourself to."

It was starting to get dark. We talked with our friend Da Shin a little longer and told him about our yearlong journey for self-discovery, then said our goodbyes. "Thank you for sharing your knowledge with us," I said.

"Anytime, my friends. May your quest for meaning bear fruit."

Brian asked him for a hug. Da Shin laughed and gave us both one.

"Enjoy the California surf. You are privileged to live in such a beautiful part of the world. Don't ever forget, with great privilege comes great responsibility."

I looked at Brian. "Where have I heard that before?"

Da Shin gave us one final wave and walked back into the main hall.

We left the monastery. Brian said, "That was the coolest monk I've ever met . . . even cooler than Thelonious Monk."

"I don't know who that is," I said.

"Of course you don't. And that's okay."

I punched him in the arm playfully like we did when we were twelve years old wrestling on the Santa Cruz beaches with our junior high girlfriends. We walked back to our hotel that night and my myriad of earthly problems seemed small when compared to the steps we were taking on our spiritual path.

But when all can seem at its best, you never know when life will take a turn for the worst. My fate was about to change and I wasn't prepared.

I had forgotten the old adage Jack taught me: "When you least expect it, expect it."

I had no idea the next sunrise would be my last in Tibet.

It seemed unfathomable at the time. We were so close to achieving our spiritual goals—then the "ghosts of our past sins" and the magnetic force of our fatal flaws pulled us back into the eternal samsara and doomed me to hell.

The day started early and we were full of life. We woke for breakfast then took a bus to the Potala Palace, which overlooked all of Lhasa. A huge monastery that was built in the seventh century, it was the spiritual headquarters of Buddhism right up until it was taken over by the Chinese.

We toured Norbulingka first. It was the summer palace of the Dalai Llamas and was founded by the seventh Dalai Lama in 1755. They call it the Jeweled Park for its sublime beauty. Legend has it the fourteenth Dalai Lama made his escape disguised as a Tibetan soldier from Norbulingka in 1959 to save himself from the invading Chinese.

Something seemed off with Brian while we toured the Jeweled Park. Maybe it was just me but he felt far away, deep in his own thoughts. His freshly shaved head and face made him seem like a different person. With no wild hair and scruffy stubble, his coarse Neanderthal side was long gone. He seemed to be evolving into some spiritual alien presence before my eyes.

Brian and I spent the morning praying with the monks. We would pray in one prayer hall, then walk to another and do it again. At around eleven o'clock, we were on our way to another prayer hall that was at the top of this huge staircase.

Brian was carrying this kid on his back (who he picked up after seeing he was out of breath walking up the stairs). I commented, "Walking through here makes me want to become a born-again Buddhist," I said, trying to tap into his mind game.

He didn't respond, so I just kept climbing the stairs. "Do they have born-again Budd—"

I turned around and Brian and the kid had vanished before my eyes. It stopped me in my tracks. "Whoa! How'd you do that??" I did circles on the stairs like a dog chasing his tail.

My logical side was malfunctioning. This could not be happening. There was nowhere they could have gone—we were in the middle of the stairs, the only way was up or down and each had about a hundred stairs to go before you reached the top or the bottom.

Was this magic? Is there a trap door I'm not aware of? Was I having some mind-altering flashback? Was that kid the future incarnation of the next Buddha? Was Brian ever even here?

I walked around the palace looking for him, calling out his name, until it occurred to me that maybe he didn't want to be found. Maybe he planned this escape just like the fourteenth Dalai Lama did back in 1959. But who were the invading Chinese in this scenario? Who was he escaping from? Me?? My mind was entering rational meltdown.

I gave up looking after an hour. I bought a Tibetan bracelet and prayer wheel and left.

I walked alone to the Sera Monastery talking to myself. I tried to learn about the monastery like nothing had happened. I learned five thousand monks used to live here back in the days before the imperial overthrow. After the Chinese invaded, most of the monks were murdered, castrated, and tortured, and the ones whose lives were spared weren't allowed to worship here anymore until recently.

The Chinese did anything they could to sweep these poor people under a rug. Just like Brian is trying to sweep me under the rug.

I couldn't stay Zen anymore. My mind was racing with questions:

Why did Brian ditch me? Does he think I'm dragging him down? Is he really better off without me, or did he just get lost? Couldn't he see by going to all these monasteries and learning their way of thinking I was trying to be a more perfect person by increasing my virtues, perfecting my intellect, and meditating along with him? I was learning their Four Noble Truths!

While I was walking and ranting to myself like a crazy person, something compelled me to stop walking. I was in the middle of a large open area. The sun was setting and only a few rays of sunshine were piercing through the lattice of the complex wall. I looked down; the last rays of sunlight were still warming the grass. I saw a cricket hopping in front of me. Suddenly a boy's hand grabbed the cricket and picked it up.

I looked up at the boy's face. It was the same Tibetan kid Brian was carrying on his back. How did he get here? He certainly didn't walk; he could barely make it up the stairs of the Norbulingka palace.

While I pondered the re-emergence of this little boy, he gently lifted the cricket up to his face with an open palm then he blew it a kiss and the cricket hopped away. The kid looked at me. Then he extended his palm toward the right part of the monastery where I heard a loud bell ringing in the distance. He motioned for me to go to the sound of the bell. So I did.

I walked past the bell that was calling monks into prayer. Some were already kneeling in deep meditation. I kneeled down to pray and noticed that at the front of the hall there he was: Brian, praying with the monks in the Sera Monastery. It was hard to miss him—sunlight was reflecting off his extremely white shaved head and he had his T-shirt wrapped around him like a Buddhist robe. He appeared to have been meditating here for a while. Had he teleported with the kid from Norbulingka?

Now I felt like I was the one in the dream. I stopped trying to understand.

I prayed a few feet behind him for at least two hours. If he would just open his eyes he could see me, but he never did. I started to get restless; I tried to use telepathy. And suddenly it worked. He opened his eyes and smiled at me.

When night fell, most of the monks left the prayer hall. Brian was still in there with a few others. I moved up and sat down quietly beside him. He didn't seem to notice I was there. Either he had experienced total consciousness, or he had gone insane . . . I couldn't tell which.

Finally, he opened his eyes and looked at me. I tried to interject, "Dude, where did you go? Do you want me to leave you alone? I don't want to bother your frame of mind, but you can't just ditch me like that."

He smiled and took my hand, "I wish I were me all the time, Rob. Did you know Tibetans never divert their eyes?"

He began speaking in proverbs. I just let him talk. "If I see you all at once . . . can you handle it?"

"I . . . think so."

"Is there ever a moment in life where you can only be awakened by the beauty of the rain?"

". . . Yes?"

"Whoever taught me to look down when I walk never saw my face . . ."

He seemed to be having multiple *satoris*, multiple spiritual kicks in the head. It may have given him a cosmic concussion. He kept going with his proverbs for a while. Then he closed his eyes and went back to meditating, totally ignoring me.

After a half hour of silence, I said, "I think I'm going to go back to the room for a while."

He just nodded with his eyes closed, "Hear much, speak little."

"Okay . . ." I left Brian to meditate in peace. I was happy for him; I really was. He seemed to have gone to the other side and reached some kind of ultimate nirvana. He was out of his body without the use of drugs or alcohol. How that is possible long term still escapes me, but I figured he would be okay by himself.

Walking out of main hall to catch a rickshaw is when evil incarnate appeared out of the miasma. He came up from behind, his huge paw grabbed my back. "You asshole, I told you I'd kill you!"

The big hand shoved me hard. Off-balance, I stumbled down a few stairs and banged my head into the giant gong by the prayer wheel. All the tourists and monks suddenly stopped to look; the sound of my head hitting the gong reverberated through the monastery.

Embarrassed, I rubbed my head and turned to get a glimpse of my assailant. It was not Satan, it was bloody Ted—the crazy chain-smoking Brit who we'd lost on the Annapurna Trail. He was smiling a big devilish smile, just like he did after banging that Nepalese mountain cougar. I had a feeling I'd see him again. It's a pretty common occurrence to meet backpackers in one part of the world then run into them somewhere else since everyone's on the same world walkabout.

"You again. Did your friend die on the mountain?"

Ted was smoking inside the monastery and was clearly very, very drunk. "You wanker! Where's your little friend!?" He slurred, "Tonight I'm gonna drink you faggots under the table. C'mon, let's get outta this shithole. This is no place for us hellbound blokes. Let's go grab us a couple of jars!"

While this was happening, I thought, who is he talking about? I'm not hellbound. Am I?? Is that why Brian ditched me?

Ted was causing a scene. I shot up and tried to wrangle him, "Shhhh man, calm down, this is a sacred place of worship and you're being very uncool." I pointed to the room Brian was praying in. "Brian's in there becoming a freaking monk."

"Monk? They don't let party animals like you sots become monks! Where's that SOB?!" Ted gave me another shove and went rambling up the stairs toward Brian, "He promised me some of that good dope he stole from that plantation!"

It all happened too fast for me to stop it, all I could do was say, "No-no-noooo!" I ran after him but it was too late.

Ted barged into the prayer room, saw Brian kneeling and lunged at him like an inebriated bear, bowling over a few old monks who were deep in prayer. Ted pancaked Brian, exactly like he did his buddy on the trail whenever he was out of breath, cursing up a storm. *"You wanker!"* He shouted.

Brian never knew what hit him. By the time I got in there, Brian was buried under two hundred and fifty pounds of smoked English brute. A few monks rushed into the room to help the three old monks who had been knocked silly.

Ted was bear-hugging Brian on the mat and laughing at his new appearance, "What the hell? Who shaved your bloody melon! You look like a goddamned cantaloupe! C'mon, where's that good hash? You got it stashed in there somewhere—I know it!" Then he began to tickle Brian.

Brian tried to keep his composure until he couldn't take it anymore and screamed, *"Get off of me you stupid idiot!"* The word "idiot" echoed through the monastery. *Everyone* could hear the commotion.

It seemed like that one word summed up this entire affair . . . Maybe our entire lives.

Ted, sensing Brian's colossal unhappiness, got off him quickly. Tears of rage welled in Brian's eyes; he was mortified. It took this moment for Brian to realize he could never escape his sordid past—not so easily, not with me and "ghosts of debauchery past" like Ted haunting him.

Like a recovering addict who has to break ties with all his user friends, Brian stood up, bowed to the other old monks who were still bowled over like a bunch of bald crimson-robed bowling pins, and said, "Please forgive them . . . I'm sorry."

Then Brian set his gaze on me and gave me a death stare to end all death stares. He said quietly, yet firmly: "You led him in here. You just want your little buddy to stick around and be your 'drink monkey' forever. You never wanted us to have a personal renaissance. You just wanted to run away."

"What?? That's not—"

"You'll never find enlightenment, man. Go home . . . I was right; you're not ready. It's over." Brian turned his back on me and disappeared into the night.

I was stunned. His words hung in the air and felt like daggers in my heart. A part of me knew he was right. A couple of idiots had invaded heaven, and this time Brian wasn't one of them. But I was one . . . I always am. Would God ever forgive me?

Ted, my new idiot sidekick, could see I was upset. He came over and draped his meaty paw around me like nothing much out of the ordinary had happened. "Was it something I said, mate?" All I could say was, "Dude . . ." which must have triggered his conscience because he hung his head in humiliation.

I felt another hand on my shoulder. This one was gentle. I turned around hoping it was Brian, but it was the head monk who did not look pleased. "Please excuse, we must ask you two to leave the monastery at once." Ted and I made the walk of shame out of the Sera Monastery. A few tourists were laughing at us and taking our picture. One of them was a Swedish kid wearing a Dodgers cap who said, "Brutal," when we walked by.

It was a brutal ending.

I have been kicked out of many establishments in my life— universities, bars, restaurants, saunas, sporting events, strip clubs—but I had never been kicked out of a monastery before. It was the most humiliating experience of my life. It felt like God was banishing me from his kingdom.

Karma had kicked my ass.

When I got back to the hotel, Brian had already packed his things and left. He left no note this time. Dejected and ashamed, I couldn't stick around any longer; I just wanted to be gone, so I hailed a taxi to the Lhasa Gonggar Airport with my tail between my legs. I told the driver, who'd been shuttling us around when Brian and I were too lazy to walk, to take me to the airport.

"Hey buddy. Where's your friend?" He asked.

"I don't know. On the road to enlightenment, I guess," I said.

"Left you behind, huh?"

"Yeah."

"You need hashish?"

"No."

"Where you going now, my friend?"

I sat there for a minute, watching the traffic go by. "Back to square one."

10

Westward Bound

M Y EPIC JOURNEY WAS on life support.

I'd endured eleven months full of profound self-discoveries and painful realizations, wild adventures, and unadulterated debauchery. I was weary from all that road going, my beaten body and rattled soul yearned to be embraced by the tender bosom of the West, but all I had was a Barbie doll.

With thirty days left before I turned back into a tax-dodging pumpkin, I was officially giving up my "new experiences only" rule I'd been living by all year and heading back to the bustling anthill of the Western world to lick my wounds. No more roughing it in hellish environs. Testing the boundaries had gotten me nowhere. Had I found myself in the third world jungles? In the Asian rice paddies? In the sprawling outback? Riding the raging rivers? Scaling titanic mountains? Had I grown *at all* in a year?

I needed an introspective mirror, but it was shattered all over a monastery floor.

I dragged ass into the Lhasa Gonggar Airport. I had no idea where I was going. I was looking to book the first flight headed west, I didn't care where. All I wanted was to wipe the memory of Tibet from my mind, which was a depressing notion since I truly loved my time here.

I waded through the sea of people; the airport lady told me there was a nine-thirty flight to Munich. "I'll take it." I slapped my ticket on the counter.

I started flipping through my mental Rolodex of friends, colleagues, and semi-acquaintances. I had to know someone in Munich, right? Who doesn't know a crazy German? No Germans came to mind . . . but I did know this crazy Italian who maybe lived somewhere near there.

His name was Giancarlo, my old scoundrel of a business partner who (coincidentally) fled the US (just like me) to Germany a few years ago, supposedly. Wasn't he involved in some sort of scandal? Now that I think about it, didn't he still owe me some money?

I rifled through my pack, I'd lost all my contact numbers I brought with me. All I found was a bar napkin from Singapore with some stoned backpacker's number scrawled on it.

Then it hit me. I must have Giancarlo's number in my address book, *back home.* To find out, I finally had to bite the bullet and call Jody, my estranged assistant back in Palo Alto. I went looking for a bank of payphones to crawl into, and called her. It took eight rings but she answered, amazingly, even though it was three in the morning on a Tuesday in California.

"Rob? Is that you?" Jody sounded dead asleep.

"Yeah, *it is I.* Back from the dead . . . You pissed?"

"We all thought you committed suicide . . . or got eaten by sharks."

"I may kill myself soon. Hey, weird question—but do you still have my contact numbers? Or did you throw them in a dumpster the second I left you holding the bag?"

"You left me holding a bag of shit . . . Ya know, Rob, I'm so glad you called to wake me up in the middle of the night to ask me about some random asshole's number. If you were here I'd punch you in the face right now. You know that, right?"

"That's so sweet. Are you mad because I never dropped you a post-card, or because I stuck you with all my crap?"

"Both."

I apologized profusely for leaving her in the lurch. She said, "The only good news I can offer at this hour is that I have not burned your

Rolodex . . . But before I continue, may I remind you that you owe me six months back pay." Which made sense since I cleaned out my business account a long time ago.

"Oooh, sorry about that . . . The check's in the mail?"

Jody sighed. Then she updated me on the fallout from my escape. After I sold all my possessions except my condo, she said she closed my "virtual office" but kept all my mail because she "still has a soft spot" for my "dumb ass."

"Thank you. I owe you, big time."

"Yes, you do."

I filled her in on all the craziness I'd been up to all year.

"So I guess you're both probably wanted by Interpol. Can't believe you left the country with Brian. I bet you both have one of those mountain-man Unabomber beards . . . You do, don't you?"

"No . . . . yes . . . I do look like a hermit. I've lost a ton of weight. Brian turned into a Buddhist—he wants to kill me. It's a long story."

Jody told me no warrants were out for my arrest but "there is definitely some serious civil litigation brewing" if I ever decided to come home. "Also, not to be a total downer, but your lawyer quit a long time ago. I've got his invoice, among others. And I don't mean to be the bearer of even more bad news, but . . . Elena's been squatting in your condo all year."

"What?? It never sold? I was going to give you a commission!"

"You *left*. You're not paying me enough to handle your shit show of a life—in fact, you're not paying me at all. I should hang up—Is this a collect call??"

"No-no, don't hang up—point well taken . . . What is she doing over there?"

"She's doing what all squatters do, squatting! I stopped by a few times *while I was still getting paid* and she wouldn't answer the door—all she did was turn down the stupid samba music she had playing inside."

"That harlot . . . Someone's been screwing in my bed, and it hasn't been me."

"Don't be such a drama queen. It's what got you into this mess. You never had to leave. You just panicked."

"Don't judge me, okay? You just . . . don't get it."

"Whatever, Rob. I probably know you better than yourself."

I had to find out what was going on with Elena, so I begged Jody to get over there and serve her "eviction papers." "Write up some false documents that look legal . . . and threaten to call the INS—she's not an American citizen! Her green card ran out a long time ago. She wanted me to marry her to legalize her Columbian ass!"

"You're shouting again. Why do you care so much? The courts may have already seized your condo!"

"She's in my house!" I calmed down and whispered. "She's in my house and I wanna know who the hell she's been screwing *in my house*. I'll wire you your back pay when I get to Munich. I swear to God I've been lost in the jungle for a year, where they don't have banks." I lied. Kinda.

"You could've at least let me know you were alive. I was really worried."

"I know . . . I'm sorry. I'll make it up to you when I get back. I'll be home soon."

"Promise?"

Jody said if I promised to come home she'd whip up some false eviction papers "the second my wire transfer arrived" in her account. I promised, she promised, then she dug up Giancarlo's number and ended our call with a "be careful and come home . . . I want to be the first person to punch you in the face."

I promised I would let her be the first person to punch me in the face, then I hung up. I stood there imagining all the people who I abandoned back home lining up to inflict bodily harm on me.

My mind went back to the hot mess that was Elena. Was she screwing one guy or a string of them? Was he wearing my clothes? Does she have keys to my storage unit? I don't know why I cared; maybe I was still in love with her, whatever love meant anymore. But what really messed with my head was that I had been paying for her to screw some dude in my bed all year like some kind of reverse pimp.

I tried to call Giancarlo next; his contact information said he was in Bavaria, Germany . . . That's close to Munich, I think. Thank God he answered, too.

"Rob Binkley? Heeeey buddy, you waken me from my siesta. What is the occasion that I hear from you? I first have to tell you that I have all your money, I just—"

"I'm not calling about the money—I'm flying into the Munich Airport in twelve hours, can you pick me up??"

"Of coursssse my friend, you are lucky to be coming here now. I have many girlfriends to introduce you with—"

"Yeah, yeah, okay—my flight lands at seven thirty. . . . in the morning."

I hung up and walked aimlessly around the airport. I thought I saw Brian sitting about a hundred feet away staring me down—but it was only an illusion, a memory of what could have been. And what should have been . . .

I still had six hours before my flight departed, so I killed time drowning my sorrows at the airport bar. I was in a dark place and had post-traumatic Brian disorder. I talked to this old lady about Buddhism and proclaimed it was all bullshit. She didn't like that very much, so I told her that I besmirched a monastery and was being deported.

This got her so upset she moved to sit at the other end of the bar. I was clearly pissing off every Buddhist within earshot—mostly because I was angry and hurt. I wanted the world to feel my pain. I was in a deep and irreversible stew over Brian's shaming.

I couldn't believe he blamed me for Ted's idiocy back at the monastery. After all I've done for him over the years? Since we were kids I always looked out for him and pulled him out of a ton of jams. I was always the responsible one and *he* was the loose cannon. How come he didn't cut me some slack?? It was a shock to see him lose his Zen cool and drop that anger bomb on me.

I still kept expecting to run into him at the airport, but no dice. Where did he go? Is he up in that monastery? Did he really find nirvana without me? I hoped not. I know that's selfish, but hey—I'm a selfish American.

I slept the entire way to Munich to try and flush some of the bitterness that was churning inside my soul. I awoke just as we touched down.

I got off the plane and wandered out of the airport. Thankfully, there my flaky friend was, standing by a shiny red Peugeot.

"You like de wheels? I promise I have your money." A smiling Giancarlo took one look at me and frowned, "Jesus, what has happened to you? Have you been in a Turkish prison??"

"I've been backpacking through Asia—it has a tendency to lean you up."

"You are 'heroin chic' without the 'chic,' my friend . . . Come with me, I will fatten you up!"

He sped me off to his hood, straight to one of the pizzerias he owns in Viechtach, a town in the Regen district of Bavaria on the Schwarzer Regen river. He drove like a bat out of hell past beautiful German houses and a sea of neverending farms, I looked in the side mirror and stared long and hard at my reflection for the first time in months. I was a slip of a man, a paper-thin shadow of my former self—inside and out.

I mumbled, "Weight loss is like aging; you barely notice it when it's happening, but if you ever get a true glimpse of yourself it can be a frightening reminder of your mortality."

Giancarlo laughed, "I am supposing you want to eat like a horse?"

"I want meat, lots and lots of meat . . ."

"You came to the right place. You will eat all you want, my treat. I own many restaurants now; I do very well! You will come in any time of the day and I will take care of you. I owe you money anyway! And you will not get a hotel, you will stay with me, do you hear?"

"I couldn't—"

"Do not say another word, do not even mention it. If you want to get your figure back, you can work out all you want at the gym in my apartment building. Rest, recoup, relax—you look like you just returned from war, my friend!"

"I kinda did . . ."

"You look like someone has broken your heart recently, am I right? Who is she??"

"Um . . . her name was Brian."

"Oh . . . is he hot? Do you have the HIV?"

"*No.*"

"That's okay, that's your business, but I didn't know you swung that way. But this is Germany, you can get as kinky as you want, my friend! I have this swingers' house you will like—we must go and wet our beaks!"

"It's not like that—"

"No-no-no, of course, you want the meat, you get the meat! Who am I to judge!? But I have many sexy girlfriends for you, too." I was too tired to explain the whole story to Giancarlo. I just let him think I was gay while he took me to eat. It didn't matter anyway since Europeans are more sexually progressive than us uptight Americans.

This is when I embarked on a monthlong food bender of epic proportions—it was a nonstop eatathon. My taste du jour was copious slabs of roasted flesh. My inner carnivore was starved and I was going to feed the beast. It had been nearly a year since my taste buds had gotten a taste of a rare steak, a tender pork chop, a juicy sausage, a succulent slice of ham, a big fat greasy cheeseburger, a bite of crispy fried chicken, or a piece of bacon. Oh, how I dreamt of them all these months.

I would eat my sorrows away, devouring every mammal in my path. I didn't care what part of the monster: I wanted livers, hearts, gizzards, tongue, intestines, gall bladders. If it moved, I was gobbling it down . . . I wouldn't eat a vegetable for two weeks. And even then, it was beans sautéed in bacon fat.

I slept for what felt like two days straight in Giancarlo's guest bedroom. Luxuriating in a regular bed for the first time in nearly a year made me appreciate all the things we take for granted in the Western world. The only weird thing about the setup was Giancarlo had to walk directly through my "guest room" to get to his bedroom, so those first two nights I got a front row seat to a sexy parade of girls, which made me yearn for them even more.

When I woke, I was recharged again and ready to take on the world, but I was so stiff I could barely move—starvation fueled me to get up. Giancarlo had left me a note with directions on how to get to his restaurants. I took his note and ventured outside like a ravenous vampire seeing the sun for the first time.

I walked to the closest one on his list—which was a pizzeria that was only a two-minute stroll. I stretched my legs and breathed in the glorious air of freedom; I was back in Western civilization and it felt great. As much as I liked the challenge of roughing it for a year, it was like I had died and gone to heaven. Giancarlo was so gracious; he really treated me right.

I kept the same "morning" routine for the next few weeks. I would arrive at the pizzeria around noon and take my eggs on the terrace. When I needed more food, I'd go back in the kitchen and they would make whatever I wanted. I'd joke around with the Czech cooks and waitresses in the kitchen. They greeted me like one of their own—it was great. There were usually three or four different languages being spoken in the kitchen and I wanted to learn to speak all of them. Through my taste buds, I was slowly rediscovering my joy for life, learning, and laughter . . . and food.

In the afternoon, I had this rehab routine where I'd go to the little gym in his apartment complex and get in a workout, then go take a nap. Eventually I started taking long hikes in the Bavarian forests, then longer runs—then another nap. Later in the day, I would walk back up to the restaurant and eat more. Eat, exercise, sleep. I repeated this cycle for weeks.

Once I regained my strength, my innate "urge to purge" came back with a vengeance. Maybe I was rebelling against all the spiritual lessons Brian and I learned in Cambodia, India, Nepal, and Tibet just to spite the *spiteful bald one* who told me I was a "lost spiritual cause." Or maybe I just wanted to "rage against the dying of the light" of my lost dream of finding Utopia or having a personal renaissance. But once I got my weight back, I began going out every night so I could start destroying my body, mind, and soul again.

Eating like a pig led to me wallowing in the nightlife like a hedonistic swine. I was forgetting about my search for nirvana all over again. I can only blame myself, but Giancarlo was a bad influence on me. He was a great host, but he brought out all my demons to come and play in his dirty sandbox of vice and sin.

I fell in with his gang of Italian troublemakers like some wayward orphan from juvenile hall. I thought I partied hard, but these maniacs blew me away.

Giancarlo and I spent our days touring Bavaria, running around to all their restaurants to flirt with gals and eat and drink like pigs. All his Italian friends, Paulo, Orrelio, Franco, Diesel, Tesso—their names started to blur together—were wealthy, entrepreneurial lunatics who were girl-crazy all the time, which was great because I was chomping at the bit to have fun with a beautiful Western woman who hopefully spoke some English. I was in the right crowd; the amount of flirting that went on at their restaurants after hours was at a hundred thousand percent all the time. The only time I successfully used my broken German were the times when I approached a group of cute girls to ask if they were single and wanted to "have a date with us."

I knew I was in trouble with these guys when Franco and I brought the girls we just met back to his restaurant and he immediately challenged me (the new kid in town) to a prosecco (a dry Italian sparkling wine) drinking contest, which I do *not* recommend. No one wins a prosecco drinking contest with an Italian. Fully loaded, we all went out to the Bavarian bars and I partied my sadness away. I lost my mind and my voice, since I was constantly shouting over the loud music and practicing my German with the beautiful blonde Bavarian girls. After hours we went back to Franco's ice cream parlor and drank prosecco and ate gelato until we fell over.

One night, when the party died down, I left Heidi, my German girlfriend, passed out in one of the circle booths, and went to find a pay phone. I wasn't interested in calling Mom. This time I called Elena who, shockingly, picked up.

"Hello . . . ?"

I was so stunned to hear her voice; I couldn't really speak.

She said angrily, "Is this who I think this is?" I gave the phone to Giancarlo so he could yell at her in an Italian version of Spanish to move out of my house. "This is a message from Rob de Godfather. Turn off the samba music, you spider woman, and move out of his casa!" he yelled into the receiver. At least that's what he told me he said.

She hung up on us.

All the Italians roared when I told them I was mad because Elena was squatting in my house with her lover, boning to samba music on my king-sized bed.

They all thought that was totally normal.

The next morning I called Jody, who reminded me I still hadn't wired her the six months' back pay that I owed her. As soon as I heard the word "money," I pretended the line was bad and quickly hung up.

I was not a good man . . . not anymore.

The next night we went to one of Tesso's ice cream shops. I wanted to drink milkshakes with bourbon, but these guys had no idea what I was talking about. "Milkshakes and bourbon??" Tesso asked, "What are you, like the John Travolta in the *Pulp Fiction?*" Then he laughed like it was the funniest thing he'd ever heard.

"They're delicious, gentlemen, let me school you on an American *delight*." I jumped behind the ice cream bar and started to blend up milkshakes for everyone. Turns out, milkshakes were invented in America by some guy who worked at a Walgreens soda counter back in the 1920s. Nobody in Europe had ever seen such a thing, except in movies.

Once Tesso and the gang got their first taste of my spiked bourbon (a very American liquor, by the way) and vanilla milkshakes, they were hooked. "This is the ambrosia of the Americas—we love it, you beautiful fool! Make us a hundred more!"

"Let us all become drunk on cow juice together!" I yelled and they cheered. The next day, I smiled through my milk and whiskey hangover when I walked into the ice cream shop and noticed CRAZY AMERICAN MILKSHAKE was written on the chalkboard menu. I was leaving my mark on the European cocktail world. Was that a good thing?

At this point, I felt no shame for all my hedonism, for all my depravity, and for my lifestyle of so-called sin and debauchery. Brian was the one who believed in God, not me. The second I opened the door to having a state of grace, I got slammed into a gong headfirst and cast out of heaven with the rest of the heathens. In my anger and in my sadness,

I was turning to the dark side for comfort. Misery loves company—yeah, yeah I know.

Introducing spiked milkshakes to Bavaria was the tame beginning of my downward spiral into a full-on deep six into depravity—it was an innocent gateway drug to the hardcore shenanigans I would get into, tomcatting around town until all hours of the night with these guys.

Every Tuesday night we drove out to the Black Forest to get weird in the woods. "You are going to the dark side now, my friend," Giancarlo said. "This place really goes off." It was Revolution, a techno club in an old farmhouse in the forest, where people showed up from all over the region. It was four discos in one, underground and dark. Drinks were only two dollars all night. I stalked through the innards of the club in a blunted haze. The place was a madhouse of sweat and skin; we danced and drank. Sexy women in tight mini-skirts were everywhere, gyrating under the black lights.

"See, us sinners do have more fun!" Giancarlo shouted to me from inside a dancing girl sandwich.

Maybe it was the twenty-eight whiskey and Cokes I consumed, but in my state of alcohol-fueled imperfection I perfected my best possible dance move there. Traveling to discos all over the world, I realized it's impossible to dance appropriately in every culture. So with my "studies" I found if you just gyrate your hips in a crazy-eight motion and wave your hands back and forth, you kind of look like you know what you're doing whether sober or drunk, no matter what country you're in.

"Are you okay, my friend? You are dancing like an epileptic!" Giancarlo yelled at me while I danced my ass off.

After about the fourth hour on the dance floor, it finally occurred to me, "Why do I feel so good? Why am I perfecting dance moves? Why am I dancing so much? I don't even like to dance." Then Giancarlo told me someone had dosed our drinks with ecstasy (or MDMA), which I'd never done before.

The results of the drugging were after twelve hours of dancing I ended up in some corner booth gently caressing the face of some Polish girl like she was the most awesome thing in the world. "This is how the

Tibetan gypsies say hello," I said, then we made out in slow motion for what seemed like an eternity.

Two days later, I woke from a coma back at Giancarlo's. We went into Straubing to do something in the daylight and shake off our Revolution hangover. Located on the Danube River, Straubing was a cool town full of gothic architecture. The Romans conquered it centuries ago, which left a dramatic mark on the region. You could see traces of the four-hundred-year Roman occupation all over the place. We spent the day hanging out in the historical town center and flirting with all the girls in the outdoor cafés in my horrible broken German.

Some American guy actually told me I spoke terrible *English*. I hadn't been home in almost a year, so I had gotten used to speaking broken English that made more sense to people in third world countries.

Now I wasn't fluent in any language.

When I got tired of not understanding anything being said around me, I decided to hire a guy who was literally an old Nazi to teach me the German language. Dieter was terrifying; he looked and talked just like Laurence Olivier in *Marathon Man*. Every time I screwed up, I expected him to say, "Is it safe??" while sticking a dagger into my side that was hidden under that old musty sleeve of his . . . But instead he hit me on the head with a ruler.

Other than the sadism, the private lessons with Deiter were fun. I was having so much fun he kept warning me, "You must take *zeez* seriously." He was a self-professed mean old man.

After about two weeks of daily lessons I was able to understand most of the common phrases as long as people spoke slowly and were looking at me. I know I looked really weird trying to hold a conversation. I was concentrating so hard while people were speaking so simply. The alcohol didn't help or the fact I was in loud bars, restaurants, and nightclubs most of the time. But I was getting better.

My Italian gang and I were starting to get noticed by the local police for our late night tomfoolery. One night we got ticketed by the local police for disturbing the peace and disrupting the citizens of Viechtach and the tiny nearby towns of Sankt Englmar and Deggendorf—all quaint quiet little villages before we stumbled in the back door with lampshades on our heads.

"If we keep this up, we're all going to be deported," I whispered to Giancarlo after a police officer uncuffed our hands from the telephone pole outside the Casa Blanca club. "You boys go back to your home!" the officer said, then he cut us a ticket for public intoxication.

Walking away, Giancarlo laughed, "Forget this nuisance, my friend. Let's go to the House and wet our beaks!"

"Whose house?" I asked.

"*The* House!" Giancarlo shouted.

A few of us rambled over to the infamous "House," which was the "singles' house" Giancarlo had been raving about. He said it had all the free drinks you could drink and an indoor pool and sauna. They charged fifty dollars entry per couple and single women obviously got in for free. Problem was they charged single men a hundred dollars for entry.

Giancarlo spent a few minutes trying to talk our way in for free, but the doorman wasn't buying it. We didn't want to spend a hundred dollars so we walked back to his car.

"Where can we find dates at this hour?" I asked. "C'mon man, this is your 'hood."

Giancarlo slapped me in the chest. "I know the perfect spot!"

We jumped into his car and made a quick trip across the Czech border where we, amazingly, found three girls who agreed to come "party" with us in Bavaria. Since they didn't have their passports, we snuck them into Germany in the trunk of Giancarlo's car.

Going through the border crossing, I looked at Giancarlo and asked, "Dude, isn't this sex trafficking, technically?"

He smiled, "You think too much, my friend. These girls are coming on their own free will."

I could hear the girls banging from inside the trunk. Giancarlo turned up the music.

"You Euros are freaking crazy."

"Yes we are!"

I held my breath and the guards luckily let us through without searching the trunk. This would be the second time I participated in transporting undocumented immigrants across a border in a trunk. This is an accomplishment I'm not exactly proud of.

With our dates on our arms, we all got into the House for half price. The Czech girls seemed to be into the scene, so I didn't feel so bad about dragging them to a "singles club" in a foreign country. I was actually more nervous than they were going in. This was a new thing for me, but my nerves quickly turned to amazement. Inside everyone was just swinging away.

I saw my friends Anke and Wolfgang there making out with a girl on the pool table. They were a typical young German couple that liked to have a good time, so when they saw us they came over to give us all kisses. I kissed Anke and gave Wolfgang a manly hug. I didn't want to give anyone any ideas; I was tired of Giancarlo telling everyone I was gay, so no more joking around.

I wandered around the place and took in all the strange acts that were going on—things were getting very crazy in all the different rooms, with many people enjoying themselves all over, on every surface, all at once. I had never seen anything like it in the world.

All I can say about the House was it was a bizarre cornucopia of perverted fun. I won't go into details, but when I woke the next day—still in the House—I was in some strange person's underwear, covered in glitter with a hellacious hangover. I gathered my things and walked out into the sunlight past many passed-out swingers.

"What have I become?" I mumbled to myself. I seemed to be living that question now.

When I found my way home, Giancarlo was in the kitchen eating breakfast; he took one look at me and laughed, "Last night *proves* you like the women better."

"Last night got a little blurry. What happened to those Czech girls?"

"I drove them home this morning. They got to ride in front this time!"

The fallout from the evening was the "Rob is gay game" Giancarlo had been playing on me finally ended after my exploits at the House, most of which I do not remember. But I did notice my hormonal urges had subsided so I must have enjoyed myself.

I went back into my room and slept for twelve hours.

There I was again, stuck in my Bavarian rut.

Every night there was something else going on; it was becoming one big blur of inequity. I was on another epic bender and I couldn't get off the ride. What the hell was wrong with me? Revolution on Tuesdays, Napoleons on Wednesdays, Trim on Sundays, blah, blah, blah . . . Saturday nights we went to Casa Blanca in Viechtach, the center of our Bavarian universe, where I started to develop the reputation as the guy who was enjoying himself a bit too much.

One Saturday at Casa Blanca I finally met a Czech girl who spoke English named Hanna. I was really into her, so we talked for half an hour. Things were going well until she mentioned how amazed she was at my drinking ability. She pointed out I had pounded four beers in the time we were talking. Hanna wasn't drinking and said I was "bad" in her Czech accent.

She stopped talking to me after that.

I resigned myself to partying with some Polish guys. I ended the night in supreme wastoid fashion, grabbing two mannequins inside the bar and dancing with them the rest of the night. All the patrons were giving me the European side-eye, in which they look down their noses at you without ever turning their head. Giancarlo, of course, mocked me: "You need a real lady, my friend—not the plastic kind!" He was right.

I was drunk and alone. Not a good combination for any living organism.

I was beyond burnt out but I kept doing it again and again and again. I felt I had to partake as a ritual of the young, while I was still young. I kept telling myself when you're old you're not going to remember all the nights you stayed home and watched TV—the moments you'll remember are the blurry ones when you're out with new friends, doing new things . . . Still, my brain was scrambled, my liver was in rebellion, my soul was in a tailspin, and my resources were running low.

I tried to clean up by going to a wholesome festival by myself in one of the farmer's fields. It didn't work. They had rides, and *bier* gardens of course . . . I ended up drinking lemon beer all day, and riding on all the rides alone like a lost child. It was pathetic.

The good news was my German was coming around with my Nazi tutor; it had been almost a month and I could understand a lot but could only speak a little—just enough to get me in trouble.

I was dying a slow death. Death by alcohol . . . Death by amusement park . . . Death by milkshake . . .

One night, Petra, an old girlfriend who I'd met on my first trip to Europe, had a party at her place. Afterwards, we went out and drank rum after rum at Casa Blanca with some Polish girls. At the end of the night, one of the Polish girls and I ended up in the bushes throwing up together—so naturally, I brought her back to our apartment, and we ended up "sleeping" in Giancarlo's bunk bed, which he kept in the corner of the living room . . . Very public.

A week later, now there were two Polish girls staying with us in Giancarlo's apartment; the four of us were very cozy there. When we were hungry, we'd walk over to Giancarlo's pizzeria and eat all his restaurant food for free since the girls had no money. I'd let them in the back door and make weird pizza combinations for them that we all tried over beers. After a week, they got mad at me because I was not taking them out to the clubs since it was too expensive to pay for them and myself.

They would be leaving soon.

After they left, I was sick of Bavaria and looking for an out. One day, I heard Simona and Petra, two Czech waitresses at Giancarlo's pizzeria, saying they wanted to go to Italy so I decided to tag along to get out of town and clear my head. They weren't big partiers; they were nice and had transportation.

The first night we stopped in Salzburg, a beautiful little Austrian village that was beyond picturesque. We were so cheap we didn't even get a room. Instead we slept in the car sitting up in our seats, which was not pleasant, but doable. The next day, we wandered around Salzburg having coffee and *wieners*.

Then we drove down to Venice and spent the day in and around San Marco Place. That night we drove further south to Rimini on the eastern coast off the Adriatic Sea. We didn't get a room there, either. In fact, we didn't sleep at all. We stayed up for two nights straight partying at the Embassy Bar with all the gorgeous bartenders. So much for cleaning up and getting my shit together . . . Maybe it's the curse of the young, but "the party" just has a way of finding me, or me finding it.

I needed to break my compass and start over. But I didn't know which way to turn.

On day three, the "*recherché* Rimini life" on the Italian Riviera was becoming more and more intoxicating. We were mixing with the wealthier class at these great clubs. After two days of sleeping in the car outside the "palace gates," we didn't want to go back to our little car and sit-sleep, so I splurged and checked us in at the King Hotel—money be damned.

We made a beeline for the buffet downstairs like three starving urchins invited into the king's palace to feast. Piling my plate high, I had a flashback to Tibet . . . Even though I'd been stuffing myself for weeks, to see all this food at once was crazy—I still had PTSD from starving myself.

I felt like I'd just returned to civilization after being stuck on a desert island where I ate bananas and grabbed fish from the water with my bare hands like some kind of caveman. Now here I was—magically transported to this modern spread, with all the chocolates, finger sandwiches, huge poached salmon, and mounds of fresh shrimp by the cubic ton. The champagne was flowing forever and a chocolate fondue bar was oozing liquid sweetness all over the place.

I stopped heaping food on my plate and stood there, nauseous from the excessive scene. I visualized all the times Brian and I ate runny rice or fish soup for dinner—and the contrast blew my mind. It all seemed so wasteful.

Are we all just a bunch of greedy, Western pigs?

The next day at the pool of the King Hotel, my visualization of Brian and I eating and laughing over fish stew in some third world hut became a self-fulfilling prophecy.

I was laying out with Petra and Simona on chaise lounges among a sea of oiled-up tourists—it was hard to concentrate on my "dates." The Italian girls strutting around the pool in their bikinis and high heels were driving me crazy. The sex was oozing from their skin; when they stared at you, you melted.

I tried to take a nap and forget about all the women lying half-naked around me, but just as I was about to drift off I heard an all-too-familiar American guffaw coming from the other side of the pool. I sat up and pulled my hat from my eyes to get a look. I squinted into the sun and saw the silhouette of something, somebody perched on the side of a chaise lounge, laughing with a gaggle of Italian girls around him.

It was a shadow that reminded me of a long lost friend.

The man was massaging the back of some beautiful girl in a bikini. She would "ooh" every time he massaged her. He said, "Let me open your mind to what's possible. Look around at all this conspicuous consumption. Don't you know this is how civilizations die? What if you died today, my sweet, would you say you have been following your bliss?"

I heard the beautiful girl reply, "I don't knoooow . . . Oooooh, *more, more.*"

Then the man said, "This whole scene is a perversion! Sexy ladies, join *me* while you still have souls to save!" By God, the chameleon had changed colors again . . . but his cult leader rhetoric was the same.

I leaned over to Petra, "That looks like Brian . . ."

"Who is this Brian?"

"*That* is this Brian."

Flabbergasted, I got up and stomped over to his side of the pool. How the hell did he get to Italy all the way from Nepal? How could he afford this place?? I got closer and saw he was rubbing a new lady friend I had never seen before. He was wearing a cheesy gold bracelet that had replaced his leather yak Buddhist bracelet. His hair had grown out and was slicked back like a Greek oil tycoon.

I watched him, wondering if I was going mad.

My holy friend who dumped me for not being holy enough for his rarified airspace had turned back to the dark side. He was wallowing in the samsara like a typical American douchebag.

I had to approach him. I tapped him on the shoulder, "You've got a lot of explaining to do, Aristotle," I said, and handed him the umbrella drink he was reaching for.

He took the drink then looked up at me. He stopped massaging and just stared at me from behind his sunglasses and a newly grown beard. He said, "East meets West in a most auspicious setting—sit down! C'mon girls, keep the drinks coming!"

Brian had lost his Nepalese righteousness, and that Zen smile of his had turned back into that old familiar devilish grin.

He didn't stop his banter just because I crashed his party. He kept regaling the girls with tall tales of his past adventure. He said he'd flown in a cargo plane full of live poultry over the high Himalayas under the shroud of darkness to get here—and he was now surely wanted by the Chinese government for crimes against the state. "Don't call me an outlaw, ladies—call me . . . a *Tibetan freedom fighter*."

"Oh my God, is this true? I adore the Dalai Lama! He has such amazing style and grace." His hot Italian massage woman was buying it all: hook, line, and sinker. I just watched him go. He had reverted back to his original state: a charming and persuasive bullshit artist.

I finally got him to stop talking long enough to pull him away from his gaggle of women; it felt like I was talking to a different human, yet again.

"Dude, are you some kind of schizophrenic psychopath??"

He mused, "To take a lesson from Walt Whitman, 'we are all mosaics, a million versions of ourselves, all fighting for supremacy' . . . Fancy meeting you here!"

"Are you following me?"

"How could I follow you? I had no idea where you went. This is kismet, baby!"

"When did you get here??"

"Just now! Look, baby, maybe I was hasty in relieving you of your duties back in that monastery, but that doesn't mean we can't still be friends."

"My duties?? Stop calling me 'baby.' What am I, your freaking valet?"

"Perhaps 'duties' is a bad way of putting it—how about 'responsibilities' for keeping up with me. See . . . I had an epiphany while praying with the monks. God told me to mend fences and offer you an olive branch. Girls, who wants me to oil them up!?"

The girls cheered.

I said, "I think you owe me an apology."

He put his hand on my shoulder, "Maybe I do, maybe I don't. Maybe dharma brought me here. Or, let's be honest, maybe it's the fact I'm totally broke and need your help to get home," he laughed. "Okay, okay, no seriously, I confess. I called your mom's house and found out you were at Giancarlo's—then I called him and he told me you were here . . . Are you mad?"

This was a test. Could I practice my Buddhist learnings? Could I be the bigger man?

I said, "Not mad . . . just slightly confused as to who you are, from country to country."

"Don't let that upset you. I'm a walking contradiction—I don't know who I am either! Do you know who you are after this year?"

"I've been asking myself the same question. But, I'm glad you're back."

"Oh I'm back, baby." Brian had returned to finish our journey together.

"I'll take you back. Just stop calling me 'baby.'"

"Deal."

"Are you just taking advantage of me cause you know I won't leave you hanging?"

"Maybe? Just . . . don't get pissed if I charged these drinks to your room, okay?"

We hugged it out then goofed off at the hotel resort for two more days pretending we were a couple of sultans in from the Ottoman Empire. I put everything on my tab since he had nothing. Every time I did, he gave me this knowing look, like we were both in on the fact that I was somehow paying for his forgiveness, which I wasn't. But who cares.

All that mattered was Brian had his mojo back, and so did I. All my Bavarian angst was washed away.

We had turned a corner in our personal renaissances. All the girls at the resort were magically into us, and Petra and Simona loved Brian so much we all slept in the same bed for the next two nights. It was all we could afford, considering our alcohol budget.

Brian and I fell in love the next few days, not with the girls, but with each other again, and the shiny glitz of Rimini and all its Western trappings. It had sexy women, great beaches, and sidewalk cafés galore. It made me miss having money. I wanted to buy things. I could feel the lure of Western capitalism seeping back into my bloodstream.

We explored the town and noticed the smaller highways were lined with good-looking prostitutes with cars pulled over negotiating a deal. It was fun to honk while you drove by; even the girls liked it. We called it the "love highway." When we ventured out to the beaches, they were so packed with chairs the sand was barely visible, all you saw were Italians running around in their Speedos showing off their bellies.

"What in God's name are you wearing??" Brian asked.

"I, uh, borrowed a pair of Giancarlo's underwear," I said.

"You're actually wearing someone else's purple underwear in public? Hahahaha! Perfect!"

By the third morning in the King Hotel, the fantasy had to end. We finally had to check out. I knew the tab was getting to a dangerously high level and Brian and the girls had no money. We were a tad late arriving at checkout. The snooty guy manning the front desk looked at us both wearing sunglasses to hide our hangovers, then looked at Petra and Simona, who probably looked like hookers to him, and frowned.

After some clacking on his computer, the hotel guy announced we "must pay" a thousand US dollars. We sat there, mouths agape. "Um, that was not our agreement."

He explained the extra fee was due to the fact we were an hour late for checkout. And he was also charging us an extra night, and for *four people* in the room each night, plus a parking spot for two nights.

"Whoa, whoa, whoa, nice try Emilio, if that's your real name—but we were told we were paying for two people per room (we had been sneaking Petra and Brian in after hours). Nobody told us we *couldn't* have any guests in our room."

We demanded to speak to the hotel manager who took one look at us and immediately threatened to call the police. We said, "That's a great idea!"

After staying quiet, Brian suddenly lost it. He totally forgot about his Zen teachings and started yelling at the guy, saying he was crazy—the manager went nuts. Things were deteriorating fast, so I told the manager we would compromise for this misunderstanding by generously offering to pay for "three people for one of the nights, but that was it!"

Clearly tiring of the affair, the manager finally agreed. With some quick thinking, when he turned around, I switched the exchange rate on his calculator and we got a great deal.

Great deal or not, after I paid the bill, we were relegated to the car again (now with Brian in tow), which totally sucked.

We spent the next night sit-sleeping again in the back seat with the girls upfront. The girls loved "car camping," but somehow we weren't having fun. Maybe we were tired of it all. That night, I kept fidgeting to find a comfortable spot on the window to lean on.

I moaned, "I'd rather be sleeping under a school bus in the rain."

Brian (sleep mask on) mumbled back, "When does the stewardess come by with the cookies?"

In the morning, the girls and I decided to pull the ripcord and go back to our beds in Germany. Brian said nothing; he just asked us to pull over at the bus station on the way out of town. I knew what was coming.

"You want to come to Bavaria with us? You can stay with Giancarlo and me."

"No thanks, I'm the man with a plan; it's time for me to blow this Popsicle stand."

Brian said he'd learned all he needed on this trip. "It's time to go." Meaning home. He was going to catch the next bus to the airport in Venice.

"You're really leaving?"

"What a wild ride it was . . . but I must bid you a fond farewell."

"Should I come with you?"

"No, I'm broke, and you still have the time and money to keep going. Thanks for floating me these past few weeks. I'll pay you back one decade."

"I'll put it on your bill. Thanks for coming to say goodbye. I didn't want it to end like that."

"We're brothers forever. No fight in a monastery will ever change that."

"Here," I gave him the Barbie doll I'd been carrying around since India. "I want you to have my dream girl."

"You still got that little heartbreaker?" He took Barbie and combed her filthy hair with his fingers, "Guess it's time to find the real thing, now, huh?"

"That may be harder than finding Utopia."

"Think we learned anything from all this?"

"Well . . . one thing I learned is there's something out there (pointing to the sky) other than ourselves. As for what that is—beats me. But I'm open to anything; we just have to keep searching, man. That's why wisdom comes with age . . . We're still too raw to know anything for sure. It's all so conceptual, this life."

"I guess, I was hoping for something less conceptual and more tangible." He laughed. "That only happens in the movies. Now it's time for us to put away childish things and start testing our concepts in a slightly more mature way—But we had fun, didn't we??"

"Enough to last a lifetime."

"I'll never forget it . . . what I remember of it."

I smiled. "One of us should write about it. I've been keeping this journal, maybe it will come to something."

He put his arm around me as we walked to the bus. "The wise ones say, 'Do or do not . . . no try.' If you want something, make it so."

Brian looked back. The Czech girls were in the car honking at us; they wanted to go. Brian's bus to the airport started up, people began to board. He said, "Well. I guess this is it . . . Hope you don't end up in debtor's prison."

"Thanks, at least jail would be a place to crash . . . Probably nicer than some of the hostels we stayed in."

"Fewer fleas . . . less floods . . . no old cougars looking to pounce in the middle of the night."

"Well, not too sure about *that*, but Elena's barricaded herself in my condo so I'm definitely homeless. What are you gonna do with your life?"

"Oh yeah," Brian said. "You gotta look me up, man. I got a Forestry Service gig!"

"You already got a job??" I was gob-smacked.

"I had to! I'm outta cash." He said he was going to be a fire lookout in the North Cascade Mountains in Washington like Kerouac did in his book *Desolation Angels*.

"I was looking around for jobs at this little Internet café in Tibet, so I sent them a picture of me climbing a cedar tree outside the monastery with my bare feet, bald head, and flowing robes—and they bought it!"

"Incredible. You're way ahead of me."

"Just know, I may be returning to the corrupt motherland, but I refuse to become a corporate slave."

"No, you're working for the federal government—they're not corrupt at all!"

"Dude, the Forestry Service has a clean record!"

"Okay, are the G-men gonna be mad when you don't show up looking like a monk?"

"I *may* have to shave my head again and get in my getup, just for the first few days."

"You're insane."

"If you need a place to stay, come see me on Lookout Mountain—they never said I *couldn't* have guests, and I'll be the only person up there. I got my own cabin! But no liquor, no drugs, no women. Just me, myself, and I . . . I wanna come face to face with God and find out, once and for all, about the meaning of all this inescapable samsara we're born into."

"I respect your choices, man. Stare into the abyss; find your bliss . . . But don't fall off that cliff."

"You know I never do, brother."

We hugged it out one last time.

"Thank you for opening my eyes," Brian said.

"No. Thank you," I said.

"Maybe we'll have that double marriage one day."

"Yeah, maybe . . . Now get outta here."

I watched Brian get on the bus in that same roadworn gray sweatshirt he'd been wearing ever since it got cold in Nepal. It looked like it hadn't been washed in a year, and it probably hadn't—but the man inside of it looked renewed and ready to take on the next chapter of his life.

I walked around to the back of the bus and saw him plop down in his trademark backseat on the left. He smiled when he saw me come around to his window. Always the prankster, he sneaked something out of his bag and looked around devilishly—then he held it up to the window. It was his last square of hashish chocolate he'd been drugging all of Asia with for the past six months.

He leaned over to his seatmate, an old German lady, and offered it to her. The window was up so I couldn't hear what she said, but she took one look at his disheveled state and shook her head no. He looked back at me, shrugged, and popped it in his mouth, grinning like the Cheshire cat who ate the psychedelic canary.

Then he did something I'll never forget. He put his open palm up against the window just like those Tibetan nomad kids did to us when we were stuck on that mountain.

I put my palm up to his in solidarity. We had one final high-five through glass.

I held my hand up there until the bus pulled away.

And off he went, the mad inspiration for this whole trip, setting off on another adventure of his own. We would be friends for life, but I wouldn't see him for months. The crazed rambler turned stoned Taoist-Hindu-Buddhist had to go his own way, like we all must.

That's the thing about life, you have those galvanizing moments of youth with your friends and then you grow up, start getting married and having kids, and you don't see or talk to each other much anymore. But you still have that bond that comes from the shared memories of youth.

No one can ever take that away from us.

11

Epilogue in Amsterdam

Brian would eventually get fired from his Forestry Service gig for extreme incompetence and end up back in Palo Alto working at a high-end restaurant called Strata and living in my condo. I told him he could live there for free if he kicked out Elena, which he did. When I finally caught up with him again, he was still full of glee.

"What are you learning from waiting tables?" I asked.

He said, "I'm learning how rich people eat! I want to open a high-end restaurant that only serves Buddhist cuisine! I call it 'Zen.'"

"I like your aspirations. I can see it now; write a new chapter of your life!"

And so he would. Brian would never find his bus angel from the Philippines, but he would clean up his act, get a good job, and finally find true love in the form of his current wife, a lovely Vietnamese woman who he met while living in my condo and is now the mother of his two children.

As for what happened to me . . . After Brian disappeared again, I needed someone to help me prepare for my reentry back into the states. Watching him leave made me realize my days of freedom were numbered. I must move on and head home to face my American reality. I needed to start my life again as a man, not as a backpacking juvenile, but was I the same guy? Could I still make a buck with Uncle Sam strapped to my back?

Lost and seemingly without a friend, when I got back to Bavaria, I called Jody like I always had for the past five years. First, she laid into me for still not paying her (which I apologized for once again), then she told me Elena laughed at the fake eviction papers she slid under the door—and I certainly "would have to involve the real authorities" to get her out of my house.

I sighed. Jody said, "But you know . . . if you ever actually get around to paying me, you can always stay with, um, me, if you want . . ."

I thought about that for a minute, then on a whim asked her if she wanted to come see me in Europe since I still hadn't paid her. I offered to buy her ticket and pay for everything on top of the back pay. "To make up for the past year of hell I put you through, and will continue to put you through . . . C'mon, whaddaya say, kid?"

She was silent for a good while. "Two weeks in Europe, huh. You're lucky I'm on Christmas break. (She was in graduate school.) Can we go to Prague?"

"Done and done."

Two days later, I met her at the Munich airport. She took one look at me and said I "looked like I'd been run over by a freight train full of shit," then she gave me a big warm hug. We drove out of the airport in a car I rented for the drive. After the initial chatter died down and silence filled the air, I asked her, "This isn't awkward or anything, is it? You being here."

"Just as long as you're not trying to seduce me," she said with a deadpan stare, followed by that cute sideways look she always gave me right after she lobbed an insult my way.

We left Munich and I drove us over to the Czech Republic, which was a four-hour drive, and the old capital of Prague. It is an absolutely amazing city, one of my favorites in the world. It's like the weirder, smarter, cooler brother of sexy, sophisticated Paris.

We checked in at the Golden Horse House hotel—and I got us two double beds so she didn't think I was up to any funny business, although at this point I was thinking about it. We went out to see the city. Americans were everywhere, but not so many obvious back-packers. My pack seemed out of place; Prague was quirky cosmopoli-tan and I felt like Indy Jones in the big city. Jody was definitely dressed better than me; she looked stunning, sexy even. Prague is one uniquely intelligent and beautiful town . . . I don't know if it was because I had been away from America for a year, or maybe because Jody had blossomed while I was gone, but I was suddenly turned on by her everything.

We walked all over the medieval, gothic city for days, exploring its museums, restaurants, and cobblestone streets. It's amazing to think this city has been around for thousands of years while my hometown had barely been around for two hundred.

"Think of all the ghosts that haunt this place," Jody said while we wandered our way through its hidden gardens, cool cafés, and gothic cemeteries. "This city feels important, ya know . . . I could get inspired to do great things here."

"I know what you mean," I said. "A lot of great thinkers have had moments of clarity walking these very streets . . . Kafka . . . Mozart . . . Rilke, to name a few."

"You're smarter than you look," Jody said and took my arm for the first time, like we were lovers. At the end of day, we collapsed in our separate beds and talked all night.

No funny stuff. Not yet.

The next day we just kept walking and talking. Talking and walk-ing. We knew we couldn't experience everything in one trip, but we were trying to squeeze every drop of coolness out of the experience. The restaurants were elegant yet inexpensive, so I could take her out and not blow the rest of my money on food. I didn't let myself get caught up in a drinking tour of the city, not this time.

Prague, like its sister city Paris, is great for lovers, and since I hadn't had a girlfriend in almost a year, I admit I was maybe giving off some strange romantic vibes to my quasi-former employee who I always knew had the hots for me, but I'd never reciprocated for some reason.

We visited the St. Vitus Cathedral, which might be the most beautiful cathedral I had ever seen. It looked ancient, and part of it was, but it was only officially completed in 1929, which was shocking to me.

"So, are you one of those guys who believes 'new things' lack depth?" Jody asked, clearly alluding to the fact she was a few years younger than me, yet seemingly wiser than any woman I'd been with—maybe ever.

"Never judge a book by its cover," I said.

"Are you saying there's something wrong with my cover?" She punched me in the arm and gave me that sideways look again.

"Never . . . You're lovelier than ever," I said.

"I know your game, Binkley . . . You're just trying to grease my wheels so you don't have to pay up," she smiled.

We made our way to the famed Charles Bridge; it was simply amazing to walk over. We strolled past the thirty statues of saints on the bridge; they were ghostly in the morning fog like visitors who got cemented for all eternity into the landscape.

On the bridge, I started to see Jody in a completely different light. She was so much more beautiful than I remembered. I began to wonder: If I'd had this great girl staring me in the face all this time, why hadn't I noticed her until now? Had I been blinded by the surface sex appeal and fire attraction of crazy women like Elena all this time?

We stopped to look at the river. I tried to explain all these new feelings I had to Jody, but she just put her hand to my mouth and said, "Shhh . . . Shut up and kiss me, fool."

So I did.

After we kissed, she asked, "What do you think all these ghostly saints are telling you now?"

I smiled. "They're saying . . . follow your bliss, young lovers . . . cause we only go around once."

"Bet you tell that to all the girls."

We kept strolling around town, holding hands like two lovers. I hadn't felt this happy in years. We walked past a public fountain where two stone figures were peeing in a puddle that spelled out literary quotations. "Why am I suddenly thirsty?" she asked. We both laughed. "Want to get a drink?"

We came across one of those tucked away pubs on the corner of some winding cobblestone path and popped in for a pint, my first in Prague. It was as quiet as a library and so very old. "If these walls could talk, think of all the stories they could tell. . . ."

A few lone patrons were sipping beer and reading. We sat down in a corner table. You could order beer without saying a word by just placing a beer note on the table, which we did. In a minute, the waitress came by, picked up the card and then came back with our drinks.

I looked at Jody's order. "I always thought you'd be the Cosmo kind of girl."

"Cosmos are for wussies," she said. "I like beer."

"My kind of woman."

"You ain't seen nothing yet."

"Elena hates beer."

"Forget Elena."

We took big gulps of beer and went "ahh" at the same time. "Jinx . . . So made for each other," she said coyly under her breath.

"You're tellin' me. Oh momma," I said and pulled out my journal.

"This is amazing . . . What you got there?" Jody asked.

I started scribbling, "This one's going in the book."

"Book?"

"I've been keeping this road journal and I have to mention the beer, which is by far the best in the world."

"So hyperbolic you are . . . Didn't know you could spell, much less write."

"I can't really . . . It's just a hobby."

"Don't undersell yourself, *dude* . . . You're always talking about wanting to break free from the dreaded routine of America; I mean, you *fled the freaking country* to change your life for God's sake. You gotta think outside the box if you really want to live a life less ordinary."

"Where did all this wisdom come from?"

"I'm an old soul, can't you tell? You could move to some island utopia and write—"

"Wait, wait, wait—did you just say '*Utopia*?'"

"Yeah. Really write a book about your trip . . . Stay off the grid . . . If you play your cards right, I'll even help you edit."

"That's what Brian said . . . '*do* or *do not*.' No in-between. Can't believe he missed this place."

Jody stopped me from writing. I looked up. She leaned in close and stared at me with eyes so direct I knew I'd met my match.

"Forget about Brian . . . You've got a new dance partner now."